Bodies of Evidence

New Directions in Anthropology

General Editor: **Jacqueline Waldren**, *Institute of Social Anthropology, University of Oxford*

BODIES OF EVIDENCE

Burial, Memory and the Recovery of Missing Persons in Cyprus

Paul Sant Cassia

Berghahn Books
New York • Oxford

First published in 2005 by

Berghahn Books
www.berghahnbooks.com

Library of Congress Cataloging-in-Publication Data

Sant Cassia, Paul.
    Bodies of evidence : burial, memory and the recovery of missing persons in Cyprus / Paul Sant Cassia.
        p. cm. -- (New directions in anthropology ; v. 20)
    Includes bibliographical references and index.
    ISBN 1-57181-646-1 (alk. paper)
    1. Cyprus--History--Cyprus Crisis, 1974- 2. Disappeared persons--Cyprus. I. Title.
II. Series.

DS54.9.S26 2003
956.9304--dc22   2003057831

British Library Cataloguing in Publication Data

A catalogue record for this book is available from the British Library.

Printed in Canada on acid-free paper.

ISBN 1-57181-646-1 hardback

CONTENTS

LIST OF ILLUSTRATIONS

List of Figures

List of Maps

ACKNOWLEDGEMENTS

The research upon which this book is based commenced in late 1996. What had begun as a small-scale project evolved into a much larger and ultimately emotionally draining engagement. When I began this research, I thought I would be studying politics but I soon realised that what I was struggling with was kinship, i.e., the emotional links between people, including the living and the dead, through the sharing of substance. This was ironic because my original Cambridge training under Jack Goody had revolved around the study of kinship, and like any anthropologist desiring to establish his or her own independent identity, I had been attracted to moving into new research areas. We always return to beginnings. Research should help enlighten us as to who we are as 'anthropologists', but even more so as individuals and help clarify what our work means to us, not as an aid to advancing some academic career, but in more fundamental senses, and why our endeavours should assist the people who have so generously shared their lives and concerns with us. For this reason I am immensely grateful to all the people I worked with in Cyprus, both Greek and Turkish Cypriot, who exposed their sufferings to me, an absolute stranger. When I was writing this book I had hoped that if this book would have annoyed the political authorities on both sides, I would have succeeded in my aim to expose the way states can caress the pain of their subjects. At the same time, I vehemently desired that my research would benefit the people who are the subject of this book and assist them in exploring the complexity of the situation fate and human actions placed them in. I still retain these desires. I also wished to show that this is not a localised, but an extensive, problem in the contemporary world, and that the issues dealt with in this book, such as the conflict between kinship rights and obligations on the one hand, and the rules of the polity on the other hand, are far more extensive and much older, many having been dealt with by the Classical Tragedians. For this reason I toyed with titling this book 'Heirs of Antigone', but wiser counsel prevailed over my fascination with Classical Greek literature. Nonetheless, I hope that after having read this book, the reader will understand why I had desired to do so. At the time I completed the initial draft of this book, major changes were afoot in Cyprus to bring about a settlement of 'The Cyprus Problem' of which the issue of missing persons constitutes a critical, emblematic and vitiating kernel. I therefore augur that this book will in a small and modest way assist the relatives on both sides to claim what is fundamentally theirs, and oblige the new nation state builders to pay renewed and responsible attention to the concerns of all their subjects, free from the corrosive virulence of nationalism.

I conducted fieldwork on both sides of the 'Green Line', but for practical reasons concentrated more on the Greek Cypriot missing. My greatest debt is to the relatives of missing persons, and in particular to Androulla Palma and Maroulla Shamishi without whose openness this book would not have been so effective. I would also like to extend particular thanks to Xenophon Kallis, Dr T. Christopoulos, Mr Rustem Tatar, and Mr Pierre Guberan for their genuine openness to my questions. They are not responsible for what is written here. I should also like to thank Mustafa Akinci, Huseyin Aktig, Semi Bora, the personnel at CAARI, Adonis Christoforou, Makarios Drusiotis, Sabahattin Egeli, Jana Federici, William Haglund and Physicians For Peace, Yusuf Karsulli, Louisa Mavromatis, Vathoulla Moustoukki. Michael Muller, Frida and Edmond Nanushi, Popi, Christina and Nikos Palmas, Yiannis Papadakis, Kika Michael-Papapetrou, Andreas Paraskos, Oliver Richmond, Mehmet Tahir, Secretary of the Turkish Cypriot Network, U.K., Neophytos Taliotis, Nikos Theodosiou, Tasos Tzionis, Myria Vasiliadou, Mehmet Zorba, as well as the Greek and Turkish Cypriot members of the Committees of Missing Persons. I should also like to record my appreciation of two Durham University students, Katherine Tripp and Janene Benson, who worked as my research assistants in the summer of 1998.

In the U.K., I should like to record my appreciation of the following who commented on earlier drafts: Ray Abrahams, Chris Hann, Keith Hart, Penny Harvey, Italo Pardo, Johnny Parry, the late Paul Stirling, and Dick Werbner. As always, I owe a very particular debt of thanks to Peter Loizos who has been unfailingly wise and generous in reading through the text and providing very helpful and sensible comments. I am indeed fortunate to have him as a friend. At the University of Paris (Nanterre), Georges Augustins, Maria Couroucli, and Martine Segalen provided an interested reception for the preliminary development of my ideas. Colette Piault generously provided of her time in collaborating on the joint production of a film on the topic *(Missing Presumed Dead?*, which deals with the story of Androulla Palma and other relatives in greater detail. The film is available through *Le Films du Quotidien,* Paris, email: piault@u-paris10.fr. I should also like to thank Vassos Argyrou, Isabelle Borg, Mercedes de Grado, Jack Goody, Michael Herzfeld, Juliet Mitchell, Mario and Melina Sant Cassia, Victor Watts, Master of Grey College, Durham, the University of Durham for financial support, and my colleagues at the Department of Anthropology, University of Durham for providing a congenial and warm working environment.

Pezenas, Summer 2003

1
HEIRS OF ANTIGONE:
DISAPPEARANCES AND
POLITICAL MEMORY

⊱✣⊰

Introduction

On 17 August 1998 two middle-aged Greek Cypriot women, Androulla Palma of Peristerona village and Maroulla Shamishi from Nicosia, Cyprus, went secretly at dawn to a military cemetery at the outskirts of Nicosia. They had with them two heavy pickaxes. They started attacking a collective grave, murmuring *miroloyia* (mourning songs). After an hours' hard work they had broken through the marble slabs. Alarmed neighbours called the police, but not before the forewarned women had called the private television channels on their mobile phones. When confronted by the police and the army, the women said that they wanted their husbands. They said that they did not know whether their husbands were dead or alive since the 1974 Turkish invasion of Cyprus and its subsequent occupation, and they wanted to know whether their husbands were dead (as they had been told by some witnesses), or whether they were still missing, as claimed by the government. The authorities told them that they had committed an offence, took them into police custody, where they were then questioned, but released.

The incident made national headlines. Some said that the women were crazy, and craving publicity; others that their pain had driven them to such extremes. After 24 years their husbands were clearly unidentifiable. They were frightened, proud, and defiant about what they did. What had driven them to such extreme measures? This book attempts to answer this question.

1

This book is about how representations of the past continue to influence contemporary realities in Cyprus. It deals with the case of some 2000 disappeared people and the resulting traumas that have affected the lives of the relatives. Its main aim is to demonstrate how memory can be seen as both a *political plan* used by state authorities and political leaders, and as a *political act* on the personal and local level against the very authorities that have employed it. Its main theme is the political economy of memory: its production, consumption, distribution and exchange – for memories too are produced socially, traded, countered, and used to obtain or purchase other 'goods'. It deals with interrupted mourning, trauma, attitudes to loss of memory, the ineffectiveness of traditional religious symbols in dealing with massive social dislocation and personal traumas, and how a whole category of people – the disappeared – have come to represent the political fantasies, fears, and aspirations of social groups, and their representatives.

Between 1963 and 1974 over 2000 persons, both Greek and Turkish Cypriot, went 'missing' in Cyprus, an island with a population distribution of 80 per cent Greeks and 18 per cent Turks. This represents a significant number for a population of 600,000. This was not a 'simple' case of individuals being made to 'disappear' as in dirty-war Argentina and elsewhere in South America where agents of fascist regimes executed political opponents, or ordinary citizens believed to be 'enemies' of the regime. Rather, these individuals disappeared in the course of hostilities between Greek and Turkish Cypriots between 1963–74, and during a mainland-Greek backed coup in 1974, and the subsequent Turkish invasion. Responsibility for their disappearances appears straightforward in some cases, more murky in others. It would be a relatively 'simple' matter if these individuals had been made to disappear by members of the opposing ethnic group in the course of hostilities. Indeed in some cases both Greek Cypriots and Turkish Cypriots may wish that to be the case. But the picture is much more complex. Some individuals may well have been killed by members of their own ethnic group and made to look as if they had been 'disappeared' by the opposing ethnic group. Few bodies have been recovered; most will probably not be. Some individuals, who it was claimed had disappeared, have now been shown to be alive. Others have recently been discovered to have been openly buried in cemeteries under normal tombstones with their names clearly visible, yet these same names still figure on the lists of the missing, whilst others on these lists are assumed to be alive, or at least missing and certainly not necessarily dead. For others there is strong evidence that they are dead, yet their relatives maintain their names on lists of the missing, and refuse to recognise, often with official connivance, the possibility of their death. The issue is far from closed and continues to poison relations between the two groups.

The issue of burial and recovery of people who are dead and yet kept metaphorically and literally unburied is an old and important theme in western and other literatures and cultures, and continues to exert a strong hold on our collective imaginations. The lack of proper dispatch and of narrative and mourning closure also runs through much recent history. It still continues to trouble many, including relatives of US servicemen Missing In Action in Vietnam, and the relatives of the 'disappeared' throughout many parts of the globe. It has also provided a plot for some basic social dramas, and philosophical explorations. One of the most potent was the story of Antigone:

> Antigone, a daughter of Oedipus king of Thebes by his mother Jocasta. She buried by night her brother Polynices, who had been killed in battle fighting against his native city, against the positive orders of Creon who, when he heard of it, ordered her to be buried alive. She, however, killed herself before the sentence was executed; and Haemon the King's son, who was passionately fond of her, and had not been able to obtain her pardon, killed himself on her grave. (Lemprière's Classical Dictionary, orig. pub. 1788; repr. 1984: 51)

As George Steiner (1984) reminds us in his magisterial survey, the theme of Antigone has dominated modern western imagination. It can also provide a good entry for approaching some important issues in Anthropology. As the entry to the Oxford Classical Dictionary notes, 'Antigone's role in the play has been the subject of endless dispute, with some critics claiming that she is wholly in the right, others that she and Creon are equally right and equally wrong. Most would now agree that she is no saint (she is harsh and unfair to Ismene)' (1996: 104).

Sophocles, like Plato, was concerned with the tensions that arise from the transition from a tribally based society, where ritual obligations are paramount, to a norm-based city state marked by obedience to transcendent rules. One could see *Antigone* as anticipating, in crude form, the tensions between Durkheim and Weber in their treatment of rationality, order, compulsion and restraint. Whereas Antigone represents justice (*dike*), Creon is concerned with the law (*nomos*). Antigone belongs to a Durkheimian world of mechanical solidarity. Ritual is critical for social harmony. Her *dike* is 'the justice due the dead and the gods below. It is private, exclusive, jealously guarded' (Segal 1981: 169). She is *compelled* to her actions. Creon, by contrast, attempts to anticipate salvation through *restraint*: compliance with transcendent city-based rules. He fails. Although he dares to anticipate Weber's world, he poses it not in terms of the interiorization of norms but in terms of differential access to knowledge and virtue. He believes that some individuals, especially in positions of authority, should be 'more rational' (or guided by different principles) than others. Because he belongs to a tribal world, of house and *genos*, he can only visualise this in terms of the elevation of patriarchy to a principle of government and obedience. He lacks the knowledge available to Plato's philosopher king, or the humility of ordinary men and women when facing the gods. Like most ancient Greek rulers, Sophocles' Creon is an aspiring Platonist but a recidivist patriarch. He has power without wisdom or insight. He starts by evoking abstract justice and principles but becomes increasingly personal and arbitrary: 'Creon's *dike*, like his 'laws' of earth, though it seems at first to be the impartial 'justice' that holds the city together, becomes increasingly personal and emotional, increasingly distant from the 'oath-bound justice of the gods' praised in the Ode on Man. He can even go so far as to require obedience to the city 'in what is just and *the opposite*' (ibid: 169). This is patriarchy without sentiment; Platonism without wisdom. As Segal notes 'both his private and his public life become the very opposite of his ideals' (1995: 132).

Antigone can be seen as the ancient Greek answer to the Hobbesian question of the rationalisation and concentration of power, except that tragedy follows rather than anticipates absolute secularising power. Rather than a rationalisation of power, *Antigone* can be seen as a critique of power. As Beard and Henderson remind us, drama was the ancient Athenian version of engaged sociology: 'Drama was special to Athens as an intrinsic and key institution of the *democratic* city ... In drama the democratic city was on display' (1995: 88–9 emphasis in original). Creon learns by his misfortune. All humans suffer. The play ends with retributive justice, and asks for piety, and moderation. Prideful words teach wisdom in old age. Sophocles cannot resolve the dilemma of social and logical coherence. The two are fatally opposed. This theme continued to trouble western thought. Hegel famously thought the two could eventually come together. Weber was not so buoyant. Rather than the Sophoclean disenchantment of the Gods, Weber's disenchantment of the world entails the separation of fact and value. Progress has its price.

Antigones as Metaphors

There is not one Antigone, but many Antigones. By this I mean three things. First, the original text has been subject to many interpretations by classical scholars, philosophers, etc. Each period shapes its own Antigone from the Hegelian Antigone where 'the Spirit is made actual' but is subject to division and partiality, to Anouilh's wilful, virginal, anti-bourgeois rebel. Similarly, each society creates its own Creon. He has been viewed as a patriarchal despot, a man genuinely possessed with a desire to uphold the laws of the *polis* as representing universal justice, an absolutist Bourbon, and an obsessive rational bureaucrat concerned to 'introduce some order in this absurd kingdom' (Anouilh, 1960: 43). It is this polyvalence that has enabled *Antigone* to be staged both as a critique and as an apologia of state power. We should not forget that Anouilh's version would probably not have had the impact it had were it not for the German permission to be staged in occupied Paris, thus creating a space as it were for it to be viewed as both apologia and critique. I do not interpret this polyvalence necessarily in Barthes' terms that the reader rather than the intentions of the author is important. Rather, I mean that a particular text such as *Antigone* is so architectonic, so taut, so laden with many of these issues that it is inevitable it should be subject to so many interpretations. In spite of the anti-cannon lobby in literary criticism, some texts are simply richer than others.

A second reason is that many of the themes Sophocles' text raises – the State versus the individual, law versus justice, men versus women, burial and memory, agnation versus affinity, etc. – have generated other plays and literature. There is a long tradition of using Classical Tragedy to explore contemporary problems. One need hardly recall that each re-interpretation is socially, politically, culturally and individually contingent. I explore two examples: Anouilh's, and Dorfman's *Death and the Maiden* (1994). A discussion of some of the ways authors have explored the issue can help us approach the ethnographic material of this study. A final third reason for the plurality of Antigones is that literature (as theme, as predicament, and as symbol of ethnic identity), lives in people. Many of the individuals and the actors I deal with in this study engaged in actions that not only harked back to some of the issues raised in the play. They also explicitly referred to the play as a means to explain their actions and beliefs. Skultans (1998) found similar propensities in her study of testimonies of people's lives in Latvia. The people and societies we study nowadays exist in our time not 'other time' (Fabian, 1983), and they operate in a literate and historic environment. The use of this trope is thus no mere literary or fashionable conceit. I hope to show that anthropology as an intellectual humanistic enterprise can benefit from linkage with the classics and with literature. This may be an unfashionable perspective to take. Yet Durkheim, Weber, Simmel and Marx also explored some of the issues raised by our readings of classic literature. They too dealt with the problems of justice versus law, the iron cage, its pessimism, etc. The use of classical themes as a heuristic device also has a respectable if somewhat discontinuous tradition. Fortes uses the themes of Oedipus and Job to explain West African religion. This study of the politics and religion of the disappeared is also about ancestors but in a modern world of DNA testing, exhumations, violence and memory. Yet, as I hope to show, the issues dealt with in our contemporary *Antigone* are more complex.

In line with my argument that there are many Antigones, I want to take three examples: Hegel's interpretation of the significance of the play, Anouilh's version staged in wartime Paris, and a modern play by Ariel Dorfman, *Death and the Maiden*, set in Chile in the post-Pinochet period.

Hegel is not a popular philosopher among anthropologists on account of his teleologism, his 'eurocentrism', and his exaltation of the State as the highest form of rationalism and power. Indeed one could argue that the whole task of anthropology has been to subvert his heritage, especially his rationalisation of (European nation-state) power, and the power of (western forms of) rationalisation. Hegel's belief that orderly thought and orderly society were not only related *pari-passu*, but also mutually influenced each other has been challenged since Evans Pritchard's work on Nuer social organisation and Azande thought. Nevertheless, perhaps because he was concerned with tension, dialectic, and resolution, Hegel saw clearly that the play posed fundamental dilemmas between the rights of the living and of the dead, between law and ethics, between men and women, between the State and the family.

5

Antigone was a major starting reference for his *Phenomenology* and his *Aesthetics*. The play raised the problem of how to reconcile the freedom of the individual with the demands of the state. Man was divided between a 'state-being' (*Staatlich*) and a citizen-bourgeois with familial obligations. Individually felt, ethical obligations to self, kin, and 'inner rules', conflict with rational(ised), transcendent guidelines for conduct within the city. Hegel takes *Antigone* as a critical example of conflict in (Greek) society's ethical life (*Sittlichkeit*) between two universals: human and divine law. Although state and family, divine and human law, are bound up and require each other, they are nevertheless in conflict in Greek society (Taylor, 1975). There is no need here to chart Hegel's complex development of ideas, but he recognized that Antigone as a supremely ethical being posed a challenge to his conception of the progress of rationality. Through her action Antigone engages in an authentic act of self-realization. In her, 'the Spirit is made actual'. Yet her act, itself an actualization and partial realization of rationality, pits her against the rule of the state. As Steiner notes, 'the ethical substance which Hegel's *Antigone* embodies represents a polarization, an inevitable partiality' (Steiner, ibid: 31). It is a polarization through its opposition between the individual and the state; it is a partiality because, for Hegel, it is the state rather than the individual that is both the guarantor and the realization of rational and ethical conduct. Thus both the state and the individual in the personages of Creon and Antigone aim in two opposing directions, rather than in a collaborative venture. Antigone's acts, emanating as supremely ethical, assume a self-destructive autonomy 'an imperative of and for the self alone' (Steiner, ibid: 30). Likewise, the law rather than embodying the most ultimate form of rationality becomes 'formalized', violently empty. Hegel resolved this contradiction through an ontological splitting: 'the Absolute suffers division as it enters into the necessary but fragmented dynamics of the human and historical condition' (Steiner, ibid: 31). In effect the Absolute must 'divide itself and crystallize around the antinomies of human and divine law' (Hegel quoted by Steiner, ibid: 31). Hegel here offers an ontological interpretation. The tension is in Being itself. In this he offers optimism, an ultimate stage where these tensions can be resolved. We can call this Hegel Mark I: an optimism in the face of a transcendent pessimism. As Taylor so clearly puts it, the act is necessary, but 'to act, in the sense of effecting some important change on the world outside, is necessarily to incur guilt' (1975: 174).

Hegel tries to resolve this evidently unsatisfactory treatment in Part Two of his *Lectures on the Philosophy of Religion*. One can call this Hegel Mark II. Here he gives a more ethical interpretation of right against right, or one truth as against another truth:

> The collision between the two highest moral powers is enacted in plastic fashion in that absolute *exemplum* of tragedy, *Antigone*. Here, familial love, the holy, the inward, belonging to inner feeling, and therefore known also as the law of the nether gods, collides with the right of the state (*Recht des Staats*). Creon is not a tyrant, but actually an

ethical power. Creon is not in the wrong. He maintains that the law of the state, the authority of government, must be held in respect, and that infraction of the law must be followed by punishment. Each of these two sides actualises only one of the ethical powers, and has only one as its content. (*Lectures on the Philosophy of Religion*, Part Two (II.3.a) in Steiner, ibid: 37)

According to Taylor, Hegel believed that what brings down the two characters, Antigone and Creon, was more than inscrutable fate. Rather, there is a sense that 'the necessity of (their) defeat is intricated in the very purpose they espouse' (1975: 502).

Subsequent authors have separated the ethical from the metaphysical elements in the play, and ultimately evacuate the play of its ethical dilemmas. In Anouilh's version there is no doubt that the sympathies of the audience are directed towards Antigone. As Steiner points out ' her decision to defy Creon … has nothing to do with the substantive issues of the legend or of Sophocles' play. Antigone's second revolt springs from a more or less modish and contingent psychological twist. She is nauseated by Creon's avuncular, patronising insistence on happiness, on the mundane routine that awaits her in married life. Antigone flinches hysterically from domestic bliss. She elects to die in virginal immediacy, unsullied by the unctuous compromises of bourgeois life' (ibid: 193). Antigone adopts the posture of *il grande rifiuto*. Gide called it an *acte gratuite*, and suggests she suffers from *l'orgeuil d'Oedipe*. In assuming an existentialist stance (existence comes before essence), she embraces her destiny knowingly[1] to define herself paradoxically as a Platonist (essence comes before existence)[2] in what she recognises as an absurd situation.[3] This is why the play, whilst cunningly insinuating, does not quite work, in contrast to the Sophoclean original where the characters suffer their destiny blindly, not quite realising why. Anouilh's Antigone is a Platonist privileging her sibling obligations over her love for Haemon, 'one of the comeliest figure in Sophocles' (Steiner, ibid: 151). This is an odd decision for a modern heroine for three reasons. First Ismene tells her that Polyneices never loved her: '*he was a bad brother. He was like an enemy in the house*' (Anouilh, 1960: 29). Creon too wishes her to face the '*sordid little story*' she wants to die for. Polyneices was '*a cheap idiotic bounder, a cruel vicious little voluptuary*', ' *a gambler who raised his hand against his father*' (Anouilh, 1960: 53). Yet Eteocles, the virtuous brother was '*just as rotten as Polynices. That great-hearted son had done his best, too, to procure the assassination of his father*' (Anouilh, ibid: 55). Both brothers were '*a pair of blackguards. – both engaged in selling out Thebes and both engaged in selling out each other*' (Anouilh, ibid: 55). Herein lies the dilemma of 'national heroes', 'national martyrs': are they indeed heroes or martyrs? Second, as in life, so in death. The brothers' corpses, mangled as they are, are indistinguishable: '*they were mashed to a pulp (bouillie), Antigone. I had the prettier of the two carcasses brought in, and gave it a State funeral; and I left the other to rot. I don't know which was which. And I assure you, I don't care*' (ibid: 55). Third, Creon wishes to save her so long as she does not proclaim her deed and so long as she compromises with the façade of power and order.

In spite of her magnificent gesture, Creon wins. After this revelation, Creon asks whether 'it would have been better to have died a victim of that obscene story?' Antigone murmurs 'it might have been. I had my faith' (ibid: 55). This is the death of her illusions. Later, she will ask the Guard to write a note to Haemon whose love she rejected in favour of her brother's memory. She is about to admit 'and I don't know why I am dying for', but erases this, as it would be like 'seeing me naked' (ibid: 67).

If Antigone emerges as an attractive but narcissistic adolescent caught in events bigger than herself, a Juliet selecting a Thanatic destiny over Eros-alliance, Creon emerges as an obsessive pragmatist, an *etatist*, to whom compromise is essential so long as one can continue to make compromises – all in the name of order because inability to compromise always spelt disaster for Thebes. Compromises repair the planks of the ship of state when it springs a leak. This is the compact between the king and the subjects. Thebes 'has a right to a king without a past' (ibid: 43). It will soon get another one: himself. For Creon there are no individuals, just principles: 'nothing has a name – except the ship and the storm' (ibid: 51). He scorns 'religious flummery' (ibid: 45), yet exploits 'meaningless rituals' (ibid: 51) for state purposes. He likens the role of the ruler to a herder of animals, 'good, simple, tough', versus the *pater familias* he is in Sophocles.

Creon's fashioning of appearances to simulate order leaves him exposed when Antigone forces open the gap between appearance and reality. He does not wish to be the cause of Antigone's death, and orders her to connive with him in maintaining the façade upon which according to him all politics depends. He complains 'If I were one of your preposterous little tyrants that Greece is full of, you would be lying in a ditch this minute with your tongue pulled out' (ibid: 47). Exasperated, he retaliates 'the whole business is nothing but politics: the mournful shade of Polyneices, the decomposing corpse, the sentimental weeping and the hysteria that you mistake for heroism – nothing but politics' (ibid: 48). A faceless *eminence grise,* resentful at being obliged to emerge from the shadows, he accuses Antigone of having cast him as 'the villain in this little play of yours and yourself for the heroine'. He confuses power with legitimacy and is blind to other forms of legitimacy except an etatist one. Whereas he emphasises appearances, the signified, simulation, Antigone is pure, uncontaminated action, a signifier with no signified except herself and her overwhelming.

A 'quick tongue but a hollow heart', Anouilh's Creon is an obsessive who conceals his lack of vision or human sentiment in what he presents as pragmatism. He likes things 'clean, ship-shape, well scrubbed' (ibid: 48). He is an absolutist anchored in absurdity, for whom the compensatory promises offered by the establishment of political order against the disenchantment of the world can never fully overcome his inherent naturalistic pessimism: 'it is stupid, monstrously stupid' (ibid: 48). He has spent too much time in the 'backroom, in the kitchen of politics' (ibid: 54). He embodies the cunning not of reason, but of reasons of state. His addiction to order, his means of retaining sanity, is none other than an obsession for predictability, and perhaps for control. Although he presents himself as a pragmatist, he misses Machiavelli's sensible advice in *The Prince*: 'To those seeing and hearing him, the Prince should appear a man of compassion … a kind and religious man. And there is nothing so important as to seem to have this last quality. Men in general judge by their eyes rather than by their heads' (Machiavelli, 1993: 140). Antigone shrewdly recognises his two failings. First, his fastidiousness prevents him from being a good tyrant (i.e. good at being a tyrant). He fails to recognise Machiavelli's advice, that although the Prince cannot observe all those things that give men a reputation for virtue, he should have a 'flexible disposition' (ibid: 140). Second, his mania for order prevents him from understanding fellow men. As the apotheosis of a true Heglian, ordered rational thought is only possible in an ordered, rational society. He intuits both are impossible. In contrast to the Sophocles' Creon, Anouilh's ruler is more self-conscious than Antigone. But he is also less majestic, less 'tragic'. We can recognise him as closer to modern rulers.

Anouilh's notion of tragedy is far removed from Ancient Greek, and is saccharine – e.g.: 'it is clean, it is restful'. Most observers of classical tragedy would consider this a misrepresentation. Steiner perceptively characterises his treatment as 'fundamentally tawdry, … reductive' (ibid: 193), although he recognises Anouilh's 'argumentative cunning'. By turning Antigone into a latter day Jean d'Arc, Anouilh ensured that wartime Parisian audiences identified with her plucky 'No!' She brings together destiny, glory, sacrifice, purity, and uncompromising and existential self-actualisation. By committing herself to the 'traditional' bonds of kinship-agnation, of descent, metaphors for the nation, over the fragile ones of affinity and alliance, she provided an important focal point for French men and women. The fact that such bonds were and are largely invented or even imagined, is not very relevant in the case of make-believe theatre.[4] Yet Anouilh's version, limited when compared to Sophocles', highlights some critical dilemmas of the nation state relevant to this study. The first dilemma inherited from Sophocles is this: are certain bonds of belonging such as kinship (agnation or affinity), or even ethnicity, more morally compelling than obligations we have to the State? In the post-Habsburg, post-Ottoman world that Cyprus forms part, as in nearby Lebanon or the Balkans, it has often seemed that primary obligations have been to kin, village, ethnic group, and religion, rather than to the state. Does the State represent justice or merely legality? Durkheim hoped it would be the former although he offered no real examples. Weber feared the latter. This is an old philosophical problem and we cannot answer it here, but as I hope to show in this study, the two are often closely inter-linked and far from separable.

If Sophocles suggests that coherence is to be found in divinity and humility in prudence, Anouilh offers a profoundly more pessimistic view. To him there can be no transcendent justice. This is also implied in Dorfman's *Death and the*

Maiden (1994). The Prince or the State, rather than upholding justice, cynically exploits intimate symbols of morality. The state's 'morality' is a travesty of domestic morality performed in the name of a 'common good'. It fabricates both heroes and villains. Let us listen to Creon's apology for having passed his harsh rule: 'What else could I have done? People had taken sides in the civil war. Both sides couldn't be wrong: that would be too much ... Two gangsters were more than a luxury I could afford. And this is the whole point of my story. Eteocles, that virtuous brother, was just as rotten as Polynices' (Anouilh, 1960: 54–55).

As Creon cynically noted, nation states require heroes, villains, and martyrs, especially after man-made catastrophes, such as civil wars, invasions, coups, ethnic cleansing, etc. In contemporary societies, such as in South Africa, or in South America, Truth and Reconciliation Commissions enable the dispossessed to get their voices, to render the past more understandable, or even to recover justice. As the contributors to the Chilean National Commission on Truth and Reconciliation noted: 'Truth and Justice – insofar as they can be attained through the courts- are the pillars on which a reconciled society can be built, but in themselves they are not enough. The various sectors of the society affected must also be brought back together' (1993: 886).

This is a theme effectively explored by Ariel Dorfman in *Death and the Maiden*. The reader will forgive me if I briefly explore this play, because it is an *Antigone* for modern times and has a direct bearing on the themes of this book. Like classical Greek drama it is architectonic, the characters are intertwined, and there is a *denouement* at the end, except that in contrast to Greek tragedy it is open-ended. As Kristeva noted, when power is diffuse as in the modern world, how do we revolt? The setting is Chile during the transition to civilian rule. The three characters are Paulina, a damaged woman who had been tortured by the Junta, her lawyer husband Gerardo recently appointed to head the Truth Commission to investigate human right abuses, and Roberto, a stranger. Her husband who had a flat tyre (lame? Like Labdacos? Or like Oedipus, swollen-footed?), has just been given a lift home by the stranger. On learning Gerardo's identity, Roberto returns, claiming to be a supporter of his efforts. Off stage, Paulina recognises him as the doctor who had attended her interrogations, his job having been to ensure detainees would remain alive under torture. As she had been blindfolded she can only recognise him by his voice. She takes a gun and threatens to shoot Roberto unless he confesses. He protests his innocence. Her husband is appalled. He likes the Schubert-loving Roberto, he is committed to due legal process, to proper investigation and to evidence which devalue her forms of knowledge (based on sounds, smell, touch of skin), in favour of more intrusive but legally secure forms of knowledge (sight). He fears her actions threaten the orderly, legally-based, dealing with the past in favour of personal revenge, that it will unravel the Commission's work, and prejudice his position. As she is disturbed, both men take her threat seriously. Throughout the play there is no way of knowing whether Paulina is right and Roberto guilty, although the viewer inclines to this interpretation. This is indeed the critical kernel of doubt. Thus whilst Roberto seems terrified that he will be found out, alternatively it could be interpreted that he is in genuine mortal fear of being shot by a woman convinced of his guilt in spite of his innocence. Gerardo is paralysed by the potentially high personal costs of the compromise he is forced into – helping a man who may have raped his wife and, if so, how he should act: through the vengeance he feels (i.e., the law of the family), or relying on the law he embodies? As he cannot countenance condemning a man without proof of guilt, Gerardo assists Roberto in writing his confession, using information Paulina had confided in him. As her ruefully puts it, the doctor's confession is to be his wife's therapy. Roberto confesses that he began participating for humanitarian reasons, but that he slowly became corrupted and compromised by the power it gave him. His virtue and humanitarianism became functionally dependent on the barbarism of his accomplices.

On completing and signing his deposition, Paulina releases Roberto who immediately denies the truth of what he had written saying that details were supplied by Gerardo. Paulina discloses she is now certain he was the doctor in question because she had concealed certain details of her detention and torture from her husband, mainly in order to protect him, which Roberto had actually elaborated and corrected. His elaboration of an partially concealed story is actually the concealed detail. Throughout the play we can never be certain whether this is Paulina's paranoia or the truth, but from the perspective of fixed, legal procedures, this evidence is inadmissible, never having previously been disclosed or confided to anyone. A lie can be used to discover the truth in the intuitive world of men, but it can never be overtly acceptable in the transcendent legal fantasies of the state. Gerardo is now faced with the dilemma of either exacting revenge on a man who tortured his wife who never betrayed him, but who is also the source of his domestic disequilibrium (unsurprisingly, Paulina is not a happy woman), and thus overturning his beliefs and role in society, or releasing him, knowing that the deposition could never lead to a prosecution. Like all Creons, Gerardo is consistent even if as a modern he is acutely aware of the costs of his compromises. He decides on the law. No longer the harsh pater-familias of Sophocles, to which he is ironically compared by Roberto as ineffectual ('can't you impose a little order in your own house' (Dorfman, 1994: 31)), nor Anouilh's cynical ruler, he is a lawyer. Like other Creons, he asks Paulina to forget the past so that she can 'live'. But what if her life has grown in such a garden of evil? And, like other Antigones, she scorns compromise: 'Compromise, an agreement, a negotiation. Everything in this country is done by consensus, isn't it. Isn't that what this transition is about? ... The Commission can investigate the crimes but nobody is punished for them? There's freedom to say anything you want as long as you don't say everything' (ibid: 26–27). Like other Antigones she is committed to the past and wants justice and repentance but is disillusioned by the costs of men's rule: 'I'll leave you men to fix the world' (ibid: 32). She gets neither justice nor repentance. Indeed she begins to realise that she will not own the past, and it will be taken away from her: 'why does it always have to be people like me who have to sacrifice, why are we always the ones who have to make concessions when something has to be conceded?' (ibid: 44).

The theme of concessions as the major price for the progress of civilisation runs throughout this play and echoes Walter Benjamin's prescient Faustian observation that for every progress in civilisation there is an equal regression into barbarism. Roberto appeals to Gerardo: 'she isn't the voice of civilisation; you are'. Paradoxically both Paulina and Gerardo recognise this even if Gerardo's 'civilisation' will be wrought out of the collaborative, compromised, silence of his wife. It is Gerardo's 'civilisation' of law that gives a guilty man a fair hearing even at the costs of not having justice done. The play has no narrative closure. The figures freeze just before Paulina could possibly shoot Roberto. The last scene has Paulina and Gerardo at a concert. Gerardo is holding forth about the success of the Commission and how it has given the ex-oppressed a hearing. Paulina is silent. Roberto sits down close looking at both of them: 'he could be real or he could be an illusion in Paulina's head' (ibid: 46). They do not see him. Gerardo takes her hand. Both look forward. She then turns to look at Roberto. Their eyes interlock for a moment. She then turns away. The musicians begin playing Schubert's *Death and the Maiden*. As Goya's famous set of etchings indicated, 'The sleep of reason produces monsters'.

There are certain similarities and differences between Sophocles's *Antigone* and Dorfman's *Maiden*. Gerardo and Paulina echo Haemon and Antigone. They have almost a sibling-type relationship. Like Haemon and Antigone, Paulina and Gerardo cannot have children (i.e. a common future). They want to adopt children but are prevented by the oppression of the past on Paulina's psyche. Like Antigone (whose name literally means anti-generation), she cannot commit to the future, because she is oppressed by her past. Similarly the Sophoclean antinomies and pairing of seeing/ignorance and blindness/intuition which are absent in Anouilh, reappear in Dorfman. In the latter, the senses and synaesthesia are key elements. All knowledge is incomplete. Both tragedies explore the opposition between theoretical knowledge reached through plans and concepts, and intimate knowledge grasped through the senses or intuition. Just as Paulina's cries were not heard when in jail, she stuffs Roberto's mouth with her knickers to prevent him from talking. Whereas he had refused to listen to her pleas, she now prevents him from pleading. When she interrogates him, she undergoes a gender shift (her voice assumes male tones) to extract a deposition acceptable to the state (through writing). By contrast, Gerardo becomes incapacitated, passive, 'like a woman'.

The dominance of the past and the difficulties of coming to terms with it, even the case of capitalising it, as with the recent debate over Finkelstein's work on the Holocaust, is one which has increasingly dominated recent decades. In many countries such as Chile and South Africa it is ongoing. In others, such as Peru at the time of writing, it has barely begun. In others, such as Cyprus, it has been ongoing whilst never being resolved. If one were to continue to use the metaphor of Antigone, in Cyprus Creon and Antigone are not ranged against each other. Rather they are engaged in a complex political choreography, at some times collaborating, at others in opposition. At times, the rulers may know where the bodies are, but manipulate relatives to clamour for the return of the bodies for proper burial. At others, the rulers may have buried the bodies too quickly and concealed them to oblige the relatives to interpret the past in a certain way.

This book on the Missing in Cyprus is a contribution to the growing anthropological literature on violence and survival (Scheper-Hughes, 1992; Nordstrom and Robben, 1995; Taussig, 1992; Feldman, 1991). It has four main aims. First, it shows how continuing differences between Greek and Turkish Cypriots over the Missing is a function of their conflicting views of recent Cypriot history and of the future, and has thus far prevented collaboration in resolving the issue. Second, it explores how the state in Cyprus has been actively and passively involved in giving expression to, and harnessing, the complex feelings of loss (material, spiritual and personal) that followed the invasion. The recovery of the Missing thus becomes a signifier of recovery and redemption. In this respect there has been passive collusion between the relatives of the Missing and official government propaganda. Third, however, I show how the process of the disappearing of the missing raised profound traumas for individuals which official accounts have not managed to assuage. Finally, I suggest that the state itself has been able to skilfully manipulate gossip and rumour.

Throughout this book I will be referring to certain scenes from various versions of the Antigone plot. This is not a Levi-Straussian attempt to explain present day realities by reference to some underlying structure – least of all in people's heads. Rather, I use these examples because they help us understand the predicaments people feel, and they re-sensitise us to the need to take ethics into account. Of course, Antigone had no offspring, but both we as readers (and anthropologists) concerned with trying to understand the world, and the people depicted in this book, are faced with the similar predicament of how to deal with the past and the compromises (including silences) we have to make – usually at the cost of ordinary peoples' lives or their happiness. In this respect we are all heirs of Antigone – and of Creon – as characters having to make ethical and existential choices. But there is another sense in which we are heirs of *Antigone* as plot and as structure, and in a manner not envisaged by many of the romantic readings of Sophocles' tragic heroine. According to romantic readings, in Sophocles' play the actions of the two dead brothers, Eteocles and Polynices, are unambiguous: one was 'good', defended the city; the other was 'bad' and attacked it – even if the dilemma presented in the play for the living is between one right and another right. Sophocles' world seems mono-perspectival. There is no ambiguity between Creon and Antigone over the role and significance of the corpses. But there is another sense in which the tragedians still have something to tell us about this type of violence and which has relevance to the modern world. This is a predicament we encounter when faced with acts of violence so extensive, so sustained and so dominated by what appears to be 'irrationality' and hatred that we find it difficult to resort to simple 'Manichean' interpretations, as for example when trying to understand contemporary ethnic violence in the Balkans, and to a lesser extent Cyprus in the past. Here some insights of Girard may be useful. He observes that 'the tragedians portray men and women caught up in a form of violence too impersonal in its workings, too brutal in its results, to allow any sort of value judgement, any sort of distinction, subtle or simplistic, to be drawn between 'good' and 'wicked' characters' (Girard, 1995: 47). Indeed, how can one salvage such simple ethical positions when faced with such reciprocal violence as in the contemporary Balkans?

The additional dilemma faced by us as heirs of *Antigone* as plot is that we are uncertain not just about the ethical identities of Eteocles and Polynices, but also about the ultimate fates of their corpses. If we were to render Sophocles' tragedy from a Pirandello perspective, both Antigone and Creon may have an existential investment in having to face such stark choices. It gives them a space to act out their destinies, however much they both regret them. But Anouilh's cunning argumentation introduces a corrosive element of uncertainty that has echoes in an insight of Rene Girard. Girard notes: ' [In] Greek tragedy violence invariably effaces the differences between antagonists ... The more a tragic conflict is prolonged, the more likely it is to culminate in a violent mimesis; the resemblance between the combatants grows ever stronger until each presents a mirror image of the other' (ibid: 47). Anouilh's suggestion, however, rests on the cunningness of power: in spite of this absolute resemblance (and perhaps because of it), political leaders require violence to salvage the effectiveness of the sign, but we are complicit in this enterprise. Nowadays we can never be that sure whether the protectors of the polity were actually worthy of the honour, just as we question the guilt of those condemned to remain unburied, un-commemorated, 'forgotten', or 'disappeared'.

'Burial' can be seen both metaphorically and literally as an active ongoing relationship with the past through ancestors. Political authorities often intervene between us and the commemoration or otherwise of the past. Just as we are Antigone's heirs, the nation state – as Creon's heir – is the supreme producer of illustrious corpses. The Tomb of the Unknown Soldier is the modern equivalent of Eteocles' tomb. In some cases there is no ambiguity – as with victorious Britain and France after the First World War. In Germany in this period there was much greater difficulty and ambiguity: 'The absence of any consensus on the meaning of the war, the origins of the defeat ... ensured that the idea of burying an unknown soldier ... had a divisive as much as a unifying effect' (Winter, 1995: 28), a situation which also obtained after the Second World War. In some cases, as in communist Yugoslavia, Tito imposed an anti-Anouilhian solution. The un-commemorated tombs of the Second World War dead (killed due to complex overlapping internecine, political and ethnic conflict) were left officially unrecognised because of the dangers they posed to the project of building a new socialist order. In short, they were not really buried. I take 'burial' in both a literal and metaphorical sense to mean an identification by the living of the dead as ancestors, and a ritualised interaction between the two continuing after interment in the earth. The 'rediscovery' of the nameless dead in late 1980s Yugoslavia and their ethnic reburials provided an emotional, cultural and historical framework for nationalist politicians to re-map the past and navigate the future according to their agendas. In other societies such as Cyprus, both among the Greek and Turkish Cypriots relatives do not know where their missing relatives are buried and thus cannot perform the necessary rites. The same occurred until recently with victims of paramilitary murder squads in Ulster.

Throughout this book I will be referring to Antigone and Creon, not just as characters from the play, but also respectively as the kinswomen of deceased/missing persons and as the political authorities. They can be seen as metaphors for the roles as well as for the predicaments people face in society. I hope that the reader will both understand and (if necessary) forgive this device. It serves my purpose not just to show the relevance of the issues raised by the play in its different variants for contemporary society, but also because if we can understand and fully appreciate the dilemmas people face in society, we can more fully understand the play. The French psychoanalyst Andre Green justified his exploration of the Oedipus and Orestes tragedies: 'It is the privilege of masterpieces to be embodiments of both the signifier and of the power of the forces that work upon it, to be the product of the work of the contradictions that they set in opposition' (1969: 17). Coleridge once wrote that between us and the text runs a 'draw-bridge of communication'. I should like to encourage traffic along that drawbridge.

In her survey of the political lives of dead bodies in former socialist states, Katherine Verdery notes that 'burials and reburials serve both to create and reorder community' (1999: 108). She also emphasises the interconnection between gravesites, ancestors and nation-state formation, an interconnection that both Antigone and Creon struggled over in the Greek city state. 'Touching as they do on matters of accountability, justice, personal grief, victimization, and suffering, dead bodies as vehicles of historical revision are freighted with strong emotion' (ibid: 115). Finally, there is additional sense in which we (and the people dealt with in this study) are heirs of Antigone. In many societies in Eastern Europe (including Cyprus), there are supernatural sanctions against leaving the dead improperly tended. This is no quaint custom. It is an important belief in many societies, and has political and ethical implications. The Serb nationalist Vuk Draskovic proclaimed 'Serbia is wherever there are Serbian graves' (quoted in Verdery, ibid: 95). In February 1996 when Serbs were forced to leave five Sarajevo suburbs, they dug up the graves of their kin who had lived there for generations and took the remains with them. They had to pay huge fees to cross 'state lines'. For modern Creon (i.e. the contemporary nation state), borders are first and foremost symbolic boundaries, whose transgression is signalled by the production of dead bodies (defending borders against enemies), and their post-mortem treatment (such as rights to freely cross state borders, or their proper burial). In short, land as territory and as earth, and dead bodies, are intimately related.

I thus believe that Anderson was mistaken when he began his celebrated study of nationalism by suggesting that the cultural roots of nationalism lay in death (1991: 10). Clearly they do, but that is not an exclusive feature of nationalism. As Sophocles indicated, other political orders such as the ancient Greek *polis* also drew upon such cultural roots. It could be argued, *contra* Hegel's teleological optimism, that both the city state and the modern nation state have similar roots because kinship is still concerned with the production, reproduction, and consumption of bodies, and it uses an idiom of the relatedness of substance that is prior to, and more potent than, the relatedness of sentiment of law pushed by the state. It is the harnessing of such sentiments in new ways that explains the state's immense hold over the imaginations of its subjects. Verdery has suggested that 'because the human community includes both the living and dead, any manipulation of the dead automatically affects relations with and among the living (ibid: 108). I would go further than this. I suggest that whilst the ultimate ambition of political power has always been a transcendental one – the manipulation of dead bodies as the ultimate sanction of power and, like Cerebus, as a means to control access to the underworld – it is individuals and groups who produce other individuals whom they need to recover at death. Whilst the state tries to define the community in terms of its control of the living and the dead, individuals and groups resist attempts to control the dead, partly because as Bloch and Parry (1982) pointed out, having given of themselves and their 'substance' (however defined), individuals linked by this shared substance need to recuperate it. Perhaps the clearest and most notorious example was Argentina in the 1970s under the military junta that waged a massive assault on its own citizens through state sponsored disappearances. Admiral Massera asserted in 1976 that 'We are not going to fight till death, we are going to fight till victory, whether it will be beyond or before death' (*La Nacion*, 3 November 1976). Robben observes 'Not only was victory more important than life, but the battle continued into the land of the dead' (2000: 82). Nor is this battle between the state and society over the dead restricted to repressive regimes. It underlies most societies. In France after the Great War there was an intense dispute over where dead soldiers were to be buried. The state and the army wanted to leave the men where they had fallen as sacrifices to land as territory, but the families desired their repatriation (Winter, 1995: 27) or, to be more precise, they desired their re-filiation, their reburial in family tombs. The state finally relented, although parents and widow associations then contested who had the right to reclaim the bodies. The parents won – a clear example of the recovery of the regenerative power of the natal group.

Burial has a double significance. It is community-making and it is linked to land claims (i.e., affairs of the state) on the one hand, and with the making of ancestors and recouping what society gave of itself, on the other. This is what Antigone and Creon struggled over. This is also what Androulla Palma and

Maroulla Shamishi did when they broke into the military collective graves in Cyprus. Creon is scornful of supernatural sanctions – although there are differences between Sophocles' Creon and Anouilh's. The classical scholar, Segal, notes that there is a double meaning of earth in *Antigone*: 'for (Sophocles') Creon "earth" is a matter of political boundaries, a territory to be fought over, protected and ruled. Belonging to the "earth" of Thebes means adhering to the "laws of the earth" in the political sense. But for Antigone "earth" is her "ancestral land", *patria ge,* her bond with the inhabitants of Thebes, an inalienable right transmitted to the family' (Segal, 1981: 172–3). *Patria ge* it certainly is, but that identity is also exploited by the nation state, and therein lies the problem and the perversity of modern politics. In Cyprus along both sides of the ethnic divide, political authorities as heirs of Creon fabricated either a missing Polynices, or a bodyless Eteocles. In the Republic of Cyprus for many years, Creon claimed to speak for Antigone. The missing remained metaphorically and literally unburied, as the state claimed to speak on behalf of its Antigones to recover its missing-unburied, in its project for the recovery of ancestral lands as homes. The state thus utilized the language, sentiments, and history of Antigone to maintain Creon's rule. In the Turkish – occupied north, by contrast, the state fabricated its missing as Eteocles, but without the bodies. The women were encouraged to mourn because the state, as Creon's heir, needed not so much a Polynices, but Eteocles – heroes as sacrificial victims for the newly established polity, the Turkish Republic of Northern Cyprus. The female relatives of the missing were encouraged to mourn in the absence of bodies. The political authorities were not so much interested in recovering the bodies of the missing to give them proper burial, but in monumentalising their deaths to be mourned and buried, if necessary without their bodies. The Turkish Republic of Northern Cyprus must be one of the few places in the world where there are literally hundreds of officially sponsored private cenotaphs – tombs with names but no bodies – a perverse inversion of the two classical forms of public monuments: cenotaphs as public tombs of all those who died, or the Tombs of Unknown Soldiers which have bodies but no names.

Modern Creon wears many masks. But do we, as Antigone's heirs, 'assist' Creon in this masquerade?

NOTES

1. 'He will do what he has to do, and we will do what we have to do' (Anouilh, 1960: 18).
2. 'We are of a tribe that asks questions , and we ask them to the bitter end' (Anouilh, 1960: 58).
3 'Yes it is absurd; for nobody, for myself' (Anouilh, 1960: 46).
4. It is equally not difficult to understand why the German authorities permitted the play to be performed. Perhaps they believed that like the obsessive Creon they too were there to 'introduce some order in this absurd kingdom'; that once they 'took on the job', they 'must do it properly' (Anouilh, 1960: 48).

2
SUPPRESSED EXPERIENCES

∽ঞ৵৹

His brother Polynices
Who came back from exile intending to burn and destroy
His fatherland and the gods of his Fatherland,
To drink the blood of his kin, to make them slaves –
He is to have no grave, no burial,
No mourning from anyone; it is forbidden.
He is to be left unburied, left to be eaten
By dogs and vultures, a horror for all to see.

Creon in Sophocles' *Antigone*
(Lines 198–209. Translation by Watling 1947: 144)

Brief History of Inter-ethnic Relations

Cyprus, the third largest island in the Mediterranean, has had various rulers. The island was generally ethnically homogeneous, Greek – speaking Christian Orthodox, until the Ottoman Turks captured it from the Venetians in 1571. Gradually the population became more complex with some conversions to Islam and the immigration and transfer of Turks from mainland Turkey. In 1878 the island was transferred to Britain and Greek Cypriots began a political campaign for *enosis* or union with Greece. In the 1950s a Greek Cypriot secret organisation, EOKA, under the command of George Grivas, a Greek of Cypriot origin who had organised a right wing armed group in Greece in the Second World War, initiated an armed struggle against Britain, in favour of *enosis*. Instead of union with Greece the island was given independence with power sharing between the Greek and Turkish communities under the 1960 Zurich agreements, with Britain, Greece and Turkey as Guarantor Powers. The island was to have a Greek Cypriot President and a Turkish Cypriot Vice-President. Greek Cypriots elected their ethnarch, Archbishop Makarios, a charismatic figure who had led the anti-colonial political struggle, as their President. The Turks selected Dr F. Kuchuk as the Vice-President. Relations between Makarios and Grivas cooled and the latter, who had a huge following, left Cyprus for Greece.

Relations between Greek and Turkish Cypriots, generally peaceful for decades had plummeted when, during the 1955–59 'Emergency', colonial authorities uncertain of the loyalties of Greek Cypriots began recruiting Turkish Cypriot auxiliary policemen in place of the former to suppress Greek civilian demonstrations in favour of *enosis*. Turkish Cypriots alarmed at the prospect of becoming a minority in a potentially Greek state, insisted that if Greek Cypriots were given their *enosis*, they too should be allowed to form part of Turkey in a *taksim* (division) or double-*enosis*. A Turkish Cypriot underground armed organisation (*Volkan*, later *TMT* – the Turkish Cypriot Resistance Organisation) was established in 1955. Communal fighting broke out in summer 1958, and both EOKA and TMT soon attacked not just members of opposing ethnic groups, but also members of their own group. EOKA assassinated left-wing Greeks as 'traitors', and TMT murdered left-wing Turks because they were in alliance with left-wing Greeks who were far from keen on union with a then 'monarcho-fascist Greece'.[1]

Following the 1955–59 EOKA struggle, many young Greek Cypriot men who had taken up the gun were lionised and given government jobs of all sorts. But demand for government posts far outstripped the supply of educated young men, and the more (usually British-) educated newly-emergent middle class soon began to monopolise government posts – a source of great prestige in Cyprus, then still a largely rural society. Many Greek Cypriots were unhappy with the 1960 constitution that they considered gave an inordinate amount of power to the Turkish Cypriots. Relations between the two communities soon worsened over interpretations of the Constitution. Following a crisis in December 1963 when Makarios attempted to modify the Constitution, Greek Cypriot irregulars attacked Turkish Cypriot villages, and violence flared for a number of months. Violent clashes re-emerged in 1967. By early 1964, Turkish Cypriots began withdrawing to armed enclaves where the Greek Cypriots also blockaded them. In a considerable number of cases, they were ousted from their villages. Indeed some 25,000 Turkish Cypriots became refugees (or 'displaced persons'). According to the figure published by the Turkish Communal Chamber, the number of people receiving some assistance from the Red Crescent Relief amounted to about 56,000, including 25,000 displaced persons, 23,500 unemployed and 7,500 dependants of missing persons, disabled and others (TCHRC 1979: 75). In effect, Turkish Cypriots withdrew from the Republic of Cyprus, set up their own administration, and refused to pay taxes. They argue they were expelled from the Republic. Greek Cypriots imposed an embargo on 'strategic materials' which severely affected the quality of life, further strengthening the position of extremist elements among the Turkish Cypriots. The first disappearances (mainly of Turkish Cypriots) date from this period.

As union with Greece had not been achieved, many activists felt their efforts had been betrayed or unrecognised by the state, which was still largely neo-colonial in structure and sentiment. Many villagers and those who lacked a sophisticated political culture believed that *enosis* would remove the problem of being hostage to the Turkish Cypriots, as well as give them the power and status they believed they deserved. In the 1960s, it was unthinkable and traitorous to be anything but a Greek nationalist, and the military junta-dominated Greek government that seized power in 1967 expected total obedience from Nicosia. By the early 1970s the Greek Cypriot community split vertically between those in favour of immediate *enosis* and those in favour of it in theory but not in practice. Makarios seems to have became increasingly aware of the internal and external dangers that *enosis* posed for Cyprus (in particular, an invasion by Turkey which had been threatened in 1967, but was held back by U.S. President Johnson), but found himself unable to take a very firm line. Internal discontent by those largely excluded from power and government employment was skilfully exploited by mainland Greek army officers stationed to train the Greek Cypriot National Guard. With CIA funds they armed a new secret organisation called EOKA-B and Grivas returned secretly to Cyprus in 1971 to train and organise a destabilising campaign against the Republic. EOKA B found febrile support among the young, impressionable and marginalised. Bombings and assassinations were common. Massive amounts of money were funnelled secretly into the island. Uncertain of the loyalties of the mainland Greek-officered National Guard and of the police, Makarios was obliged to rely on unofficial *omadhes* (groups of armed men) linked to ex-fighters and politicians loyal to him, as well as on the large unarmed communist party and a smaller, but highly activist and armed socialist party (Panteli 1984: 392, Hitchens 1989: 61–100, Sant Cassia 1983).

With the death in hiding of Grivas in February 1974, EOKA B fell totally into the Greek junta's hands. On 2 July 1974, Makarios publicly accused the CIA-supported Greek military junta of attempts on his life, ordering the expulsion of Greek army officers from Cyprus. The Junta did not respond, but on 15 July the National Guard staged a coup, fierce fighting broke out between the Greek-officered army and right-wing *Griviki* nationalists on the one hand, and democratic *Makariaki* forces on the other. Fighting spread from Nicosia to other towns. Makarios was whisked away from the island by British forces. For some three days Kalashnikov-toting Greek Cypriot young men strutted around the villages imposing curfews on their fellow villagers, whilst mainland Greek officers conducted more ominous operations, imprisoning known Makarios supporters and communists for a fate unknown. A puppet regime was established under Nikos Sampson, an anti-Turk nationalist and ex-EOKA gunman. In the 1960s Sampson had become the owner of a virulent nationalist newspaper, and posed as a Greek patriot. He had led assaults on Turkish enclaves in 1963, and was widely feared by the Turkish Cypriots. Greece, a Guarantor Power of the constitution and territorial integrity of the Republic of Cyprus, had taken over the country. This was bound to provoke a response by Turkey, which on 20 July 1974 interpreted its role as the other Constitutional Guarantor Power to invade and restore the previous constitutional order, as well as to protect Turkish Cypriots. Ecevit, the Turkish Prime Minister, recalled 'the coup was the green light for our invasion' (Panteli, ibid: 232).

The invasion had two phases. The first invasion, effectively resisted by Greek Cypriots, lasted from 20 July to 30 July 1974 and resulted in the capture of a small area from Kyrenia in the north to Nicosia. There was then a cease-fire, but the Turks unilaterally abandoned negotiations on the 8 August and started their second invasion effectively sweeping everything before them in the north from Pirgos in the north west to Famagusta in the south east, cutting Nicosia in half. All resistance collapsed, but this was David taking on an army of Goliaths without his sling. The Greek Cypriots were demoralised, leaderless, and hopelessly outgunned. Turkey fielded a huge army, had total air and naval control and deployed heavy weapons, Greece 's junta had collapsed, the United Kingdom (the other Guarantor Power) did nothing. Kissinger's State Department actively supported the Turkish invasion, which effectively resulted in the partition of Cyprus – a plan that had long been mooted by U.S. politicians. Greek Cypriot disappearances date from the 1974 coup and invasion.

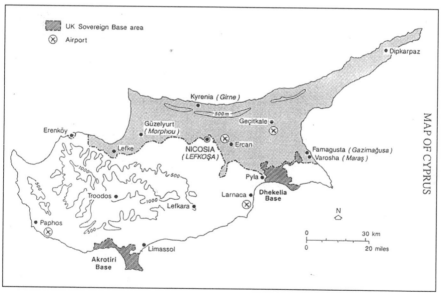

Map 1 Map of Cyprus showing Current Division due to
Turkish Occupation and Turkified Toponomy.

Turkey interpreted her role as Guarantor Power to allow her the right to a military intervention and occupied some 37 per cent of the island in the north (see Map 1). Turkey's ostensible aim was to protect Turkish Cypriots, but whereas she had the right to restore the *status quo ante*, it is highly debatable whether she had the right to effectively partition the island, occupy 36 per cent of the territory, expel its 200,000 (Greek) inhabitants, a third of the island's total population, and eventually install a puppet regime. During the coup an unknown number of Greek Cypriots were killed in internecine fighting. Irregular Greek forces then killed unarmed Turkish Cypriots in various villages. The killings accelerated after Turkish invasion. Turkish Cypriots were justified in feeling seriously threatened. In turn, during the Turkish 'peace operation', some 1600 Greek Cypriots went 'missing' behind the advancing Turkish army, presumed killed by the Turks or irregular Turkish Cypriot paramilitaries. In 1976 Greek Cypriots in the North, fearful for their own safety, moved South, and Turkish Cypriots in the South, similarly fearful, but also under threat from Turkish authorities, moved North. The two communities are now separated and there have been ineffectual attempts at unification within a new constitutional federal framework. At the time of writing (July 2002), new talks under UN auspices have begun between the leaders of the two communities.

The Missing

The case of The Missing in Cyprus is a highly political issue not just between the Greek and Turkish Cypriots and Turkey, but has domestic repercussions in Greek Cypriot society which I explore in this book. It raises issues of the allocation of responsibility and culpability, and the tension between civic-political transparency and ethnic responsibility, but is also a means to talk about the past, present and future.

There are major differences in the manner in which the Greek and Turkish Cypriots regard the Missing. Briefly put, whereas the Turkish Cypriots regard their missing as *kayipler* (disappeared as dead or lost), the Greek Cypriots regard their missing as of unknown fate, *agnoumeni*: as not-(yet)-recovered either at best as living prisoners, or at worst as concealed bodies requiring proper and suitable burials. In normal Greek usage, the term *agnoumenos* is often used immediately after natural disasters (e.g., earthquakes) and largescale accidents (e.g., accidents at sea) to mean 'fate unknown' when there is still some hope for survival. Significantly, whilst the English rendition of *agnoumeni* now also includes 'disappearances', the Greek Cypriots do not use the proper Greek word for this (*ksefanistikan*) which implies a finality and non-recoverability, like the *desparicidos* in Argentina and elsewhere, although they tap the nuances of the affinity to this term for political reasons. They prefer to employ the nuances of 'not known' (as yet), but-potentially-knowable. The continued use of the term is thus a marker of, and insinuates, uncertainty. There is no sense of this in the Turkish word *kayipler*, which means dead, fallen, lost. Turkish Cypriots lost a considerable number of civilians between 1963–64 and in 1974. By contrast, the Greek Cypriots claim their Missing date from the 1974 Turkish invasion. The Turkish Cypriots therefore lost their people over an 11-year period with two intense periods, whereas the Greek Cypriots lost the majority of their missing in a single short period, a traumatic couple of months. This was bound to affect the perception of their losses. Propaganda leaflets from both sides gave the following figures for missing persons: Turkish Cypriot, 803, and Greek Cypriot, 1619 persons.

Although the Greek Cypriots claim more than double missing persons, the proportional percentage of the missing is much greater for the Turkish Cypriots whose community was approximately a quarter the size of the Greek Cypriots. Proportionally therefore, the Turkish Cypriots appear to have suffered at least double the losses of the Greek Cypriots. This would further have exacerbated their sense of insecurity and loss. The theme of insecurity is one that is emphasised by both groups. For a beleaguered minority group like the Turkish Cypriots, the disappearances of 1963–64, often a series of unrelated vengeful attacks on individuals, could easily have appeared like a pattern and an ominous plan for their destruction. Indeed, there were disclosures of reputed plans, such as the AKRITAS plan which purported to project a plan at ethnic cleansing. To the Greek Cypriots, a minority of some half a million on the borders of 60 million mainland Turks, the sudden loss of all these men is a harbinger of the destructive potential of their historically hated erstwhile oppressors. Both groups thus capitalise on the power of powerlessness in order not to make concessions, especially over constitutional matters, and they cite the issue of missing persons as an example of their victimisation.

The Turkish Cypriots claim that 99 per cent of their missing were innocent civilians, whilst the Greek Cypriots lost mainly military casualties. For the Turkish Cypriots the problem of the missing began not in 1974, the year of the coup and the Turkish invasion, but in 1963, the first year of intercommunal troubles in the Republic of Cyprus. By contrast, they claim the majority of missing Greek Cypriots (61.19 per cent) are military personnel, and that the majority of Greek Cypriot missing were casualties of the coup and post-coup violence.[2] The Greek Cypriots have long officially claimed that their missing were captured by Turkish army and seen alive, and that they disappeared in captivity.

There are further differences in perception. On one hand, the Turkish Cypriots perceive their missing as dead, and have long been encouraged to do so by their leaders who wished to distance the Turkish Cypriot community from the Greek Cypriot community, whom they blame as the aggressors and culprits. The Greek Cypriots, by contrast, have long maintained that their missing might be alive as they were captured alive, and that the main culprits are not the Turkish Cypriots but the Turkish army occupying half the island. Turkish Cypriots maintain that these men died in the hostilities or in the coup, but have refused to return their bodies for reburial. They state that the issue 'is a smoke screen for covering the terrifying cost in human life during the Sampson coup' (TCHRC 1979: 92). For the Greek Cypriots the Missing, together with the enclaved still living in the north, and the refugees, constitute a power and semantic field for talking about the past, and their contemporary predicament. The Greek Cypriot bypassing of the Turkish Cypriots as the culprits is consistent with their general claim that difficulties between the Greek and Turkish Cypriots were (and are) an internal matter, that 'we got on like brothers in the past'. The Greek Cypriots have largely cast the problem of the Missing as an unresolved international problem, a humanitarian issue, and a means to talk about their political oppression: the occupation of a sovereign state's territory by another state, and the creation of refugees and the enclaved in occupied territories which are presented in official maps as 'temporarily inaccessible because of the Turkish invasion'.[3] By contrast, for the Turkish Cypriots the issue of the Missing is a closed chapter: an example of their oppression by the Greek Cypriots in the Republic of Cyprus, a state of affairs that the Turkish 'peace operation' ended. Thus whereas the Turkish Cypriots appear to wish the matter closed in its present manifestation, but keep the memory and memorials of their oppression alive, the Greek Cypriots wish to maintain the issue open in a present continuous tense, as an issue that is very much alive and will only be buried when the missing are finally laid to rest, when their bodies are returned.[4]

The two groups employ different persuasive strategies to convince listeners of their case. Turkish Cypriots appeal to 'reason' or 'rationality' to convince third parties that the Greek Cypriot missing are actually dead and war casualties, and that the Greek Cypriot leadership has concealed the truth for propaganda purposes. They quote testimonies of Greek Cypriots to show that there were far greater casualties during the coup than was admitted by the Sampson, Junta-controlled, government, and that the Greek Cypriots are blaming the Turks and Turkish Cypriots for Greek Cypriot induced crimes. By contrast, they emphasise that their missing are dead because of a conscious policy of genocide. Greek Cypriots deny that their missing persons died during the coup, claiming that these casualties were low and that they know who was killed during the coup. They tend to appeal to 'emotion' and 'sentiments' to convince third parties of evidence from organizations such as Amnesty International, and the European Commission of Human Rights (Council of Europe) that their missing are victims of the crime of enforced disappearance by Turkey: 'it is a crime which perpetuates the sufferings of the missing and their families, a crime which constitutes the most flagrant violation of the basic and fundamental human rights of both the missing persons and us, their families' (PCC: 7). Parallel persuasive strategies were employed in post dirty-war Argentina (Robben 1995). As we shall see, the situation is much more complex. Greek Cypriot claims that their missing disappeared after the invasion are not as watertight as they initially claimed. Over the last twenty years, evidence has become known that many died during the invasion and were buried hurriedly. However, there is equally strong evidence that a good number of men disappeared after being captured by Turkish forces.

Such widely divergent official interpretations suggest not just a lack of trust between the two communities, a passive mistrust of the other, but an active *trust in distrusting* the other. Trust is not just a social relationship, it is also a culturally informed perspective and expectations that one brings to bear in dealing with others (see Gambetta 1988). This is not merely an inability to agree on events in the past, but rather a tendency to be so profoundly attached to the paradigmatic explanatory value of one's official interpretation of the past, that it must be critically important for the community's navigation of itself in the future. In addition, it suggests that the Missing are not merely casualties, but means to talk about the past, present and future. Writing about post-socialist politics in Eastern Europe Veredery has pithily observed: 'Dead bodies ... have properties that make them particularly effective political symbols. They are thus excellent means for accumulating something essential to political transformation: symbolic capital' (1999: 33). One can imagine how much more over-determined as symbolic capital absent or hidden dead bodies are. Disappearance is a political act. So too is the disappearance of the evidence. It follows that the disappearance of individuals is not just the pursuit of political struggles in the present. It is setting the stage for a series of stories that make the past and emplot the future. In the next section I examine how the problem first emerged in 1963–64 to sour relations between the two communities.

First Disappearances

Although international awareness of the problem of missing persons in Cyprus emerged in 1974, the problem dates from 1963, the year of the first serious intercommunal clashes. Despite Greek Cypriot claims then, and to a certain extent nowadays, violence did not emerge 'spontaneously' between the two communities in December 1963. Unhappiness by the Greek Cypriots over the Zurich agreements and the Constitution had predisposed both sides to view the current situation as unsatisfactory. The Greek Cypriots believed that the Constitution gave the Turkish Cypriots a disproportionate power relative to their demographic strength which had held up the workings of government, whilst the Turkish Cypriots insisted on a strict interpretation of their constitutional rights even when this proved impractical. Patrick, who conducted geographical fieldwork in 1970, notes that 'both communities expected the 1960 constitution to prove unworkable, and that they anticipated and planned for an armed clash' (1976: 37). The veteran Greek Cypriot politician Glavkos Clerides wrote in his memoirs:

> Unfortunately, what were to be contingency plans, should everything else fail, became the priority and the answer in the search for a way to break the deadlock. It is true that both paramilitary organisations were defensive in their origin, but unwittingly, once intransigent attitudes prevented solutions, the defensive position was slowly abandoned and both sides were ready for offensive action to achieve their aims. (1989: 196)

25

Clerides is perhaps too coy to acknowledge that politicians on both sides were reluctant to hold back paramilitary forces that had been established during the EOKA campaign. There is evidence that nationalist politicians, both Greek and Turkish Cypriot, had strong links to their ex-comrades in paramilitary groups, and may even have aided and abetted them. As the debate between Blok (1972) and Hobsbawm (1985) over violence and banditry indicates, prolonged violence by illegal elements usually requires protection by powerful individuals.[5] Nevertheless Clerides notes the potent dynamic mix between the desire by each side to display victimhood (and thus assume intransigence in dealing with the other side), and that certain interests on both sides desired confrontation.[6] As Patrick noted:

> There were in existence a number of armed Greek Cypriot gangs who refused to become integrated into the 'official secret army' .... These groups did not formulate any cohesive political and military strategy. Their prime objective was to exact revenge on Turkish Cypriots for events which occurred during the enosis campaign of 1955–59, to indulge their fantasies for adventure, and to enhance their own local social and political ends. (1976: 36)

Turkish Cypriots subsequently claimed that the violence was the expression of a secret Greek Cypriot plan (the AKRITAS plan) to exterminate them. Whilst 'Secret Plans' were prepared by both sides to deal with (and anticipate, according to one's perspective) a rupture between the two communities (in a conspiracy culture that is both the product and the creator of conflict, the signalling of secrecy further valorises and authenticates that which is signified as secret), they could be seen more as expressions of intent by key individuals within both communities. An examination of newspaper reports at the time suggests that the situation was far more unmanageable than any purported plans could have envisaged, anticipated, or even capitalised upon. Patrick confirms this: 'Chaos prevailed; it was more a matter of persuading, rather than ordering, independent [Greek Cypriot] captains to follow directions .... The various dissident armed gangs remained a law unto themselves for at least six more months' (ibid: 36). Yet, from the perspective of the Turkish Cypriots, such unanticipatable arbitrariness must have exacerbated their uncertainty.

Hostage-taking emerged as a central feature of Greek, then Turkish, paramilitary activity. The essential feature of hostage-taking is that it is a complex, multi-dimensional practice subject to conflicting interpretations. It is usually found in situations where two opposing groups are intermixed, and uncertain about the future development of hostilities. It is found where there is a lack of distinction between combatants and non-combatants, because of fear, or because of the 'unofficial' nature of the conflict. From the perspective of the victim, it is an aggressive act towards 'civilians', but for the perpetrators, it could be 'justified' as an attempt to 'move civilians to safety' or to isolate potential supporters of one's enemies. It could also be an attempt to remove hidden enemies from hostilities, an insurance against future attacks, and a discouragement to opponents. Hostage-taking is both the seeding and the harvesting of fear.

The above situations can equally be described in terms of detaining opponents. Hostage-taking however has a specific 'anthropological' significance. It could be seen as a travesty of *filoxenia*, or hospitality, the idea that a stranger is safe from attack at the host's home (Pitt-Rivers 1977), a central feature of Mediterranean culture since Homeric times. It also implies the shedding of blood of disarmed individuals. It thus bears comparison to sacrifice, of which it is an inversal. It is a taxonomic seizing of the other, a means to create 'otherness'. Through the simulation of 'substitution', it works in an opposite way to sacrifice. In sacrifice, substitution is a signifier. In hostage-taking, substitution is the signified. Its referent, in contrast to sacrifice, is not specific. Whereas in sacrifice, 'A', the substitution-signifier, stands for 'B', the substituted-signified, in hostage-taking the referent is general and diffuse, and can be interpreted in different ways. The hostage, 'A', seems to taken as a substitution-signifier, but the taking without an agreement or certainty on the substitution-signified is actually a sign to simulate substitution. One never fully knows for what type of (past or future) substitution hostages have been taken, or what will happen next. It is a simulation of 'exchange' to subvert exchange – a patterned and relatively predictable relation between persons or between things. By breaking down the distinction between persons and things, the whole 'exchange' is rendered unpredictable, not pursued with an aim of parity, or 'getting even', but rather with the aim of keeping one's opponents off-guard. All the cards lie in the opponents' hands. 'A' thus becomes the substitution-signified. Hostage-taking becomes a pure sign without a referent; it indicates that for your opponent anything is substitutable. It thus generates open-ended rather than specific fears. As Zur notes for Guatemala, 'kidnapping is discontinuity personified' (1998: 224).

There is little evidence from the statements of the participants at the time that the 1963–64 violence between the two communities was viewed then as the enactment of long-term plans,[7] although in Cyprus it is always possible to find different views. Such interpretations emerged later, partly in the light of memoirs and released official documents. They should not necessarily be discarded as the products of a febrile imagination. However, information then was restricted and tightly controlled. The press was neither independent nor investigative. There was a premium on the management of information. The Greek Cypriot leadership wished to present Turkish Cypriot violence as arbitrary, criminal, vindictive, and as a revolt 'fomented to provide an excuse for Turkey to invade and impose partition'.[8] Patrick notes this generated an 'intense Greek Cypriot enmity against the Turkish Cypriot community and encouraged a number of revenge murders'.[9] Greek Cypriots were always worried that Turkey would find an 'excuse to invade'.[10] Turkish Cypriots presented violence against them as the actions of murderous anti-Turk Greeks from which they required protection by Turkey. Clearly both sides wished to present themselves as victims. Because of information management, the numbers of deaths and wounded was uncertain, hostage-taking was presented as a 'removal to safety', and events that appeared in press reports to be spontaneous, unconnected, localised acts of violence, were related in agency, in response, and in the narratives the participants employed to guide and legitimise their actions.[11] On Christmas Eve, 1963, the newspaper reporter Gibbons claims 21 Turkish in-patients in Nicosia General Hospital disappeared.[12] In Kumsal 9 people were killed and 150 people were taken hostage; 'some of the hostages were never seen again'[13] although he gives no figures. By Christmas Eve 1963, 59 Turks had been killed. At Omorphita on 27 December, 550 were taken hostage and kept at the Kykkos school,[14] where they joined the 150 Kumsal hostages. 550 of these were released on 31 December 1963. Gibbons, a somewhat jaundiced and unreliable observer, claimed that the remainder of these 700 (i.e. 150 Turks) were selected and shot. He claims that an English woman teacher who witnessed the shooting was immediately put on the first available London bound plane by the High Commission, and 'her story was never made public'.[15] There is no other evidence of this, so the story is somewhat suspect. A day later, when news started emerging of the killings, the Turks complained about organised murder. Yorgadjis, the Minister of the Interior, rejected this and displayed the disfigured bodies of Greeks to the press.

Because of the difficulty of communication and the dispersed nature of the Turkish community which had not yet moved to safe havens, the Turkish Cypriot leadership lacked information on what was happening in those crucial first days. As Patrick noted, confirmed by my own fieldwork, 'outside of Nicosia, the Turkish Cypriot community was completely bewildered by the course of events' (ibid: 49) The following interview indicates that initially individuals had no real inkling how things would develop, that some Greek Cypriot gunmen ran amok, and that initially Turkish Cypriots' relatives received (ineffectual) protection as well as information from Greek Cypriot friends.

> My father disappeared in 1963. He was one of the first people to be declared missing. On Sunday afternoon on the 22 of December 1963, he went to work as usual at the factory on the Greek side of Nicosia. By this time most Turkish men had been discouraged by both Greek and Turkish Cypriots from going to work there, but my father liked his job and continued to work there. On the evening of the 22 December a fight broke out at about 10.00pm in the centre of the city. Four people were killed and many more were injured. The fight was near the factory and my brother and I were worried that my father might become involved when he went on his inspection of the factory grounds. We telephoned him and told him that there had been trouble. We told him to come home as he may be injured if Greek Cypriots identified him as a Turk. He said he would leave straight away, but we have never seen him since.
>
> I did not discover what had happened until a few weeks later. A friend of my father, who was also a Greek Cypriot, told me what had happened. Shortly after we had spoken to my father, a gang of EOKA men went into the factory and asked if there were

any Turkish Cypriots working there. The factory owner said that there was only one, but that he had just left. The EOKA men went onto the roof of the factory and shot my father. We went to the factory to confront them about my father, but they said that all they knew was that he had gone missing on duty.

Thankfully, due to the Turkish Cypriot government's mercifulness my mother is supported by the money that they give to her. Turkey is like a parent to us, and has given us the justice we demand for our people. My mother has been very ill since my father's death. Look at her; see how her skin has lost all its colour. She was once brown but now she is so white and old. Did you know that on the Greek side the teachers tell the children that the best Turk is a dead Turk?

Here we teach the children peace.[16]

I have obtained independent verification from Greek Cypriot sources about the veracity of this account. It is even more ironic and tragic that it was individuals who had good relations with Greek Cypriots who were killed.

Map 2 produced by the Turkish Cypriot leadership for the United Nations, shows the distribution of Turkish Cypriot missing persons. Although the missing are distributed throughout the island, the majority were concentrated in the centre and the north of the island. There were comparatively few missing Turkish Cypriots from the Paphos district, which had a large Turkish population. What is of interest is that the missing appear to have come from villages and certainly not cities. The map shows that a considerable number of Turkish Cypriots disappeared on the roads. Thus seventeen persons disappeared on the Nicosia-Limassol road in 1963–64.

In Christmas 1963, the British High Commissioner in Nicosia foresaw the need to bring the ICRC (International Committee of the Red Cross) to Cyprus because a conflict situation was developing fast. Article 3 of the Geneva Convention specifies that in the case of internal disturbances the International Committee should offer its services. On 1 January 1964, the ICRC sent a delegate to Nicosia. Two weeks later, owing to the spread of the troubles, the ICRC increased its representation. The ICRC did much important humanitarian work. It is probable that its presence dampened the initial enthusiasm for hostage-taking, and enabled the release of the majority of missing persons who were then in captivity. This account is based upon their written reports, published material of the period (including newspapers), and interviews on both sides of the island. Apparently, as with other cases of official records, the records of the ICRC went missing in Cyprus. One must not minimise the fact that ICRC officials also experienced considerable difficulties.

The ICRC did two major things. First, it looked after displaced persons. Many Turkish Cypriots were moving from mixed neighbourhoods and villages to the safety of more ethnically homogeneous areas such as northern Nicosia. They were also being pushed out by the aggressive actions of irregular Greek Cypriot paramilitary groups, as well in some cases by the Turkish fighters. Many displaced Turkish Cypriots were living under tents and in very difficult conditions. The

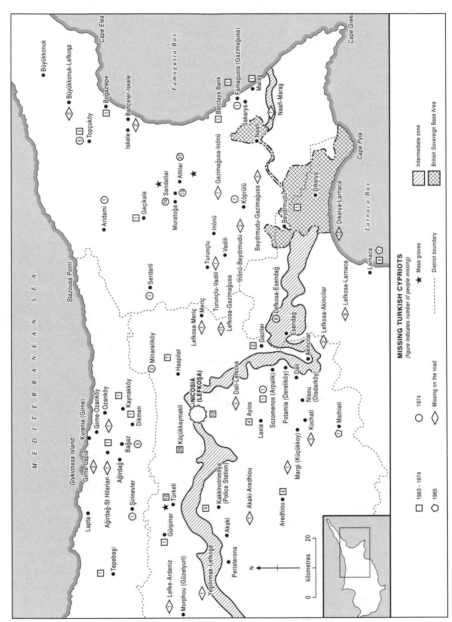

Map 2 Distribution of Turkish Cypriot Missing Persons, 1963–74.

ICRC conducted surveys to prepare relief operations for the displaced Turkish Cypriots.

Second, they visited detainees and tried to trace missing persons. This was much more difficult to effect. Here, it is important to discuss briefly the situation which was very confused to the participants as the issue of Missing Persons slowly began to evolve. It is also important to recognise that the bland language of academic political history and the highly charged language of propaganda leaflets and press releases by both sides, as well as accounts published later, rarely capture either the complexity of a series of events that occur over a particular territory, or the evolving consciousness of the participants, including how they responded to those events. Social life is predictable only insofar that the structures we establish, including patterned anticipation of other people's actions, permit us to recognise current situations and collectively emplot the future in ways where even what is unknown is considered collectively unproblematic and 'natural'. Between 21 December 1963 and May 1964, and particularly at certain times within that period, social life in Cyprus became highly unpredictable, uncertain, and unmanageable, not just for ordinary people, but even for politicians who in some cases were just responding to events. In other cases, they may well have been creating situations in order to simulate that they were in control. We need to try to grasp how individuals perceived the situation, how some responded to the immediate situations they found themselves in, how others pursued (or even thought they were pursuing) hidden agendas, how some others cynically took advantage of the uncertainty to pursue their own (petty or even criminal) aims, how others genuinely thought that their actions were meritorious, necessary, and good, and finally how such actions were interpreted. It is important to try to understand what occurred in 1963–64 as it unfolded to the participants, because the experiences of this period had a fundamental bearing on 1974. The experiences of 1963–64 were not just an incident of inter-communal conflict including the meddling of Greece and Turkey. They were also a response to events and their mismanagement by various actors in the two communities that created anticipation, fears, and experiences to guide future responses. They established a pattern of action, interpretation, and counteraction based upon readings of the past that guided actors in 1974.

According to Gibbons, Turkish officials such as Osman Orek, the Defence Minister, did not know of the hostage-taking. At a meeting between Makarios, Orek and the UK High Commissioner, Sir Arthur Clark, Makarios as representative of the Greeks was accused by the St John's Ambulance representative, and the ICRC delegation, of condoning the keeping of hostages.[17] Makarios agreed to supply a list of names and to have the hostages released as soon as possible.[18] Gibbons claims that the Turks decided that they could not implement the cease-fire until the hostages were released. This is doubtful, and illogical. He is more justified in his claim that the Turks had no idea initially how many hostages had been taken.[19] Gibbons further claims that the Justice Minister, Stella Soulioti, a confidante of Makarios, phoned Orek on Christmas Day and promised to hand over the list. Mrs Soulioti was the Honorary President of the Red Cross Society of Cyprus and a person of high moral and personal probity. Orek demanded to know the fate of some Turkish nurses at Nicosia General Hospital, who it transpired, had been personally brought to safety by Makarios, alarmed by some earlier disappearance of Turkish in-patients. Orek claimed to Gibbons that Mrs Soulioti 'assured him that they and the hostages were safe and under Red Cross supervision'. This seems like a genuine mistake. Gibbons notes: 'Assuming that Mrs Souliotou was telling the truth as she knew it, she must been unaware that 150 of the hostages had been taken away, lined up, murdered and their bodies disposed of.'[20] There seems correct insofar as Soulioti was talking about some hostages. However, there is no independent evidence, including from the ICRC published reports, that 150 hostages were murdered and disposed of. Certainly their bodies were never found, and the do not appear in the lists of missing persons subsequently presented by the Turkish Cypriot leadership.

It is also clear, however, that the authorities were not in control of the situation. Many Greek irregulars and ex-EOKA militants were either in the police force under the control of Yeorgadjis or donning policemen's uniforms. Some other bodies were found. On 14 January 1964, 21 bodies were exhumed at the Turkish Cemetery in Ayios Vasilios (near Nicosia). The newspaper accounts were confused and suggested that they were the 21 patients who had died in hospital. The Greek Cypriot authorities claimed that as the Turkish Cypriot leadership had refused to take the bodies back, they had to be buried quickly. It seemed that some of these bodies were hostages taken from the village of Ayios Vasilios, who had been buried with the patients. The next day, three Greek Cypriots were abducted. A pattern was quickly developing of an exchange which consisted of abductions that followed a disclosure of killings through previous abductions.

By the time the ICRC arrived in Cyprus, patterns of violence had already taken shape. By the end of January 1964, the ICRC had obtained the release of 30 detainees. The delegation had also visited 27 other persons under detention in various places of arrest and prisons. However, the Annual Report for 1964 noted that this activity 'came up against increasing difficulties'. It pointed to the complete separation of the two communities which 'together with the extreme tension existing, gave rise to a considerable number of tragic situations' although it did not specify. On 23 January 1964, Jean Pierre Schoenholzer of the ICRC noted that some 20–25 Greek and 200 Turkish Cypriots were reported as missing. Throughout January 1964, there were drip-feed releases. But on 12 February, 1964, Dr Kuchuk's allegation that 150 Turkish Cypriot missing must have been killed by Greek Cypriots in cold blood was rejected by the Government as fantastic and he was accused of wanting to 'fan the flames in an effort to justify the recent callous Turkish ambushes … his aim (being) to keep tension high in order to promote sinister political ends'.[21] Over the next days some Greek Cypriots went missing. Many of those who went missing in January were isolated, vulner-

able, individuals – either (Greek) shepherds tending their flocks in remote coun-
tryside (animal and tractor theft thrived in such conditions), or itinerant Turks
picked up at roadblocks, tradesmen carrying cash, etc. Kuchuk renewed his claim
on 27 February as a 'massacre'. On 2 March, he listed Turkish Cypriot losses as
36 dead, 196 missing and 603 wounded. On 7 March, Makarios repeated his
order for the release of Turkish Cypriot hostages by the Greeks while Kuchuk said
that 207 Turkish Cypriots were still being held, which suggests uncertainty over
their fate. On that day the leaders agreed to an exchange of hostages. The Greek
Cypriots turned over 49 Turkish Cypriots, and the Turkish Cypriots 4 Greek
Cypriots, but the Turkish Cypriots expected more releases and presumed that an
additional 176 Turkish Cypriots had been killed. Fighting was still breaking out
in different places. The ICRC report for March noted that there were still
hostages, especially in the Nicosia region. A highly placed third-party source told
me in 1997 that the ICRC representative had confided: 'the real problem was that
the Turkish Cypriots disappeared practically in front of us. The policemen were
around but they told us nothing'. On the other hand, the ICRC representative
admitted that there were Greek Cypriot policemen who protected Turkish Cypriots. It was evident from the releases that 'many of the hostages of both communities had been cruelly treated by their captors. This exchange, which had been
negotiated to reduce inter-communal tension immediately increased inter-communal enmity. Within 24 hours of this exchange, a number of shooting incidents
had occurred. It seems clear that Turkish Cypriot anger over the hostage issue may
have fomented some of this violence'.[22] The day of the exchange Turkish Cypriots took as hostages hundreds of Greek Cypriots who were shopping at the
Paphos municipal market.

On 27 April 1964, Turkish Cypriot women, relatives of missing persons,
demonstrated against the UN in Ataturk Square. In that month 49 hostages were
released, welcomed, and met by more than three thousand people. Soon after Mr
Kuchuk announced to (the ICRC delegate) his intention to make a similar gesture with respect to Greek hostages.[23] The pattern was that when killings took
place some abductions followed.

In May following an incident in Famagusta, where three mainland Greeks
and one Greek Cypriot policeman were killed, 32 Turks were abducted. The UN
representative Galo Plaza made representations to Makarios who denounced the
taking of hostages on May 16. On 27 May 1964 Kuchuk again repeated that 223
Turkish Cypriots were still missing since last December: 'I shudder to think that
these innocent Turks, among whom there are women and elderly men have been
murdered in cold blood ... The act of taking hostages and murdering them is
worse than cannibalism'.[24] In response Makarios admitted that Turks had been
abducted by irresponsible Greek elements and had probably been murdered. He
also asserted that individuals who were against the present Turkish Cypriot leadership had been murdered and their names included on lists of missing persons as

persons abducted by Greeks. He appealed once again against the taking of hostages. The ICRC report for May noted:

> After long and difficult setbacks the ICRC delegation was able to have released 4 policemen and a Greek civilian who were being kept as hostages in the Turkish sector of Nicosia. Also in March, four Turk hostages were released by the Greek Cypriot authorities. This brought respectively to 16 the number of Greek and 96 the Turkish hostages released.[25]

In June, the ICRC made systematic investigations in various villages of the island. This resulted in the discovery alive of thirty-six missing Turkish Cypriots. It noted however that the situation remained troubled, and the taking of hostages continued despite the presence of UN troops and the efforts of the ICRC delegation. Consequently, the ICRC addressed an urgent appeal on 28 May 1964 to the interested parties and particularly to Archbishop Makarios who replied that the Government of the Republic totally disapproved of any taking of hostages, as well as all reprisals.[26] On 20 June 1964 the ICRC found that three Turkish Cypriots on the missing list were living at home. By the end of June, 251 Turkish Cypriots were still missing, reduced to 208 Turks and 38 Greeks by the end of October. In his report to the Security Council on 15 June 1964, U Thant concluded that 'Little hope remains that they are alive'.

The following is an interview with a Turkish Cypriot teacher from Yeni Bogazici whose father disappeared. It brings out some important themes.

> My father disappeared on 16 March 1963 from Pervola together with his brother-in-law. He was a gardener. My father used to deliver vegetables every day to Nicosia. My father had a lot of guts. He had already been captured twice by the Greeks. He had a Greek friend who had saved him. When he was stopped at checkpoints he used to give sacks of artichokes as bribes to let him through He wasn't involved in any fighting or any organisation, or anything like that. He just did his job. One day when returning from Nicosia (probably carrying money from some sales, PSC) they captured him and he spent the night in a cell where he was seen by another Turkish Cypriot who was saved. The UN traced him to Aradippou where the trail went cold. They believe he was killed and his body dissolved in lime kilns ... .
>
> After about four days, we ceased hoping that he was kidnapped or alive and gave up all hope. If my father had been taken prisoner by the army then there would have been a chance, but as irregulars and bandits picked him up, we did not think he had much of a chance. We went to the (British) UN forces but we could not go to the Police because they were linked to EOKA. At that time, we could not travel out of the enclave so we could not leave and talk to our MPs. It was tit for tat then. There were ultra-nationalist Greeks murdering Turks. Maybe they were enjoying what they were doing, like the Klu Klux Klan. Perhaps they were getting a kick out of it. Although we had a Communal Chamber, we were completely unprepared for what happened. The Turkish Cypriot Communal Chamber was stuck in a room. We were completely under siege so we could not communicate with each other. It was still very 'hot' in March at

that time; when there was a skirmish the (Turkish Cypriots) would also shoot at the UN, almost to provoke them and get them involved. The British took down the details of the missing persons. It took one and a half years to get the £5 monthly cheque (for my father) because it was so difficult to get anywhere. ... We never got any information or serious news. I know I had a father because his photograph appears in an English book with his name and his date of birth .... Inside, I want to believe he is alive. We want to know where they are buried and to carry out our religious duties. It gives us great pain that we cannot do so.... We still hope. Logic tells me he is dead but my heart tells me something different ...We also find it very hard to accept that the *shehitler* (TMT fighters) were and are treated as heroes, but the *kayipler* (missing) are not.[27]

Conclusion

The missing in 1963–64 were primarily hostages who disappeared over a relatively long period (some four months). This period was one of great collective uncertainty for the Turks who constituted the majority of the missing. There was a climate of mass fear. 1963–64 seems to have consisted of two periods, and created two categories of missing. The first period, from 21–31 December 1963 was the 'hot', uncontrolled, phase of major clashes and collective disappearances. The majority of Turks disappeared during this period. Here whole groups disappeared, members of villages. These disappearances were consciously designed to intimidate the Turkish Cypriots. The second period from January to June 1964 was more cautious and marked by the disappearances of individuals or small groups, spread over a longer period. These were opportunistic exploitations of the situation by paramilitary groups for banditry and for self-aggrandisement. It was thus difficult for the Greek Cypriot leadership to control the situation. Because hostages were being released gradually right up to March 1964, relatives continued to expect that their missing kin could still be alive. Disappearances were a reflection of, and influenced by, military clashes occurring in various parts of the island. Usually a major clash or a killing was followed by a disappearance of a member of the opposing group a few days later. They can be seen as part of a negative exchange or negative reciprocity between the two groups. Yet some individuals on the Greek side took advantage of the prevailing climate and used the cover of confusion and uncertainty, and the legitimisation of 'patriotism', to rob and kill ordinary Turkish civilians in the course of their business. Many of these disappeared were individuals who travelled from one community to the other in the course of their work (e.g. butchers, petty traders, etc.). They carried cash, but were also suspected as peddlers of information, as runners or members of TMT. Suspicion of being a member of TMT legitimated killings, and it was easy to plant information that someone was a member of TMT to pre-justify a planned killing. Greek Cypriots disappeared more as vengeance attacks on isolated individuals. By contrast, the pattern of disappearances in 1974 was different.

By 1968, the Turkish Cypriot leadership appear to have considered missing Turkish Cypriots as dead. As far as I could ascertain, the Turkish Cypriot leadership never published a list of missing persons in the press. On the Greek Cypriot side by contrast, there was never a judicial or police investigation into the disappearances of the Turkish Cypriots. Nor did the Greek Cypriot authorities fully recognise the fact that there were thirty-eight missing Greeks, as that would have been tantamount to an acknowledgement that the authorities did not fully control the island.[28] They were erased by the leadership. By the end of 1965 the ICRC representatives could do no more and returned to Geneva.

NOTES

1. Ironically the use of Turks not only provoked the inevitable Greek complaints of collusion but they were ineffective in the policing of the Turkish community.

2. This figure corresponds to the number of reservists/soldiers submitted by the Greek Cypriot authorities, men between the ages of 16–39. The statement is correct but is somewhat disingenuous. Until 1974 the Turkish Cypriots did not technically possess an army, although many men were involved in military activities as members of irregular paramilitary groups. Nevertheless, it appears correct that a number of Turkish Cypriots were chosen taxonomically as victims of Greek Cypriot aggression and were innocent civilians.

3. Thus, the Greek Cypriots appear largely uninterested in the pre-1974 casualties, mainly Turkish Cypriots.

4. For a discussion on views of history see Papadakis (1993).

5. See also Sant Cassia (1993). Martin Packard, a Royal Navy officer seconded to the UN in Cyprus at the time, also noted the lack of central government control over local strongmen in the outlying regions (1966: 230).

6. Clerides (ibid: 196–97).

7. Patrick (ibid: 36).

8. Patrick (ibid: 38).

9. Patrick (ibid: 49).

10. S. Panteli, (1990: 198).

11. Patrick notes that the published or claimed casualty figures were massaged. Some figures or Turkish Cypriot deaths include some who were killed accidentally by their own hand or by other Turkish Cypriots. Greek Cypriot deaths are probably understated (ibid: 46).

12. H.S. Gibbons (1997: 113); Panteli (1990: 199). *The Guardian* later quoted a secret report from Commander Packard sent to Cyprus to trace missing persons: 'One of Packard's first tasks was to try to find out what had happened to the Turkish hospital patients. Secret discussions took place with a Greek minister in the collapsed government. After a brief investigation, he was able to confirm local rumours. It appeared that the Greek medical staff had slit the Turkish patients' throats as they lay in their beds. Their bodies were loaded on to a truck and driven to a farm north of Nicosia where they were fed into mechanical choppers and fed into the earth' (2 April 1988) (also quoted in Gibbons, ibid: 204). It is highly doubtful that the killers were the med-

ical staff. Other accounts point to EOKA men who forcefully entered the hospital. The identification of hospital staff transforms them into exterminating angels. The Turkish Cypriot
authorities made much use of this story, but it appears it was much more complex. Three people had been killed at the Nicosia General Hospital – two men sheltering in a nurse's flat and
one other person who died of a heart attack. Ironically, the father of one of the two killed had
refused to heed Denktash's call to withdraw from collaborating with the Greek Cypriots. During this period the hospital was receiving anonymous calls to collect bodies of Turkish Cypriots who had been killed by Greek Cypriot armed teams (*omadhes*). The bodies were taken to
the hospital and the Turkish Cypriot authorities refused to collect them, or were afraid to do
so. Apparently there was need for more space in the morgue and the bodies started to smell, so
the bodies were taken to Ayios Vasilis and buried there. At the same time some persons, including a young woman, a grandmother and a child who lived in the end house of the village, had
been killed and buried in a collective grave. The bodies from the hospital were then buried on
top of the family and a bulldozer was used. When Packard began his investigations he was told
by Yorgadjis, the powerful and ominous Minister of the Interior, an ex-EOKA fighter, who
reputedly had links to British Intelligence and the CIA, that the bodies of the Turkish Cypriots had been chopped up and fed into the ground. Yorgadjis' motives in doing so are obscure.
My interlocutor suggested he said this to terrify the Turkish Cypriots assuming that the story
would have reached them. However Yorgadjis then discovered that the three Ayios Vasilis residents had also been buried in the grave, so there was a secret hurried night exhumation to withdraw the three bodies. The exhumers made a mistake and picked up three bodies (not the Ayios
Vasilis residents) from the top of the pile instead of the bottom. The story suggests a cock-up
rather than a conspiracy. On a later visit to Cyprus, Packard accepted that he had probably been
deceived by Yorgadjis.

13. Gibbons (ibid: 128).
14. (ibid: 137).
15. (ibid: 139).
16. This interview was conducted by Katie Tripp, my research assistant, in 1998, in the presence
    of a translator provided by the Turkish Cypriot authorities.
17. This information comes from Gibbons. If that is the case then the meeting must have hap-
    pened after 1 January 1964 as the ICRC representative arrived on 1 January by which time the
    Turks were well aware of the hostage taking.
18. Gibbons (ibid: 149).
19. (ibid: 150).
20. (ibid:153).
21. *Cyprus Mail* (12 July 1964, p.1). Presumably this meant to provoke Turkish intervention.
22. Patrick (ibid: 60).
23. *Revue Internationale Croix-Rouge*, Avril 1964. *Comite International* (p.179).
24. *Cyprus Mail*, (29 May 1964).
25. *Revue Internationale Croix-Rouge*, Mai 1964. *Comite International* (p.255).
26. *Revue Internationale Croix-Rouge*, Juin 1964. *Comite International* (p.290).
27. Private interview with author, (3 August 1997).
28. The Government of Cyprus considers these Greek Cypriots as an internal matter and has
    decided not to present these cases to the Committee for Missing Persons.

3
TESTIMONIES OF
FRAGMENTATION,
RECOLLECTIONS OF UNITY

And we stand patiently, by the hour, by the day, counting those who have returned, thinking about those who have not ...
How frightful! To count the living so as to be able to estimate the dead ....
Dear God, maybe today he'll come ...
Maybe he'll come ...
I don't know: Missing? Prisoner?
Dead? No, not dead ...
He's a prisoner. He must be ....
He's being held ... and maybe he'll come today ....
Maybe.
But there are so many. How will I be able to find him? How will I know him? His hair will be longer, his beard will have grown. His clothes will be torn. His face will have a new, strange look...
Dear God, maybe today he'll come ....
Maybe he'll come ....

(Andros Pavlides, *Cyprus 1974, Days of Disaster, In Black and White*. 115)

Introduction

In this chapter I examine the events of 1974: the coup inspired by mainland Greeks against the legitimate government of Cyprus headed by Archbishop and President Makarios, and the subsequent Turkish invasion which divided the island. I concentrate on reactions to loss among Greek Cypriots, because with a few notorious exceptions that affected the Turkish Cypriots, most losses and disappearances were Greek Cypriot.

Figure 1 *L'enlevement des Sabines*, by Nicolas Poussin, c.1637 (Musee de Louvre, Paris. Reproduced by kind permission of the Trustees).

A number of issues arise when looking at the problem of missing persons. First, one can look at it in terms of what happened. This is important from a historical, legal, and therapeutic perspective, for the survivors and relatives. This is the most opaque area for investigation. Many have personal and political interests to conceal events. But the issue also raises epistemological and methodological problems. Here we can turn to art. Let us look at a painting of a 'reconstruction' of a single traumatic event such as Poussin's *L'Enlevement des Sabines* (Figures 1 and 2). This profoundly disturbing but brilliant painting depicts the moment the Romans, lacking spouses, acted on a prearranged signal to capture the Sabine women. The reader will forgive this attempt at drawing parallels between the writing of ethnographic reconstruction and the composing of a painting, but my purpose here is to suggest that we can learn from such an exploration. Traumatic events affect an ordinary, quotidian, routinised collectivity and atomise society. A single threatening outside event, such as a war or a collective abduction of women (even if 'mythical'), shatters routinised life between individuals. To describe such events as ethnographers we therefore have to concentrate on individual experiences. Yet we also need to convey the larger picture. We cannot do that just through a grouping of isolated snapshots of individual experiences. We also need to engage in a reconstruction that requires artifice, much like that employed by

Figure 2 *L'enlevement des Sabines* (Detail).

an artist constructing his/her painting. Poussin's painting is powerful because although it appears 'realistic', it aspires to convey something more than a snapshot of a particular incident. The painting's figures are structured in a way that can never be captured by any imaginable photograph/s of such a particular incident. The event, like a war, is too total, encompassing, multidimensional, and traumatic in the emotions it generates and its effects, to be encompassed by a series of photographs or testimonies. They have to be combined together creatively. In Poussin's painting, the figures are too impossibly crowded to convince the viewer that such an abduction could really have happened that way, yet its construction possesses an immense depth, giving the viewer the impression that the action could equally be comprehended if viewed from within the picture. Like any cunning artist, Poussin strove for effect, and effect requires the staging of drama. Poussin built up paintings such as this through arranging little clay figures in strategically placed groups in a small boxed theatre set to enable him achieve the most effective fluid dramatic combination of bodies within a three-dimensional space. He then sketched the resulting combinations of figures. The brilliance of this painting emerges out of its exploration of time and space-volume. A single traumatic event is captured diachronically, beginning with the trigger (the signal given by the single silent standing Roman figure to the left), and its result, the various abductions of the Sabine women. The painting insinuates a diachronicity which we as viewers grasp intuitively as an unfolding event, whilst being led away from it. And we are led away by the cunning artifice of the artist in his intention to choreograph movement to depict a collective internal condition (fear) kaleidoscoped through the motions of various bodies. He links the interlocked flailing bodies through the movement of arms which give direction, the backward fearful glances, and the complex triangular dispositions of colour. Although the canvas is filled with figures, each cluster is self-contained in its fear and their key source of terror lies behind them, invisible or glimpsed at. Terror emerges from the cracks of uncertainty. The centre of the picture is an empty space from where ripples of fear emanate. It shows the precise moment when an interacting assembly, a community, is dissolved into individuals each locked in by their fear, trying to escape from the canvas. The artist's genius is that he *structures confusion* for the eye of the beholder when we know that in such a situation, just as the entry of an army into a village, there were no spectators, only participants, and that the participants were all imprisoned in their own worlds trying to escape from a source of danger.

I give this digression through a reference to a work of art and its construction because in dealing with such traumatic events when social order breaks down, we as ethnographers have to work with individual stories. But we are also concerned with how these individual stories can be linked together, much like an artist, knowing that there is no observer who has to work backwards as it were, to create in the mind's eye of the beholder a totality like in a work of art. We have to structure confusion, isolation, and fear. To effect this in words is probably more difficult than in images. But we can draw inspiration from the problems faced by artists when attempting to deal with the violent breakdown of order and pattern, and we can be stimulated to recognise that artifice can sometimes enhance our appreciation of events. To try to capture what happened after a single traumatic event that atomises society through fear is analogous to what Poussin suggested in this picture. Each individual has his/her own story – in some respects they are all similar – but they have also disappeared. As we shall see, sometimes we have the look on their faces, which can tell us what was going to happen to them, but we can never be sure. Sometimes we have photographs, which I will examine. But in most cases we just have to piece together what happened, and there seems to be little information. Nevertheless what people think (or fear) happened is critically important because it affects how they perceive their situation, their actions, and how they represent themselves. As Zur noted 'chaos enters the memory as an impression of chaos without taking on meaning. For traces to remain in memory, the experience must be structured; what is well remembered is what is found in memory as organised units, and ordered memories hang on ordered experience' (1998: 161).

Nor is our knowledge of the events and the disappearances fixed or complete. During my periods of intermittent fieldwork from 1996 to 2000 new information was coming to light, and is still emerging, that helps explain certain actions by various participants, including official representatives of the relatives of the missing and state officials throughout the whole sorry period after the invasion and during the coup. This book also deals with the twists and turns of the negotiations over the missing because it helps explain the political manipulations of Creon's modern heir, the nation state.

A second issue concerns how individuals reacted to their losses. This is a huge topic dealing with matters of memory, representation, therapy, and narratives. I will be dealing with this throughout this book. The final issue concerns the diplomatic and political efforts to resolve the issue – or keep it alive. In short, with the relationship between Creon's heir, the modern state, and Antigone's heirs, the relatives of the missing, or the unburied. As Cyprus is a small country and a modern western democracy, individuals are keenly observant of the actions of state officials, able to represent themselves, and generally able to speak out, in contrast to, for example, certain central and south American countries, and Turkey which has a huge list of disappeared persons. Thus we cannot treat the relatives purely in terms of their often-concealed responses to loss, as Zur (1998) was obliged to do when she worked in incredibly difficult conditions among Guatemalan widows. Thus the three clusters of issues (what happened; how relatives reacted to their losses; and the diplomatic, bureaucratic, and political attempts to deal with the issue), cannot be treated either analytically discrete, or as causally unrelated. What relatives then thought happened affected how they responded to their losses, and what they now think they were *made* to believe also currently affects their actions, with implications for the diplomatic and bureaucratic efforts to resolve the problem. Rather than presenting the current contemporary understanding of what happened in 1974, I begin with how relatives perceived the situation *then*. I will then discuss how subsequent disclosures in the mid-1990s about the 1974 events raised some serious questions about the motives and positions taken by the political representatives of the relatives of the missing. We can be stimulated by the efforts of artists, such as Poussin, to structure confusion to understand how unrepresentable traumatic events experienced by participants can be presented to outside observers, such as a reader of a text or a viewer of a painting.

Experiences and Reactions to Loss among Greek Cypriots

We need to examine how Greek Cypriots 'disappeared' or went 'missing' (i.e. the actual situations and their representation), and how the disappeared or the missing emerged as a distinct mental, social, and political category. The major initial difference between the Greek and Turkish Cypriot experiences of loss is that the former disappeared in a short period (less than four weeks) in a context of massive and total dislocation. Due to the confusion and the close concatenation of events it was sometimes difficult to specify whether individuals died during the coup and the first invasion, although disappearances during the second

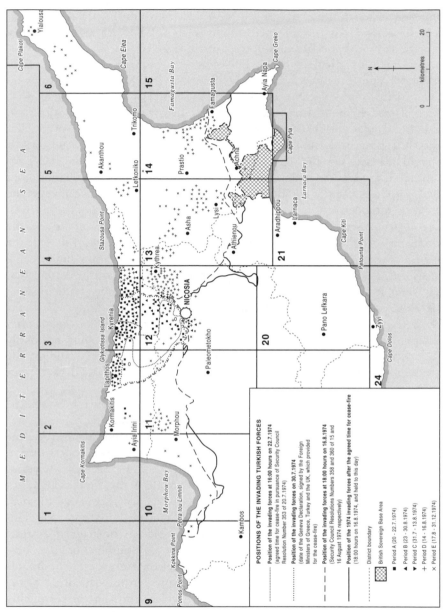

Map 3 Distribution of Greek Cypriot Missing Persons, 1974.

invasion are much clearer to identify. Nevertheless even during the second invasion it was (and is) uncertain whether individuals had died as a result of military engagements with the Turkish forces, or disappeared after being taken into custody. Thus was particularly the state of knowledge for many years among Greek Cypriots, and this uncertainty was exploited by the Turkish Cypriots who claimed that Greek Cypriot missing were casualties of the coup which were then blamed on to the Turks. As will emerge, there is some element of truth in this, but Greek Cypriot authorities vigorously contested this claim. Nevertheless the truth is probably somewhere in between these two positions, although it should be stated from the beginning that both I and investigative Greek Cypriot journalists experienced major difficulties in obtaining precise information from both the Greek Cypriot authorities and the representatives of the relatives of the missing. Although officials claimed to be protecting the interests of the relatives, the degree of secrecy surrounding the details of the disappearances and the problems over the lists, coupled with their apparent eagerness to present the issue at international fora, raised serious questions which are only slowly being answered. It also weakened the credibility of the Greek Cypriot authorities. However, it has to be acknowledged that a substantial number of the missing Greek Cypriots were civilians in areas overrun by the Turkish army, whilst others were young men in the National Guard. It is indubitable that the majority disappeared during the second phase of the Turkish invasion. This profoundly influenced how Greek Cypriots visualised their situation. Map 3, produced by the Republic of Cyprus for the UN, indicates the distribution of Greek Cypriot missing.

One should begin by treating such maps with some caution. It should be recognised that they are political documents as much as humanitarian ones, and therefore potentially contentious. This is particularly important because the Turkish Cypriot leadership has claimed that the missing Greek Cypriots died in the coup and invasion and not in custody, and therefore that Greek Cypriot claims are baseless. Greek Cypriots have not, since 1974, cast similar doubts on Turkish Cypriot claims on their own disappeared, and consequently the map submitted by the Greek Cypriots requires a more agnostic initial approach. This map can be seen in assisting the scientific scaffolding constructed by state authorities around a particular issue, but built out of testimonies of loss. There is no doubt that the greatest number of missing persons were located in the area around Kyrenia and Lapithos, the stretch of coast that bore the brunt of the resistance to the amphibious landings by the Turkish army. The map explicitly links the advance of the Turkish army with the disappearances. The map is unclear as to the disappearances in the south of the island. These could have been individuals whose origin was in the south, or individuals last sighted in the south. Alternatively it could be that the disappearances occurred there. My own knowledge of specific cases suggests origins or last sightings rather than location of disappearance, which is impossible to ascertain by definition. We should therefore take the map to indicate last sightings. Although we are dealing with testimonies, this is what the authorities and we have to work with. It is worthwhile to correlate the missing with specific events in specific periods:

Table 3.1 Numerical Distribution of Greek Cypriot Missing Persons by Period

Period	Number of missing	Major contemporaneous events
20/7–22/7/74	267	First Turkish landings. Intense resistance by Greek Cypriots
23/7–30/7/74	170	End of 'first round' of the invasion; cease fire on 30 July
31/7–13/8/74	131	Turkish army begins second round on 8/8/74. Greek Cypriot resistance collapses. Civilians start fleeing *en masse* ahead of the Turkish army, but many are left behind.
14/8–16/8/74	596	Turkish troops reach their final positions and cease-fire declared on 16 August 1974
TOTAL	**1011**	

These figures must be treated with caution. They are nevertheless indicative. It could be argued that the majority of army casualties (437) occurred in the first phase of the invasion (from 20 to 30 July 1974) and that the Turkish army faced much less opposition in the second phase, in particular in the last two days when the Greek Cypriots claim that 596 persons disappeared, or more precisely were last seen alive. This could support the Greek Cypriot claim that they suffered disappearances when the Turkish army faced little resistance. Tables 3.1 and 3.2 based upon Greek Cypriot official data correlates period of last sighting, number of groups, and number of independent cases. They also claim that 329 individuals disappeared after the cease-fire was declared on 16 August 1974. Another key issue concerns the geographical distribution of missing persons. In the first invasion, the Turkish forces carved out a corridor to Nicosia; in the second invasion they drove southeast to Famagusta initially bypassing the whole northeastern part of Cyprus that was later occupied by the army. If the map is correct, it indicates that a considerable number of individuals disappeared not just in villages, but also in these areas cut off by the Turkish army from the rest of Cyprus and which were certainly not areas of military resistance or engagements. This would include the segments 4–14 on the grid map (the north east of the island), in particular areas 4 and 13 in the Karpass area which include 42 missing persons who disappeared after the second cease-fire on 16 August 1974 (see Maps 4 and 5). The maps are consistent with events, as we know they evolved. We therefore have to take these maps as bearing a strong and verifiable plausibility.

	■ Period A 20–22/7/1974		▲ Period B 23–30/7/1974		▼ Period C 14–16/8/1974		+ Period D 14–16/8/1974	
Map Box	Number of groups	Number of Independent cases	Number of groups	Number of Independent cases	Number of groups	Number of Independent cases	Number of groups	Number of Independent cases
1	–	–	–	–	–	–	1	3
2	12	28	3	4	11	75	2	2
3	48	157	25	72	17	50	8	55
4	1	1	–	–	–	–	16	55
5	–	–	–	–	–	–	5	15
6	–	–	–	–	–	–	2	3
7	–	–	–	–	–	–	–	–
8	–	–	–	–	–	–	–	–
9	1	2	–	–	–	–	–	–
10	–	–	–	–	–	–	1	1
11	–	–	–	–	–	–	9	20
12	21	79	22	94	3	6	51	341
13	–	–	–	–	–	–	25	71
14	–	–	–	–	–	–	14	31
Total	**83**	**267**	**50**	**170**	**31**	**31**	**131**	**596**

	x Period E 17/8–31/12/1974		◯ Period F 1975		Total	
Map Box	Number of groups	Number of Independent cases	Number of groups	Number of Independent cases	Number of groups	Number of Independent cases
1	–	–	–	–	**1**	**3**
2	1	3	1	2	**30**	**114**
3	4	7	–	–	**102**	**341**
4	3	5	–	–	**20**	**61**
5	3	3	–	–	**8**	**18**
6	13	40	–	–	**15**	**43**
7	1	1	–	–	**1**	**1**
8	–	–	–	–	**–**	**–**
9	1	5	–	–	**2**	**7**
10	3	8	–	–	**4**	**9**
11	12	19	–	–	**21**	**39**
12	20	39	1	1	**118**	**560**
13	24	134	–	–	**49**	**204**
14	26	62	–	–	**40**	**93**
Total	**111**	**326**	**2**	**3**	**411**	**1493**

Table 3.2 Greek Cypriot Disappearances by period.

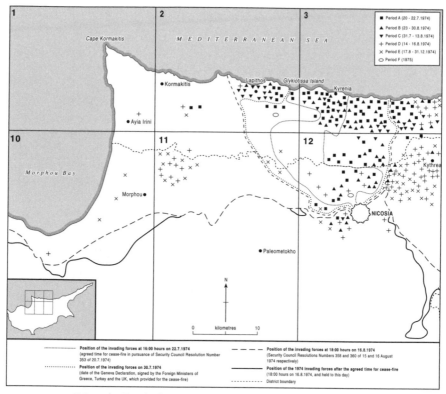

Map 4 Greek Cypriot Missing Persons, 1974 (Detail).

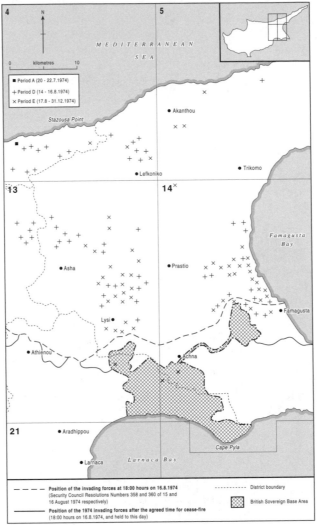

Map 5 Greek Cypriot Missing Persons, 1974 (Detail).

Greek Cypriot Missing Persons can be divided into the following eight groups. The list is based upon what is known, and what Greek Cypriots believe could have occurred:

1. Individuals who died as a result of the coup. This includes National Guardsmen, pro-Makarios paramilitaries, and civilians.

2. Individuals who died when engaged in military encounters with the invading Turkish army in the north of the island, and whose bodies were buried hurriedly there.

3. Individuals like the above whose bodies were returned to the South during the cease-fires and buried hurriedly in collective graves.

4. Elderly or incapacitated individuals including women, and children suffering from Downs Syndrome who were executed by Turkish soldiers in cold blood, to be saved from the trouble of having to take care of them.

5. Individuals who were captured alive by the invading Turkish army, some of whom were known to have been executed in cold blood, and whose bodies were returned as in 3 above.

6. Individuals who were captured alive by the Turkish army but handed over to Turkish Cypriot paramilitaries who then apparently executed them.

7. Individuals who were captured by the Turkish army and last seen alive in Turkish POW camps in mainland Turkey.

8. Civilians who disappeared in the area occupied by the Turkish army either in the first few days of the invasions or later.

The major point of disagreement concerns the last five categories, and there is uncertainty over the numbers involved. Turkey has resolutely refused to get involved in the issue even though these individuals disappeared in another sovereign state's territory which it forcibly entered. The evidence and testimonies contradict the claim by the Turkish Cypriot leadership about the Greek Cypriot missing. One could view such claims as absurd as best, or as deceiving at worst. Nevertheless there is uncertainty over the numbers involved. In 1974 many relatives of those individuals who have subsequently been classified as missing, believed they were prisoners. At the end of hostilities in August 1974, both sides (the Republic of Cyprus and the Turkish Army) gave prisoner lists to the ICRC. The Cypriots had a handful of prisoners; the Turks had thousands, including people enclaved in the north. When the Turkish lists were checked it emerged that some 2,500 had an unknown fate (*agnoumeni*). The lists were known not to be comprehensive, and were treated with deep scepticism and suspicion by both sides. If a person whose whereabouts was unknown did not appear on such lists, it was not necessarily assumed that that person was dead or missing in action. Relatives immediately started to try to trace them through photographs in the newspapers, radio announcements, and visits to army camps to speak to their comrades. Not all the missing men were, properly speaking, soldiers. Many were reservists, called up during the mass mobilisation. A reservist might be seen as a soldier by an opposing army, but his family normally sees him as a civilian, and a father or husband, obliged to fight. It emerged later that many such men, aware of the hopelessness of the odds against them having to fight tanks and aircraft with rifles, changed out of army fatigues (also the type of clothing that they as farmers would use in their fields) into civilian clothing. It would seem that some of these were treated with extreme suspicion by the Turkish army and shot.

For 3–4 months until October 1974 there was mass confusion, dislocation, and displacement of people. Official suppression of information and misinformation thrived together with rumour. Many Greek Cypriots were still in the Turkish-occupied north, in hiding, or displaced as refugees in the government-controlled south unable to make contact with their kin, including their sons in the National Guard. The term *agnoumenos* emerged as a colloquial term, employed as an *ad hoc* category by the local workers of the ICRC (International Community of the Red Cross) to designate those individuals whose fate had yet to be clarified.[1] The word *agnoumenos* is employed after major (natural and man-made disasters, such as in the immediate aftermath of an earthquake or a ship sinking) to denote missing, fate unknown. It contains an expectation or anticipation of future or imminent clarification, and indicates that as long as the term is used the present is abnormal. The use of the term thus signals a situation of continuing abnormality. The initial list of individuals whose fate was unknown was inevitably extensive containing some 3–4,000 Greek Cypriots (including some 2,015 prisoners in Turkey) and 106 Turkish Cypriots, and had many mistakes (e.g. individuals whose names were entered twice, because of different spellings). In 1975 the Red Cross wrote to all those relatives to confirm that their people were still missing. Some, but not all those who should have, replied and the number fell to 2,100. During that time families were still being united. Relatives were thus encouraged in their hopes that they would be reunited with their missing.[2] Indeed initially the Government authorities grouped the *agnoumeni* together with the enclaved as there were some two hundred thousand Greeks in the north under military rule, and to whom the authorities could not gain access. This suggests that the missing were perceived as a residual category of the enclaved, whose whereabouts would eventually be identified, or that they were being held by the Turkish Cypriots as hostages, but did not appear on the official Turkish prisoner lists. As Loizos pointed out 'the patchwork nature of the dispersal of the two ethnic groups throughout the island made many combatants think in terms of hostages, and counter-hostages' (1981: 95). The Turks claimed that they held no others except those on the lists they had published. In a climate of intense suspicion, hostility, anger, and confusion, with stories spreading of mass rapes by Turkish soldiers and the anticipation then that the situation might change and the refugees would return to their homes by the end of the year, these claims were not believed. It was feared that perhaps more prisoners were being held secretly as a bargaining counter, or even as a means to further torment the Greek Cypriots. Another belief was that they might have been in hiding. Clearly, experiences of 1963–64 were critical in influencing the climate of anticipation. This suspicion was reinforced when the ICRC discovered some prisoners in northern Cyprus in October 1975 not on the official Turkish list of prisoners. By the end of 1976 the ICRC considered the emergency to be over and withdrew from Cyprus.

It is thus important to appreciate how bureaucratic knowledge was produced, as this can help explain the differences between the two sides in the evolution of their perception of the problem of the missing. The process of information-gathering was assumed by outside organisations as a crisis management measure, in a situation of extreme confusion. The Red Cross lists were compiled as a humanitarian effort to help individuals discover what happened to their loved ones, ideally to facilitate family unification, and were given to both sides. This information was gathered deductively with increasing precision across time. Yet the reception and subsequent use of such lists was not so much oriented towards the gathering of information on what was known or knowable (casualties, deaths, etc.), but on what was still unknown or unknowable (as it was believed information was being withheld). The Red Cross list, from which the *agnoumeni* list was derived, was not so much a definite list of casualties, deaths, etc, but rather a list of question marks attached to names. The list of *agnoumeni* was thus a list of people whose fate was still undetermined after enquiries. Greek Cypriots assumed that this was a list of question marks to which the Turks held the answers. They feared the Turks would never answer these questions unless pressured by international opinion. Yet as we shall see, the Greek Cypriot authorities were somewhat lacking in checking their information, and in some cases they were responsible for promoting an interpretation through omission or commission, which should have been corrected. This was a grave mistake as it worked against the interests of the relatives in the long run.

Until 1980 it was claimed that the number of missing was around 2,000 (Drusiotis 2000: 13). That year however the Committee of Relatives of the Missing Persons presented a list to the UN. This had 1,510 names and it included the names, dates of birth, nationality, the place where they were last seen alive, and the conditions under which they were last seen. It seems the original 2,000 names included double entries. However the journalist Drousiotis notes that there were inconsistencies. Of these 1,510, 7 are entered twice. Another 355 do not have their Identity Card number, and details of disappearances are given for 425 only, 'and these are in many cases very vague' (ibid: 15). Around 1981 for the first time the number of 1,619 was mentioned. However from then until now other lists appeared with different numbers. Drusiotis notes that the Government Service for Missing Persons stuck to the number of 1,619 from 1981 to 1999, but the various lists had various names, even if the number remained the same. His experience, echoed by my own, was that until 1999 Government Departments refused to indicate when or how the number of 1,619 was reached. Similarly, the Committee for Relatives of Missing Persons was far from forthcoming in supplying lists locally to local journalists or myself. It is significant that up till the time of writing (June 2000) the Republic of Cyprus has never published an official list of casualties of the invasion. In March 1998 it presented a series of 'files' (or more precisely a list of names) to the UN-sponsored Committee for Missing Persons (CMP), which was not published until March 2000, in the face of much opposition by the Relatives of the Missing, which I explore elsewhere. Indeed both Government agencies and NGOs representing the relatives of the missing have long resisted making public the names of the missing whilst asserting that the number was known to be 1,619. Whilst Cypriot society has known precisely the number of missing (until very recently), neither the public nor government officials appear to know the number of casualties. Many say 'about 5,000' or 'about 6,000'. Logically one would expect the reverse: a specific accounting of casualties and an indeterminate list of those missing. It almost appears as if the only 'factual' official list of casualties is primarily the list of the missing, whilst the factual list of casualties has never been officialised and given official veracity. This is consistent with the Greek Cypriot belief that 1974 was not just a defeat of Hellenism, but an injustice which has not yet been resolved, an 'open' history in Papadakis' terms (1994). The Missing have become the society's official collective casualties of 1974 mourned continuously, to recover a past that many would wish to recover differently.

The upshot is that apart from the State's management of the issue for nationalist purposes, the process of how people knew what they knew (their epistemology) was far from emotively neutral. The process of information production was pursued and managed in a manner that generated hope and openness, rather than finality and strict accounting of casualties. This was not a list for 'historical' or accounting purposes, but a working document consisting of a series of question marks. The Red Cross list was not so much a list of casualties, but a list of individuals whose fate, and ideally whereabouts, had to be ascertained. Yet the list of the missing, to adopt a chemical analogy – the liquid from which various precipitates (i.e. categories) have been progressively extracted through the application of various tests – has become implicitly a list of casualties of the Turkish invasion. Exposure to the process of information production especially in the early stages appears to have encouraged hope, and was reinforced by experience. Many relatives claim 'But we know who took them away, and we know their names'. There is no reason to doubt that these beliefs were genuinely held.

Testimonies of Fragmentation, Recollections of Unity

Paulina: All right then, I'm sick. But I can be sick and recognize a voice. Besides, when we lose one of our faculties, the others compensate. Right, Doctor Miranda?
(Ariel Dorfman: *Death and the Maiden.* 1994: 16)

I now examine the testimonies of relatives. There are a number of common themes. To begin with, individuals faced a total disruption in their world which they were not initially aware of, although many were collected enough to take precautions. The women present their narratives in terms of a collectivity. They responded to events not individually but with their loved ones, as family members. Although these interviews were conducted mainly in 1998 (i.e. 24 years after the events), they have lost none of their detail, nor their poignancy. Two types of testimonies are presented. First, there are those women who had some evidence that their men were alive when they were captured and in good health. Then there are those women who did not see their men taken away. Indeed their accounts could very easily indicate that they recognise their men-folk lost their lives in battle. Nevertheless their testimonies are included, because from their perspective, they are wives of missing persons. They, too, attend protests, commemorations, etc, although they may do so for companionship, support, succour, etc, rather than to make an overtly political point. Some of these latter accounts indicate that relatives continued to hope that their menfolk may be alive, and how during the extreme chaos and dislocation that accompanied the invasion, many were led to believe that their menfolk might still be alive. Many rely on intuitive evidence, such as Paulina's type of evidence in *Death and the Maiden*. For example, many claim to have recognised their sons in the photographs and news clips that were taken then. Others claim certain knowledge by virtue of being mothers. This constitutes the most difficult and grey area of all the cases, and is a major bone of contention between the Greek and Turkish Cypriots with the latter insisting that they were MIAs (missing in action). This raised complex problems in the relations between the relatives and the Greek Cypriot authorities. It also raises important issues over the nature of intuitive knowledge and whether it is acceptable for legal evidence. Intuitive beliefs can only be sustained through a cultural scaffolding. The fear that such men might still be alive has deep cultural and historical resonance in Greek culture, such as fears of the old Ottoman custom of *paidomazoma*, the collection of Christian boys as Janissaries.

1. Maria

Both Maria's father and husband are missing. Her family lived in the village of Afaina, which is near Asha. Maria still lives in refugee housing.

> One morning we spotted Turkish tanks heading for Afaina. We were afraid so we decided to go to another village where we thought we would be safe. When we got there we found that the Turkish tanks were already there. We hid in the orchards near the town hoping that the Turkish soldiers would not find us. We were there for two days when some Turkish Cypriots learnt of our whereabouts and persuaded us to surrender. We were taken to a mixed school and were assured that we would be safe, that we had all lived together for many years and they wouldn't let anyone hurt us. We stayed in the school for five days after which we were told we could go to the free areas. Everyone got on the buses provided to take us to the free areas except eight men, as the Turkish Cypriots said they had to hold them for further questioning. My husband and father were among these eight men. At this time my husband was only 35 and I was left alone with my four young children.
>
> It was only when prisoners started to be released that I really worried about the whereabouts of my husband and my father. I didn't know what information they could have that the Turks would want. I heard from some soldiers that the Turks wanted an airport built and that my husband was among those building it. I went to the Red

Cross with my information and asked them to investigate it. The said they had heard similar reports. When the Red Cross asked the Turks where the men building the airports were, they moved them. Now we have no information and don't know what to think. The government didn't really help us at all. At first we were given a basic food allowance but when we began to receive the eight pounds per month payout they stopped the food allowances which made it virtually impossible to survive.

The children reacted very badly to losing their father. This was made worse by our financial position, loss of our home and their grandfather also. We didn't receive this house until six years after the war and were living in the houses of strangers for many years. Even I, their mother, was no use to them as my nerves couldn't cope under the pressure.

There was a scheme set up shortly after the war where people in other countries, the States and England where families could pay money to help a child with their education. This helped my daughter. A lady in the States wanted to adopt my youngest son but he did not want to go.

The children were always sad. They were all old enough to remember their father and missed him and their home. This affects even my grandchildren. My little grandchild often asks why we can't send her granddad a message.

2. Pelayia

Pelayia's husband is missing. She comes from Neo Chorio, Kythreas (new village of Kythreas) and still lives in refugee housing. This is an example of an individual who disappeared before the Red Cross was able to gain access to the Turkish-controlled north immediately after the invasion:

On the 14 August we heard planes bombing the land around our village. We ran out and hid in the orchards. At that time my four children were grown up. Three were married and the youngest one, who was single, was twenty. Luckily they had all gone to the mountains (Troodos) a few days before the invasion began. My husband, my brother-in-law, and I went in my brother-in-law's car to Asha. When we got to Asha we realised that the tanks were already there. A lady on the outskirts of the town offered us a hiding place in her house. We hid there for four days with the woman, her son and her husband. After four days the Turks came and found us. My brother in -law and the woman's son were registered by the Turks and taken to Turkey. My husband and the other woman's husband were taken, we don't know where. All we know is that their names were not registered. On the 22th August we saw our husbands pass by the house where we were being kept prisoner. They had their hands tied behind their backs. A few days after this we were set free into the free areas of Larnaca. They said they would free our husbands a few days latter but they never returned. Only my brother-in-law and the woman's son returned from Turkey.

I went to live with one of my daughters who lives in Larnaca. As there were so many refugees in the area there were over twenty-three people also staying with my daughter's family. Immediately after I was released I went to the Red Cross to demand that the whereabouts of my husband be investigated. The Red Cross say that they did not know where he has been taken, but someone must know and those persons can be traced.

3. Fostira

This harrowing example shows that men who changed into civilian clothing to escape maltreatment were paradoxically more at risk of being killed. Ironically, farmers in Cyprus wear army fatigues for work in the fields. Fostira's husband is missing. She comes from Kythrea. This example also shows the systematic use of rape as a means of 'softening up' resistance as well as clearing areas of civilians through fear. It is also claimed that the Turkish army executed the mentally retarded and invalids. Similar situations were corroborated later by a Kurdish officer.[3] In the chaos where Turkish soldiers were receiving different orders, Turkish Cypriot militia took away some Greek Cypriot men who are now untraceable. Rauf Denktash, President of the TRNC, acknowledged this general phenomenon in a recent TV interview. The account also shows that in spite of fear, women had the presence of mind to record names, which probably saved lives, and to collect photographs, which helped trace them. The Pavlides Garage referred to in the testimony was a big open space in the northern part of Nicosia where detainees were collected. It has been claimed that some men were taken from there by Turkish Cypriot militia (TMT) and disappeared, probably as revenge killings either for losses sustained in 1963–64, or more likely in response to atrocities committed by EOKA B during the first Turkish invasion.

After the first invasion the Turks took my brother because he was caught providing food for the Greek Cypriot soldiers [these were soldiers caught behind Turkish lines during the first Turkish invasion – PSC]. Although my husband and I realised that a second phase of the invasion was likely we were desperate to find my brother. We heard the night before the second invasion that he was being held in a house nearby. On the 14th August the second invasion began. We woke up to the sound of bombing. We had no car to escape in but the neighbours did. They didn't have space for everyone but they were able to take my thirteen-year-old son. We stayed in the village but because the bombing continued my husband thought he should take the other two boys in case the Turks arrived. He had heard that the Turks had tortured and killed many boys and felt that the Turks would be less likely to kill us women.

With my daughter (who was 14), my mother and my sister in-law I moved up nearer the main road in order to hear some news. By the 15th August we didn't know what was happening or where the military lines were. Later on that day we saw Greek Cypriots coming down the mountain who told us that the lines had been broken. They asked us for civilian clothes in case the Turks found them. My daughter wisely recorded all their names in case the guards later arrested them. When the prisoners were released during the exchange, after the war, she found that all of the men whose names she had recorded were free.

On the 16th August the Turkish troops arrived so we waved a white cloth on a stick from the house so they would not attack us. Women and children were lined up on one side of the road and men on the other. On the 17th all the women and children were taken to a church in Neo Kythreas. That night many of the young girls were raped. The next day we were told that we were free. We didn't know where to go so we started to walk back to Kythreas. While we were walking we saw a bus. The bus stopped and one

Turkish Cypriot said that we should all be killed. Another man got off the bus and told him not to talk like that. Instead of killing us, we were told to get on the bus. We got on the bus, which took us towards Nicosia. It was getting dark and when we approached some farms we were told to stay there for the night. When we entered the farm we saw that some male prisoners were already there. My brother was among them. That night we women were given some bread but the men were given nothing.

The next day we were all put on the bus. We women had to sit at the back. The men were blindfolded and had their hands tied, and put at the front of the bus. The Turkish soldiers treated us badly. They threw stones at us throughout the journey to Pavlides Garage. A Turkish Cypriot who was handing out bread to us told us to ask the guards to be allowed into the free areas. We asked, but instead we were taken to Kythreas. It was terrible to be back there. There was no water or food and my house had been partly demolished. Luckily I was able to recover my photographs of my husband and boys.

On the 21st August the Turks (i.e. Turkish soldiers) came. They asked us to stand in a line and just walk. We were able to, but some of the sick and elderly couldn't and were asked to stay behind. As we moved of we heard the soldiers shoot them with their rifles. We were taken to a house where a high Turkish officer, members of the Red Crescent, and TV cameras were waiting. The Turkish officer told us to line up in front of the camera and tell the interviewer what a nice time we were having and that we were being treated well.

At this point she began to cry as she recollects what happened that evening. Despite an offer to stop the interview she insists on continuing.

Later that evening some Turkish soldiers came and told us to line up. As we were afraid of being raped, all the younger women, myself included, tried to make ourselves look older, rubbing our faces with charcoal, wearing headscarves and any old baggy clothes that we could find. Despite our disguises the soldiers took us into several houses and began to rape us. Everyone was screaming and crying. I will never forget the screams of the women in all the houses surrounding mine. They even raped the pregnant women and the young 13 and 14 year old girls. Just before I was to be raped, the High Official we had met that afternoon entered the house. I ran to him and begged him to help. "You promised that you would not hurt us, look what is happening, what are you doing to us. My own little girl is being raped now by one of your own men". The official sent the soldiers in our house away and went with me to the other houses where he told the guards to go back to their duties. I was so glad when I found that my daughter had not been raped. She had bitten the hand of the guard as he tried to rape her and he had beaten her instead. Although her face was bleeding badly she had not been raped.

The next day they were taken to another village. It was here that I found my ten-year-old boy hiding at the outskirts of the village. He told me that his father, my husband, was being held in the village church. My son told me that when they reached Asha they met some UN men who told them not to be afraid, or to leave, as they would return the next day and take their names. My husband trusted them to return and help them but the next day the Turks came and arrested them. My eldest son was separated from my husband and my youngest son because he was so big and tall. Only my husband and ten-year-old son came to the village where we were also taken as prisoners.

When I saw my son I asked him if the women were allowed to go to the church to visit the men. My son asked the guard and he said that it would be possible the next day. For the first night since they had left me I felt positive. I had one son next to me and knew that I would see my husband the next day. I was the first woman at the church but when I got there was nobody. A Turkish Cypriot told me that the Turkish soldiers in the middle of the night had taken my husband and six other men, the other men he had been with had been killed.

We were enclaved in that village for three months. Each day I asked the Red Crescent to investigate the disappearance of my husband but they did nothing. The only thing that I found out was that it was Turkish Cypriot men who took away the seven men and that two known Turkish officers were also there. Surely these Turks must know the names of the men who took away my husband? ...

You ask me if I found out the whereabouts of the son that had escaped with my neighbours. By this point I believed him to be dead as I had seen the car of my neighbours filled with bullet holes at the side of the road when we were being taken to Pavlides Garage. Although I had heard nothing I believed that he must have been killed. However, during the time that I was captive I heard on the radio that he had been taken prisoner and that he was well. Another day I also heard a message from my eldest son who was being held prisoner in the Technical School in Nicosia. When the Red Cross finally arrived, my son, daughter, and I were able to put our name on the Red Cross list and send a message to my sons.

At the beginning of November the Turks began to release us into the free areas, although my family and I were not altogether until mid-November. My sister found the other two boys and my father and brother were also released. With the exception of my husband we were united again. My sister accommodated us in her house in the free area but my only concern was for my husband. All I wanted was for him to return. I went every day asking about my husband but I have never had any news.

My major problem after we were released was to provide for my children. My children suffered a great deal. They had all been close to my husband and loved him dearly. I think that my youngest son in some ways suffered most, as he was the last one to have seen his father and was under pressure at the time to remember every last detail about what had happened. After we were released into the free areas he became very sick with rheumatic fever. Ever since then his fingers have been deformed and he walks very badly. I also developed rheumatoid arthritis.

Even now my children believe that he is alive somewhere and will come back to us. I remember that when my youngest boy was 14 his class was going on a week's holiday to Greece. We all wanted my son to go but he wouldn't. I said 'But why won't you go? You'll have a great time'. He said 'I can't go *mitera*, when my father comes home I want to be able to greet him. What will he think if I'm not here?' Do you see how my children have suffered?

The following interviews were with mainland Greek relatives of missing persons. Missing mainland Greeks were mainly, but not exclusively, Greek army officers. Their testimonies highlight an area of uncertainty. Some individuals who were reported injured are believed by their relatives to be alive. Parents claimed to have recognised them in news reports. Photographs become critical means of harvesting belief through the sowing of doubt. In the testimonies of Eleni and Evridikhe (interview nos. 4 and 5 below), photographs assume a potent persuasive inducement to belief in the face of black nothingness as in Michelangelo Antonioni's film *Blow Up*. They come to indicate not just the absent object, but also traces of presence. In short, that the loved one is absent because he was present, and thus may well be present. *Pari passu* they also insert a corrosive mistrust in the webs of significance society spins around individuals. A common feature of these testimonies is that these photographs and evidence originate *outside* the national territory of certainty and attribution – foreign newspapers, documentaries, even the Turkish Cypriot radio station. There is a suggestion of betrayal by superiors in Evridikhe's testimony (interview no. 5). Many Greeks and Greek Cypriots believe that the 1967–74 Greek Junta connived with U.S. policy to induce the Turkish invasion, neutralise Makarios' non-alignment, and split the island. Finally, Dimitra's account (interview no. 6) questions the evidence because there is so little evidence. She was faced with a photograph of part of a body which it was claimed was her husband's. She never saw the body. The photographs of her husband's body were so disturbing that she was unable to satisfactorily identify him. The frame moves from grainy newsprint distant picture in a foreign newspaper of men huddled together, to a close-up Polaroid of a body part, an eyebrow. We move here from metaphor (where one person stands for someone else) to metonymy (where a part stands for a whole). In both cases doubt is sown. After this interview it emerged in 1999–2000 that these bodies were buried hurriedly without being returned to the relatives, and became the focus of DNA testing (Chapter 9).

4. Eleni

My son was a soldier fighting in Cyprus when he went missing on the 16th August during the second invasion. As he was a wireless operator I believe that the Turks kept him alive for his technical skills.

I have proof that he was alive for some years after he was arrested. I identified him from a newspaper picture of people being taken by boat to Turkey. He has also made contact twice since then through a wireless unit to let me know he is OK. The first time he made contact was straight after he was captured and then again, about eight months after that. The fact that he contacted me almost a year after the fighting ceased contradicts the Turkish claims that all prisoners of war were released safely or died during the conflict. I know, having heard my son's voice, that this isn't true. I know that they wouldn't have killed him. My husband believed that they would have kept him alive to crack the codes of the National Guard. He could also speak five languages and is a graduate of English literature.

58

My husband died of grief over my son. He became very ill one year after we learned that he had disappeared. He was in hospital for one year and then died. My health also deteriorated after we heard the news.

(*Crying*) Tell me, how can so many people disappear and never be heard of again. Is it right? Why can the governments not do anything? I don't care about politics. It's a humanitarian issue. I don't care about anything other than the well-being of the children that have been taken. We want nothing you know, no compensation. We would pay for the cost of the food they had during captivity if we could have them back.

5. Evridikhe

My son was 24 when he disappeared. He had been serving in Cyprus for six months when the invasion began. The last time that I talked to him was on the 13th August. He phoned me and told me that he loved me. He said that he would phone again in a few days. That was the last time that I spoke to him.

It appears that on the 15th August there was an attack on his camp. His army superiors were warned and fled the camp, but my son and many other young soldiers were killed or captured in the attack. It is unclear who were killed and who were captured, as it was the local people who buried the bodies. It was only when I saw him in a photograph of the prisoners of war, in a German newspaper, that I knew he had survived the attack.

I feel that my son's superiors knew of the attack because the soldiers' base was near the airport, which the officials knew that the Turks wanted to attack. They didn't remove the soldiers because it would look like they had tried to protect the airport if the Turks attacked. One of the soldiers who survived told me that this was the aim of the Greek army officials.

I feel that in every way the Greek government has let down our children that went to fight on behalf of their country. They have only recently officially acknowledged that there was actually a war in Cyprus and that many lives were lost.

6. Dimitra

My husband was only twenty-six when he disappeared. He had recently qualified as a doctor, after studying in Greece. He had received a job offer in the United States and we had planned to start a new life there. I was very excited because my brother and his wife had moved there some years earlier.

We were on holiday visiting our families before leaving for America when Dimitris was enlisted.

He survived the first invasion but went missing on the 16th August during the second invasion. I don't know, even now what happened to him. A few days after I was told that he was missing I spoke to one of the soldiers who had been fighting with Dimitris. He said that they had tried to leave the battlefield together but that the smoke and noise was so bad that he lost sight of him.

The UN visited me a few days later to tell me that they had identified some of Dimitris's personal items on the battlefield. They had found his watch, which they say had been forcibly removed from his wrist. I couldn't believe it when I saw that it had stopped fifty minutes before the cease-fire. They had also found his glasses. They were all misshapen, with heat bubbles inside the plastic.

The UN said that they had collected many bodies from the battlefield. They suggested that I went to the hospital nearby to see if I could identify him. I couldn't bear it, so I did not go. Eventually my brother in-law took me. We looked at many Polaroids of the dead bodies. I saw a picture of half a head, which I thought, may have been his. All I could really see was the eyebrow. I thought it looked like his. The photographs were terrible. They were taken in a dark room, without much care. I think it would be impossible to identify anyone from those pictures, but I still sometimes wonder if that picture was of Dimitris. Then sometimes I think that he was captured and taken away by the Turks. He was a captain, so maybe he was treated differently.

The Bureaucratisation of Uncertainty

Members of the International Committee of the Red Cross arrived in Cyprus on 22 July 1974. Their main priorities were to cope with the relocation of families and the disastrous situation that had emerged. Missing persons were not high on their list. It took them weeks to obtain permission to gain access to the occupied territories and they travelled under Turkish military escort. ICRC delegates also began visiting prisoners, and internees held in Turkey were granted the status of 'prisoners of war'. They also directed private talks with the prisoners or their spokesmen and with the commanders of the three prisoner of war camps in Turkey. The ICRC statement of 11 March 1976 noted that 'In the course of all these conversations, no case of escape, death or disappearance of one or more prisoners was ever brought to the attention of the ICRC delegates'. They added:

'This statement, however, does not cover the cases of nine prisoners of war who have been listed on August 28, 1974 by a delegate of the ICRC and about whom nothing further has been heard. Nor does it solve the problem of prisoners of war whose families believe that they can identify them in photographs that have appeared in the press.'

This is the crux of the issue. All the prisoners Turkey acknowledges capturing were returned. But many more people went missing than the ones who returned. It was claimed some were captured in small groups, and there were also sightings of apprehended individuals who disappeared. The list of prisoners Turkey acknowledges was drawn up in Turkey many days after the hostilities. In other cases as indicated above, parents or spouses claimed to have seen their loved ones in photographs or newsreels of detainees. Mr Denktash has acknowledged that some men were taken away by Turkish Cypriot militia after they had been apprehended by the Turkish army, and killed. Some of these killings appear to have been revenge killings for earlier disappearances in 1963–64. Others appear to have been triggered by a mass killing of Turkish Cypriots in the village of Tochni in August 1974. On the pretext that they were to be taken to safety in the Turkish occupied North, EOKA B men transported the men of Tochni on two buses, and they were never seen again. One man escaped the massacre but the mass graves have never been officially identified and the bodies exhumed. In short, we have a gap here between official certainties and private doubts. More precisely, there seems to a gap between the certainties created by the military organs of the state in a situation of extreme dislocation, war, violence and fear, where the military was imposing its own order through the controlled application of violence, and ordinary individuals' experiences and perceptions of that situation. It is important to appreciate that we are dealing with differing levels of reality, not just a 'political propaganda' issue, which it also indubitably is.

There were thus powerful, subtle, and sometimes hidden pressures and incentives to encourage relatives of the missing to weave together their experiences and hopes in an epistemological framework that encouraged them to believe their relatives were alive and recoverable. The demand for information on the missing cannot thus be treated as the cynical exploitation of the emotions of the relatives by the State (the Republic of Cyprus) as a means to blame Turkey. There certainly was exploitation especially where the authorities had credible evidence that some individuals were probably dead, but this does not cover all the cases. The authorities were also reacting to grassroots pressures, and as will be shown, the political representatives of the relatives of the missing also appear to have wanted to keep the some cases alive when they should have closed them. Nor does the fact of exploitation render the issue a false one. The closing of the issue by the Turkish Cypriot leadership was, and is, likewise politically motivated. Equally, one must be suspicious of treating the issue solely as the 'natural' expression of emotion by the relatives of the missing, as their representatives and politicians maintain. That it has elements of both is to be expected. But the nature of how people came to believe what they believe, and how experiences were woven together with hopes and fears in a determinate cultural climate which set limits on what was anticipated (suspicion of the Turks, belief in the stories of their being taken away) is critical. Knowledge, anticipation, fears and hopes were embedded in a cultural framework. Between 1974–76 most Greek Cypriots do not appear to have believed that the missing were dead, nor actively entertained that possibility. They may even have feared thinking this. Loizos, who conducted fieldwork among refugees in 1975, noted that 'it was common for a family to refuse to believe that several witnesses had seen their boy killed' (1981: 116). There are other examples where witnesses feared to tell relatives that they had seen their boy killed.

One cannot thus explain the persistence of the refusal by relatives to accept the deaths of the missing merely in terms of the state's cynical political exploitation of the issue, although there certainly was this. Indeed many government officials now recognise that the Government should have acted more decisively in this matter, in not having connived in such a complicated manner in presenting the missing as a puzzle for which it asserted only the Turks held the key. Nor is this persistence merely an 'unrealistic' refusal by relatives to 'face facts', although unofficially some officials appear to suggest this as a means to both create more space for political manoeuvring in its dealings with the UN Committee for Missing Persons, and at the same time 'explain' why the Government cannot appear to be 'more realistic', 'because this would offend the sensibilities of the relatives'. The political representatives of the relatives of missing persons also wished to prevent closure. It then emerged that these representatives may have known what happened to some missing persons but wished to keep the matter concealed and blame the Turks. Thus the matter is complex. What is certain is that the way relatives learnt gradually about their missing, in a context of the recovery of individuals, encouraged them to view their relatives as recoverable, not as a bureaucratic euphemism for the dead. Rumours abounded. In the words of the novelist Angeliki Smyrli: 'It was a overcast period in the midst of an orgy of rumours and spreading rumours, which in reality was nurtured by the suffering [*pathos* – used also to refer to the Passion of Christ – PSC] of all those who had missing relatives' (1989: 36). The radio was an important means to trace kin, and names of prisoner exchanges were read out.

In the late 1970s and early 1980s any suggestion that the missing might be dead, or that the hopes that they might still be alive conflicted with logic, or even that few counter-examples were available from other countries, were not voiced at all. Right up to 1998 the suggestion that they might be dead was still expressed *sotto voce* as an individual belief against the officially sanctioned view, and rarely in the self-censoring Greek Cypriot press. It thus appeared to remain on the level of unofficial knowledge. Interestingly, contemporary resignation does not question the official presentation, but assumes rather that after so much time one would expect the missing not to be still alive (rather than to have been dead/killed in 1974), e.g., 'According to my opinion there is no *agnoumenos* who is alive. Perhaps the young ones … If these lived, they would have done something to make friends with someone to send a letter to an Embassy, or done something else' (Greek Cypriot refugee, 1998).

Soon after the end of hostilities a series of meetings between the two sides represented by Glavkos Clerides and Rauf Denktash began on 6 September 1974. In February 1975 they agreed to establish an interim Committee on Humanitarian Issues to deal with the issue of Missing Persons in confidential meetings. Relatives of missing persons had already been active. They had begun meeting at a primary school where the IRC had established themselves. On the 11 August 194 the relatives elected an *ad hoc* five-man committee under the chairmanship of the cleric Father Christoforos. The latter and some other individuals have remained prominent political figures. Partly out of frustration that no results were forthcoming, in June 1975 the first Cypriot Committee of Parents and relatives of Unknown Prisoners and Missing Persons was established under the continuing leadership of Father Christoforos. Membership consisted of first-degree kinsmen and spouses.

This was a non-governmental organisation although it received some financial support from the State. Soon after, relief for relatives was made available by the State. On the return of President Makarios to Cyprus, the Government set up a Service for Humanitarian Affairs with responsibility for some 200,000 refugees and for relatives of Missing Persons who had to be housed, given jobs, loans, etc. The identity of a Missing Person thus became bureaucratised and a whole new field of political representation created. The nature of evidence required to qualify for Missing status does not appear to have been very rigorous – merely, it appears, statements that someone saw their relatives taken away. The lack of precision demanded might have been due to the perception that this was an extraordinary situation and that refugees would soon be able to return to their homes. The list remained relatively static for some 15 years.

This list assumed two interrelated functions, First, it became a political weapon used by the Republic of Cyprus in its international diplomatic efforts to hold Turkey to account for its actions (a list of shame), and second it created an internal interest group: a list of individuals entitled for financial relief, housing benefits, (unskilled) government jobs, scholarships, and other important resources for relatives of the missing persons, who in some cases had lost not just loved ones but all their material possessions. Many of them came from poor backgrounds. It has been rumoured that between 15–20 July 1974 some 2,000 young men from wealthy and middle class families, were flown to London to be out of harm's way. Whereas previously (in 1960) social entitlement to government resources was through active Greek nationalism, through the sacrifice of life and limb for an ideal, in 1974 entitlement was through victimhood *by* Greek nationalism, through having lost life, limb, and property. It is not surprising that the society was dispirited and confused. The Missing also became a latent source of contention between relatives of the missing and the coupists, who were popularly held responsible for the 1974 catastrophe but never legally prosecuted. This raised some dilemmas when the political representatives of the relatives of missing persons were later suspected of having participated in the coup. To revert to *Antigone* as metaphor: it is as if those searching for Eteocles' missing body to give it a state funeral are believed to have been partly responsible for his death, or at least suspected of knowing where Eteocles' body is. The implications are examined in Chapter 8. In addition the list became a list of supporters of a cause, a community of suffering.

Internationalization of the Issue

The UN General Assembly passed a number of resolutions recognising the importance of Missing Persons. Resolution 3220 noted that 'the desire to know the fate of loved ones lost in armed conflicts is a basic human need which should be satisfied to the greatest extent possible' and that 'provision of information ...

63

should not be delayed merely because other issues remain pending'. It also called for parties 'to take such action as may be within their power to help locate and mark the graves of the dead, to facilitate the disinterring and the return of remains, if requested by their families, and to provide information about those who are missing in action'. This was largely based on Resolution V adopted by the 22nd International Conference of the Red Cross. Due to Greek Cypriot pressure which fitted in with world-wide concerns about the role of the military in disappearances world-wide (such as in Argentina, Chile, etc), a number of General Assembly resolutions (including No.3450, 32/128 on 16/12/1977) were passed calling for a UN sponsored Committee on Missing Persons (CMP). Turkey resolutely refused to acknowledge any problem or to get involved, although its army invaded and still occupies a sovereign state (according to the Greek Cypriots), or intervened according to its right afforded by the 1960 constitution (according to Turkey and the TRNC). However one might term or even justify this action, it is indubitable that military intervention results in violence and loss of life. Nevertheless, Turkey still refuses to get involved. The Turkish Cypriots, in response to Greek Cypriot claims, were very specific that they too had missing persons they wanted taken into account by the CMP. Although the 105th plenary meeting of 16 December 1977 requested the Secretary General to 'support the establishment of an investigatory body ... to resolve the problem without delay', the Committee was only established four years later in April 1981. It consisted of a Greek Cypriot, a Turkish Cypriot representative and a third member appointed by the Secretary-General. This was the first such body ever established under UN auspices. Disagreements over procedural rules and workable criteria further delayed its setting up, and the CMP did not begin its investigative work until May 1984, ten years after the disappearances. Its deliberations are confidential, and it must act by the unanimous agreement of the three Members; it is a purely 'humanitarian organ', and bases its work on the files and documents submitted by each side on their own missing persons, and on the 'testimony of the witnesses interviewed by the investigative teams'.

There have been, and still are, fundamental differences between the Greek and Turkish Cypriots regarding the CMP's ultimate aim. The Turkish Cypriots want it to establish whether such individuals are simply alive or dead. It is almost as if they wish to confirm that the missing are dead and end the matter. This has uncomfortable parallels with the situation in Argentina. Robben notes that in the 1970s at the height of the repression, the military rulers made two official attempts to have the disappeared pronounced dead even in the absence of a corpse (2000: 83). It certainly is not a wise position to adopt. The Greek Cypriot side, partly in response to the relatives, have adopted a slogan which is sufficiently wide to include all of the above, but can also be used to demand more detail. The standard statement is 'We demand clarification on the fate of the Missing' (*na diakrivosoume i tyche ton agnoumenon*). This could include the situations under which the missing, if dead, lost their lives, or even were murdered either by the

Turkish army or by the TMT. A compromise was reached when it was agreed that the CMP was to specify 'as appropriate whether they are alive or dead, and in the latter case appropriate time of death'. The categories for classification were also agreed. Around this same period, the (Greek Cypriot) relatives began demanding the return of the bones for proper burial. Proper religious burial is an important aspect of Orthodoxy and Greek culture, and is justified with reference to the needs of the relatives. With the advances in genetics and forensic anthropology, exhumations can yield much information. Exhumation as conducted in Guatemala and Bosnia could provide information the Turkish Cypriots and Turkey, whose troops were imposing a 'peace operation in Cyprus', might well be reluctant to divulge. A *corpus delicti* provides literal evidence of a crime and hence opens up a whole field of criminal prosecutions and human right transgressions.

The demand for the return of the remains is more than a cynical political ploy by the Greek Cypriot authorities, as the Turkish Cypriots claim, although political considerations are certainly important. Even a political reading renders the issue complicated and far from transparent. From the Greek Cypriot perspective at least five distinct political actors are involved: the Committee of the Relatives, the Greek Cypriot CMP negotiating team, the Foreign Ministry, and political party interests. There are close links between the Greek Cypriot CMP negotiating team and the Foreign Ministry. This is not surprising given that the Greek Cypriots consider international public opinion over humanitarian issues the only weapon likely to convince the Turks and Turkish Cypriots to co-operate. Consequently, it is hard to specify whether this demand was (i) an expression of the relatives' suspicion that the state's involvement in the CMP negotiations might not fully represent their interests and investigate the conditions of death, (ii) careful orientation by nationalist political parties to prevent a sell-out of national interests by the government, (iii) Foreign Ministry interests to present the Greek Cypriot negotiating team with apparently autonomous demands from the relatives to convey to the CMP negotiations as a humanitarian issue requiring resolution, and thus present the Turks as intransigent or as having something to hide, or (iv) a 'natural', 'non-political' request by relatives as a human right. The overt high ethnic politicisation of the issue and its covert politicisation in Greek Cypriot society suggests that a combination of the above is possible. As a centrally placed observer confided, 'the relatives have been marginalised from the mainstream of society. They are exploited politically by a certain party, by the church, and by the UN'. One may add that the Government has facilitated this because it has not taken a specific and firm line. It is clear that the political alignments behind such a request are far from transparent, and there are important symbolic aspects I examine in the next chapter.

Each member of the CMP is supposed to submit names, according to mutually agreed criteria, to the other side for investigation. Each team independently presents its own cases that are then supposed to be investigated equally independently by the other side, although the third member accompanies the investigating team. Theoretically each team therefore could have access to an immense amount of highly embarrassing information, both in terms of killings committed by its own side and how bodies are disposed of on the one hand, and in terms of the corresponding information offered by the other. Such arrangements could work if trust was present, but this is largely absent. Each side invests the Other as the keeper of its dead as missing/lost, a Cerberus guarding the Mourning Fields preventing recovery of its dead. The submission of names was slow. By 22 November 1993, nineteen years after the events, 'only 210 cases of missing persons had been submitted by the Greek Cypriot side and only 318 cases on the Turkish Cypriot side'. These appear to have been those cases where the submitting side had strong suspicions about culpability. They do not appear to have been those cases where there was a greater degree of uncertainty as to the conditions of their disappearance. The delay in submissions held up the CMP's work. It was only by December 1995 (14 years after its establishment) that the CMP had before it the total files of the Missing, comprising 1493 Greeks and Greek Cypriot and 500 Turkish Cypriots. The latter had been 'revised' downwards from 803.[4] There was much resistance to the final submission of names by the Committee of Relatives of Missing Persons, who wanted more names included, and severely embarrassed the Cypriot Government by accusing it of wanting to close the issue. By 5 March 1996 the CMP had held 2364 meetings and 82 sessions, and it issued a press communiqué that stated:

> No Committee, especially a humanitarian one, can operate successfully without the full co-operation of its Members. Until now, however, the indispensable spirit of collaboration between the Parties had not been sufficient.

On 9 March 1996 the third member resigned, which led to a recess in formal meetings. It has had a formal shadowy existence since then. In his submissions to the Security Council, the Secretary-General suspended formally recommending the appointment of a third member until some progress was made. The CMP costs the international community some $200,000 annually, although the Cyprus government makes a substantial contribution to the operations of the UN in Cyprus.

Various reasons can be advanced to explain the lack of movement. First, there is the absence of trust. Negotiations are influenced by the overall climate of inter-ethnic relations. A cold or hostile phase (such as after August 1996 when two unarmed Greek Cypriot demonstrators attempting to demonstrate over the Green Line were killed by Turkish Cypriot forces), severely hinders progress. Second, if decisions can only be reached by consensus, the third member is mainly a mediator with little independent means to exert pressure. Third, whilst confidentiality formally enables the committee to operate free from overt political pressures, obtain witness statements, and exercise initiative, the overall climate is still politicised. 'Confidentiality' can also be a euphemism for secrecy. Lack of openness has permitted political considerations to intrude into the negotiations. Fourth, although the CMP is not a court, it is difficult to exclude considerations of 'responsibility', 'culpability', even 'justice' and 'retribution' both through the way evidence is collected, and in the way it is feared it might be treated by the other side. The Committee made a public appeal to 'official bodies and to private persons to furnish [it] with any information in their possession on missing persons', which would be 'treated in the strictest confidence', and repeated that 'no prosecution of any nature will ensue as a result of statements or information given to the committee'. Yet witness statements *qua* witness statements are hard to come by, although such information is widely available. As Amnesty International's report suggests, such witnesses are open to intimidation, or even liable to 'self-censure'. Many on both sides would prefer to forget certain aspects of the 1974 events. Individuals may be willing to talk 'unofficially', 'in confidence' but still display a suspicion of writing which is associated with state power, evidence, and incrimination. A member of the Greek team investigating the Turkish Cypriot cases told me that people are prepared to talk, and he had developed a subtle and sensitive understanding of the various legitimations offered by the individuals involved in inter-communal killings. But he noted that information was only forthcoming either confidentially on the understanding that this would be denied by the interlocutor if ever socially confronted, or almost as religious confessions, a catharsis evoking complex notions of personal punishment. There was little motivation for witnessing based upon civic responsibility.[5] Furthermore the issue of prosecutability is left vague, partly because both sides' rhetoric present what happened in Cyprus as proto-Bosnian and hence use terms such as 'ethnic cleansing' and 'war crimes'.

A final reason is that the State (on both sides) is too heavily implicated in the process of witness statement collection and investigating cases submitted by the other side, given the fact that both sides implicitly licensed such violence. Much information was obtained with the participation, assistance, or in the presence of the state's personnel (Police or KYP, the Intelligence Service). Some of these individuals on both sides were heavily implicated in inter-ethnic violence and even condoned it. They are known for their nationalist sympathies. It is hardly surprising that 'condemnatory' witnesses (rather than 'confessional' witnesses) would be reluctant to come forward. Condemnatory witnessing could expose a person to a dangerous labelling and retribution.[6] On 5 March 1996 the CMP issued a press communiqué saying that up till then 'the indispensable spirit of collaboration between the Parties has not been sufficient'.

In addition each party fears making concessions to reach a breakthrough because it has an *a priori* assumption that such concessions will be exploited by the other side for propaganda purposes. This establishes a vicious circle of pessimistic deadlock and optimistic unrealism. Each side accuses the other of prolonging the issue. As I was told: 'It is seen as a useless committee crippled by inadequate terms of reference and has no success in solving any particular case'.

In 1997–98 there were three important developments. First, on 31 July 1997, Clerides and Denktash agreed (i) the problem of missing persons should be considered as a 'purely humanitarian issue the solution of which is long overdue', (ii) agreed that 'no political exploitation should be made of the problem', (iii) agreed 'as a first step ... to provide each other immediately and simultaneously all information already at their disposal on the location of graves of Greek Cypriot and Turkish Cypriot missing persons'.[7] This agreement was outside the CMP framework and indicates the point made above that politicians can sometimes side-step the stage of confrontation and concentrate on resolving 'humanitarian issues'. It was clear that Denktash did not want this agreement to fall within the remit of the CMP. This may have alarmed the Turkish Cypriot CMP negotiating team who had long insisted that many Greek Cypriot missing were victims of the coup or were missing in action. For a brief moment it appeared that the issue was on the way to resolution. However on 30 April 1998 the Turkish Cypriot representative stated that he was not prepared to discuss the necessary arrangements leading to the exhumation and return of the remains of the Greek Cypriot and Turkish Cypriot missing persons until the Greek Cypriot side, as proof of its sincerity, agree to first look into the fate of the Greek Cypriot victims of the coup d'etat against Archbishop Makarios in 1974. The Turkish Cypriot side claims that victims of the coup d'etat are among the persons listed as missing. 'This position', noted the Secretary General

> deviates from the 31 July 1997 agreement ... As a result of the position taken by the Turkish Cypriot side, no progress has been made towards the implementation of the 31 July 1997 agreement. The Greek Cypriot side has since decided to begin exhumation and identification of the remains located in graves in the area under its control.[8]

Second, after intense pressure by the U.S. State Department on Turkey, which effectively controls the TRNC, a team of investigators managed to get access to the occupied North and retrieve the remains of a U.S. citizen of Greek Cypriot origin who had disappeared. The resultant report helped shed much light on the probable circumstances surrounding the fate of missing Greek Cypriots.[9] It indicated that this individual had probably been murdered. His remains were returned to the US. His friend, who disappeared with him, was not returned because he was not a US citizen, although his remains were probably retrievable. By 1999, tensions had emerged between the Government of Cyprus and the Relatives of Missing Persons, and quite independently two women tried to force the issue by staging the dramatic exhumation referred to in the beginning of the book.

NOTES

1. It was suggested to me that as the Red Cross worked through local interpreters they might have been given names of those whose fates were known in order to magnify losses.

2. 'At that time [in 1975] the incidents were still fresh and it was generally believed that there might be missing persons who were alive'. Report by Mr Claude Pilloud, representative of the ICRC/UN Secretary-General on the tri-partite autonomous Committee of Missing Persons (CMP).

3. Yialsin Kuchuk, a Kurdish captain in the Turkish army in 1974, said in an interview with Greek Cypriot TV station *Antenna* in February 1998 that soldiers killed a Down's Syndrome woman in the area of Tymbou (Drusiotis, 2000: 19). After this interview the authorities made enquiries and identified Despina Kountouro who had remained enclaved in Tymbou. Then they discovered another person whose name was also not on the government list of missing persons. Thus there were some people on the list who should not have been there, and others who should have been (Drusiotis, ibid: 19–20).

4. The 500 missing Turkish Cypriots include: 1963–64: 200 civilians who were abducted and disappeared; 21 slaughtered in Ayios Vasilios (Tarkeli), Nicosia district (13 cases of which have been presented to the CMP). 1974: 14 August: Maratha (Murataga) and Sandalaris (Sandallar) where Greek Cypriot armed elements massacred 89 persons; 37 people from Aloa (Atlilar). 15 August: 85 Turkish Cypriot men from three villages (Tokhni, Zygi, Mari close to Limassol who were arrested, transported by bus towards Limassol and massacred. One witness escaped to give testimony.

5. Amnesty International has claimed that 'its entirely confidential method of work has undermined public confidence in its work and defeated its humanitarian goal of providing information to families of the fate of their relatives'. Yet the 'confidentiality' is a function of a lack of trust between the two communities as well as the desire by both sides to exclude their own citizens from participation and consultation, partly because both sides have made political capital out of the issue.

6. It could be argued that a South African-styled 'Truth Commission' based upon notions of public confessions for forgiveness could be employed, as this bypasses the opposition between 'official' (legal, written, quotable, etc) and 'unofficial' (confidential, oral) testimony but this would run into difficulties. First, it is based upon a Christian concept and may not appeal greatly to the Turkish Cypriots. Paradoxically the Church in Cyprus has been the religion of the oppressed ethnos rather than the religion of the oppressed irrespective of ethnicity. Second, there has been much resentment in S. Africa that this has been exploited by the ex-security services to bypass judicial proceedings.

7. UN Press Release, 31 July 1997.

8. Report of the Secretary General to the Security Council: S/1998/488, 10 June 1998, p.5, para. 23. I suspect that one reason for the Turkish Cypriot CMP intransigence is that it would indicate that TMT was less under the politicians' control than was believed, and that they actually have very few records.

9. R.S. Dillon, (retired ambassador), 'The President's Report to Congress on the Investigation of the US Citizens who have been missing from Cyprus since 1974'. Washington: State Department, 1998.

4
THE MISSING AS A SET OF REPRESENTATIONS

ഏᴥᏩᏗ

It's vile; and I can tell you what I wouldn't tell anybody else: it's stupid, monstrously stupid. But the people of Thebes have got to have their noses rubbed into it a little longer. My God! If it was up to me, I should have had them bury your brother long ago as a matter of public hygiene. I admit what I am doing is childish. But if the featherheaded rabble I govern are to understand what's what, the stench has to fill the town for a month!

Creon in Anouilh's *Antigone* (1960: 48)

Introduction

The Turkish invasion and partitioned occupation of Cyprus was the single most cataclysmic event in modern Cypriot history. It was a collective trauma for Greek Cypriot society, though not for Turkish Cypriots – at least then. It shook the economy, family relations, politics, and forcefully uprooted a third of the population turning them into refugees. The economy collapsed, but subsequently made a remarkable recovery. In the long run the society became urbanised and Cyprus was transformed from a largely rural-based economy to a modern, thriving service economy with all its attendant problems. The invasion re-formed the actual space, the geography and the landscape of the island, inserting a dangerous no-go area between the two communities. It affected time: how Turkish and Greek Cypriots visualise their past, present, and future. Something similar seems to have occurred in Latvia. In her study of people's testimonies in Latvia, Skultans noted that the 1940 Soviet occupation of Latvia came to play a leading role in defining national identity. Cypriots similarly talk about the 1974 events as the central reference point of their history, space, and identity.

Michel de Certeau has perhaps rather grandly claimed that the quest for historical meaning 'aims at calming the dead who still haunt the present, and at offering them scriptural tombs' (1988: 2) This statement is useful in setting the aims of this chapter: how the missing still haunt the present in Cyprus, and how they are used by the state and society as a means to talk about the past. This complements two approaches to memory: as a strategy to cope with the traumatic experiences of the past (Antze and Lambek, 1996), and as a means to deal with ancestors and with death (Battaglia, 1992; Davies, 1994; Taylor, 1993). In his study of responses to the trauma of the First World War, Winter concentrates on war memorials 'as foci of the rituals, rhetoric, and ceremonies of bereavement' (1995: 78). I shall be looking at the memorialisation of the missing by the state as well as by political representatives of their relatives as foci not so much of bereavement, but rather of attempted recovery. It is worthwhile to visualize this within the context of *Antigone*. We shall look at how modern Creon memorialises the body of Eteocles – except that the body of Eteocles is missing. The concern here is with the missing as presences, as a series of representations. In a subsequent chapter I examine the converse: how the state and individuals represent the missing as losses and as absences.

Memory, Mourning, and Recovery: Narratives of the State

In the previous chapter we discussed how in the early years after 1974 relatives came to believe, or hope, that their missing persons might still be alive. I now wish to examine why such beliefs are still maintained at least officially on the level of institutions. This involves a study of how continuing inter-ethnic contestations over the interpretation of the past interrelate with internal Greek Cypriot politics to structure the institutionalisation of memories. In Cyprus, memory as a set of images and as process has not just been kept alive. It has been progressively manufactured, managed, and elaborated to reflect, and adjust to, the changing political programmes of the state, and the evolving complex emotional exigencies of individuals. I begin by concentrating on the former.

It is important to begin by noting that in Cyprus generally the state or political authorities on both sides of the ethnic divide does not have a programme of attempting to erase or oppress private memories, although both sides certainly want to suggest *how the past should be remembered.* Thus makes the politics of memory very different to that found in, for example, Central America. Zur notes that 'the distance between private memory and public representations is particularly wide in repressive regimes such as that ruling Guatemala during *la violencia* (1998: 170). By contrast the political authorities on both sides of the ethnic divide in Cyprus actively attempt to represent private memories through public representations in various forms, although there are significant differences in terms of the political appropriation, forming, and expression of these private memories.

Following the invasion, the Republic of Cyprus became actively involved in giving expression to, and harnessing, complex feelings of material, spiritual, and personal loss. The invasion resulted in the creation of three social categories: *the Missing, the Refugees,* and *the Enclaved.*[1] These are not just individual social identities, 'sociological' or 'political' groups, or merely political actors. They are also symbolic groups having a semiological identity as political signifiers and subjective signifieds.[2] Through their double role as political signifiers of loss and recovery, and specular signifieds of mourning and recuperation, the state harnesses individual and collective emotions articulating them in mutually reinforcing discourses about the past, the present, and the future. It is not just the past that has to be redefined, it is also memories.

The issue of the Missing and the Dead is both an internal and an international matter. The Republic of Cyprus appears to group the two, by which it means the dead as a result of the coup and the invasion, and the missing as a result of the invasion. As noted, the Missing have a greater facticity and symbolism than the Dead. Their numbers are known and, since 1995, their names published. They are evoked regularly at meetings, demonstrations, etc. The dead by contrast, that is the actual casualties, have never had their names published in lists, and there is no official statistic of their numbers. There are no official memorial services specifically for them, as they are grouped together with the fallen of 1955–59. In popular Greek Cypriot consciousness, the Missing have become the murdered casualties of the Turkish army and Turkish Cypriot irregulars, subject to a greater degree of active public evocation that the actual casualties of the resistance to the Turkish invasion. To the Greek Cypriots, the invasion was a shameful period and established an unacceptable state of affairs. Having boasted for years how one Greek could vanquish ten Turks in battle, etc, they were defeated. 'Protecting Mother Greece' betrayed Cyprus, and Greek Cypriot soldiers were routed and their women raped. The Missing by contrast are seen as victims of the invasion, and therefore legitimate subjects to mourn. Indeed as I hope to show, in spite of the fact that the Missing have not been recovered, they are in a very real sense the 'mourned' of this society. This is because perhaps the only way Greek Cypriot society has been able grapple with an unacceptable state of affairs has been through the representation of the Missing as a category of liminality. One could therefore suggest that for many years the society remained stuck in what has been called the first stage of mourning, i.e., shock, anger, denial.

The coup unleashed violence against both Greek and Turkish Cypriots, and the Republic of Cyprus in the interests of 'ethnic unity' has been reluctant to investigate this period. Consequently, no coupists have been prosecuted for murder either of Greek or, *a fortiori*, of Turkish Cypriots. This angers those on the Greek Cypriot left who have long insisted on justice for the memory of those, particularly leftists, killed by the coupists. In the week between the coup and the invasion there was much confusion and fighting between Greek Cypriots, and there were some anonymous collective burials in Nicosia. The bulldozer moves from being a secular instrument of building and reconstruction, and becomes a sacrilegious symbol of the concealment of bodies and crimes, the mechanical collectivisation of death, the travesty of burial rituals, the disassembly of bodies, and the permanent denial of identity.

Turkish Cypriots have long claimed that an unspecified large number of the Greek Cypriot missing were killed during the coup period, suggesting that most if not all of the 1619 claimed Greek Cypriot missing persons were killed during this fighting. AKEL (the Communist Party) originally subscribed to this view because leftists led the resistance against the coup, but later, in the interests of national unity, toned down this interpretation.[3] Until 1999, the Greek Cypriot side claimed that the 1619 missing were distinct from coup casualties and that only 19 died during the coup.[4] Powerful inducements sustained such claims and beliefs. Some men were murdered by coupists who hid their bodies. Others died in the fighting. Relatives of the missing not only gain social benefits and become symbols of national suffering because of their lost ones, but achieve little except social reprobation if they insist their relatives were killed as a result of internecine fighting. Claiming that one's loved ones were killed by fellow Greeks could also commit the descendants of the missing to dangerous and risky partisan political allegiances, when all political parties (leftists included) wish to remember ethnic oppression rather than political murders. The secretary of the Committee of Relatives of Missing Persons claimed that 84 people were killed in the coup and not one of these was included in the list of missing persons. The state is reluctant even to investigate this period, much less to prosecute because it would then be obliged to investigate the killings of Turkish Cypriots during the coup period. This created many contradictions, which I examine in another chapter. As one man explained to me: 'Why should Fivos admit that he killed Pavlos?' Better, therefore, to let such killings remain *agnoumeni*, of unknown origin, and therefore by implication killed by the Turks, thus directing aggression and suffering outwards. One reporter who investigated the matter in the mid-1990s noted that the dates of deaths of some of the fallen had subsequently been changed from the coup to the invasion. Better to be a hero protecting the island from the Turks than a shameful victim of an internecine tragedy; better an Eteocles than a Polynices. Finally, many survivors of fighting would be reluctant to tell relatives that their missing ones were killed whilst they survived, a guilt-inducing admission. Some witnesses have claimed they were asked by relatives of the missing not to get involved. The Communist Party, whilst eager to blame the right for the coup and the invasion, is reluctant to insist on proper judicial enquiries which would expose it to accusations that it is playing into Turkey's hands, and thus vitiating Greek Cypriot unity. There have thus been inducements to remember and forget this period in certain ways. In addition, as I show below, there was great uncertainty about what happened during the coup. By 1999 personal accounts were surfacing which threatened the hegemony of official depictions of reality. I examine this in a later chapter.

The relatives of the Missing also constitute an important electoral segment, accustomed to, and solicitous of, media exposure and manipulation. They are strongly supported by the Church and by DiKo (Democratic Party). Both take a hard anti-rapprochment line on the inter-ethnic level. As the Missing have become signifiers and signified of ethnic suffering, no political party was likely until the time of writing (2000–1) openly to question the validity of the 1619 missing, after the state has so long made use of them in its internationally oriented efforts to expel Turkey from Cyprus. By 2001, this simulation of certainty was beginning to be seriously questioned. The demands of relatives of the missing have become institutionalised and reflected in party programmes. The failure of the individuals elected to leadership positions in the Committee to satisfy demands means that they have to be seen to give something back to their constituents and keep hopes alive. Their leaders form temporary alliances with hard-line politicians, who sponsor their activities to further their careers. Many activities are expressed through ritual activism: vigils outside embassies, in public places, torch-lit processions, etc. Since Christmas 1996, weekend demonstrations have been held outside the Ledra Palace Hotel, the only recognised checkpoint to the Turkish side. The aim is to publicise the issue, discourage tourists from visiting the Turkish Cypriot side, and further re-enforce the blockade of the North.[5] Yellow ribbons with the name of a missing person were tied to a Christmas tree (Figure 3). Clearly, the act of writing symbolised that they were not forgotten, as well as perhaps a reminder to the state, as relatives were worried that some names may be dropped by the Government from the official list of missing persons, as indeed I show happened. The holding of photographs, tied by a string round the neck or holding up a frame, is a critical part of demonstrating (Figure 4).

The Committee of the Relatives of the Missing (CRM), until recently an independent powerful pressure group skilfully run by Father Christoforos a priest whose son is one of the missing, not only receives Government support and funds, but until the late 1990s actively sponsored the belief that the missing may well be alive. It has acted more as a group focussing international pressure on Turkey and keeping the issue publicly alive, than as a body concerned with representing the interests of the relatives to the state. Right-wing interests dominated it and there have been suggestions that individuals have hijacked leadership positions for access to benefits (travel, etc) and national prominence. The journalist Drousiotis noted 'Christoforos made some 200 journeys to every corner of the globe, he was met at airports by embassy cars and his expenses were met by the state and he stayed at luxury hotels' (2000: 44). He suggests that partly because of the guilty conscience of society, until the early 1990's 'the power Father Christoforos had then was so great that no one could refuse him anything' (ibid: 40). Indeed he explicitly states 'the Committee of the Relatives, which was established with the highest aim of discovering the fate of the missing, quickly became a closed organization which fell under the complete control of Father Christoforos and the brothers Nikos and Georgiou Serghidis' ... 'Thus was created a *nomenklatura* in the group of the relatives of the missing. The leadership enjoyed all the advantages of power, exploiting the pain of thousands of relatives' (ibid: 43–45). More ominously, it has also been suggested that some individuals dominated this Committee to prevent investigations into deaths of the Missing during the coup. There has been, thus, a passive and active complicity in what this society wished to remember and forget. By 1996 tensions emerged between the government and the CRM which I explore below.

Figure 3 Tying Yellow Ribbons, Symbolising Hope.

Figure 4 'The Body as Billboard'.

In addition, there is also the natural desire by the mourners, in the face of official connivance to imagine that such men may well be alive. One man, whose photograph as a prisoner in Turkey was printed in the papers, said that many parents swore he was their son. Even after 22 years, when society 'expects' a degree of 'realism' in official Greek Cypriot calculations, relatives of the missing require proof that their loved ones are dead. As one man said: 'if you don't have information, he is (still) a Missing Person *(ean dhen ehete stihia ine agnoumenos)*. There is always the hope that some may be alive. It is a human right to know what happened.' Rather than presuming such men to be dead unless proved to be alive, relatives normally presume these men to be living unless demonstrated to be dead. That this interpretation is a cultural one is brought out more clearly when one compares this to the Turkish Cypriot position. Logically one would have expected the latter to believe that their missing were alive because they disappeared sporadically and individually in contexts phenomenologically resembling kidnappings, of which there were some in the 1960s. By contrast the Greek Cypriots disappeared often collectively in groups, in a short period, and following mass hostilities and major dislocation.

A final consequence is the investment and elaboration of memories, as interiorised explorations and as collective representations. With the passage of time, memories have to be scripted and narrated by those expected to have them. In so doing, individuals can continue to make sense of their experiences, adjust them to their present situations, and confabulate them in their futures with others. Since 1974 and the population swap-over, the possibilities of an independently negotiated settlement between the Republic of Cyprus and the internationally unrecognised Turkish Republic of Northern Cyprus have receded even further. The enclaved Greek population in the North is likely to disappear within some 10 years due to natural wastage (children above the age of 18 being prohibited from remaining there), and the active memories by refugees of the loss of their homes, of their past, and of their identities, is progressively being replaced by a different set of memories. These are not so much the directly painful experiences of specific images and of specific detail which wound the heart that retells in order to symbolically recover (Loizos, 1981), but they have become more imagined memories, memories of a different sort. These are the stories that children of refugees, brought up in the South, have heard from their parents about their homes, and their villages, seen in photographs, but now part of family lore as lost patrimony and thus as denied rights. They are also officially encouraged memories of villages in the North when children were encouraged (as indeed they still are) to draw pictures of their village by school authorities to be displayed, published, or put on stamps, even if they have no direct experience of their 'paternal' (*patrigoniko* – which also means ancestral) village.[6]

Here it is worthwhile to try to relate the actions of recollection and recounting, the practice of memory, to emplotments by individuals in the past and the future. In her excellent study of narratives in Latvia, Skultans (1998) concentrates on the transformation of memory into narrative. She suggests that when individual memories are expressed in narratives, then the anthropologist should also be sensitive to the concerns of narratology. This requires a consideration of the narrative structure, and the groping around for experience. 'The transformation of memory into narrative loosens the ties with original experience and opens the way for the substitution for schematized images. Like literary texts breaking free of their authors' intentions, Latvian narratives possess commonalities of structure and theme which override individual experience' (ibid: xi). Skultans emphasises that 'as memories are cast into a narrative mould so they must of necessity conform to the conventions of story telling' (ibid: xii). She discovered this was particularly the case in the narratives of older people. She gives importance to the notion of coherence as 'central to an exegesis of narrative', but criticises Bruner's individualistic and potentially solipsistic version of narrative coherence (Bruner and Feldman, 1996). Instead, she supports the notion of an inter-narrative coherence, a type of inter-textuality practiced in literary analysis: 'allegiances are not towards the past but towards other narratives. It seeks for connections and where it succeeds in making these we as listeners and readers recognize coherence. Coherence is thus about belonging' (ibid: xiii). In the case of older Latvians, this coherence was supplied through commonalities through shared conventions in literary paradigms. Skultans was struck by the similarities between Latvian literary themes and structures, and autobiographical frames. The younger generation who lacked such common conventions experienced semantic collapse.

There are similarities to Cyprus. Individuals employ themes from classical mythology. Many talk of the 'Penelopes of modern Cyprus' (after Penelope, Ulysses' wife who waited twenty years for his return from the Trojan war, the theme of Homer's *Odyssey*, see Roussou, 1986). Alternatively, they refer to Euripides' tragedy, *The Trojan Women* (*Troades*), one of the most poignant of the Euripidean dramas which is not a narrative but a tragic situation: the fate of the Trojan women after their men have been killed and they are at the mercy of their captors, to be sold into captivity. In Cyprus, political authorities also employ Greek literary themes. These themes are employed not so much for solace or to create inter-narrative coherence, but also by political authorities as a means to explain the 'Greekness' of the national predicament and to situate it within a common European cultural framework. Indeed, and herein lies the irony, 'coherence' *as belonging* is *supplied by the state* in Cyprus. This is precisely what was absent in the Latvian case where the state was the cause of oppression and suffering. In Cyprus, the state has intervened to provide meta-(i.e., post) narratives, or master-narratives, based on a mixture of classical Greek themes and Christian symbolism. In spite of the lability of literary themes, and indeed because of it, it is an argument of this book that the similarity between peoples' experiences and literary themes can also be a subversive one, that literature can help subvert the state's emplotment of the past, present and future by providing different scenarios for individuals to enact out their predicaments. As I explore in this book, the linkage of people's predicaments to *Antigone* on the structural (i.e., the plot) level (i.e. the tension between women *qua* kinswomen of the dead in war and internecine strive, and Creon *qua* political leaders in the modern state), does take place. However, different workings-out can (and do) take place.

Memory is as much the recollection of the past through personalised narratives, as the anticipatory emplotment of the future. Ricoeur suggests that narratives do not just establish human actions 'in' time. They also 'bring us back from within-time-ness to historicality, from a "reckoning with" time to "recollecting" it' (1981: 174). He notes 'the priority given to the past in the structure of care that underlies the unity of the three dimensions of time … may no longer be taken for granted … the past is not the primary direction of care … *The primary direction of care is towards the future*. Through care, we are always already "ahead of" ourselves' (1981: 177 emphasis in original). The authorities often use the term *'I Thisies tou EvdomindaTessera '* (The Sacrifices of 1974). The vocabulary of sacrifice, a barely concealed statist secular theodicy, with its semi-religious associations of redemption and recovery, thus becomes particularly important for individuals *qua* citizens (rather than as private persons) to interiorise and conceptualise their pasts and futures in collective terms, uniting expectation, memory, and attention. Individuals as citizens navigate their future selves through voyages of recovery imagined by the state.

An example of the State collectivisation and articulation of memory, anticipation, and recovery is provided by exhibitions of children's art. The Education Ministry organises yearly exhibitions on specific themes. Most years this has been 'I won't Forget' (*Dhen Ksehno*). Consider a picture (Figure 5) from an exhibition of Children's Art held at Nicosia in February 1996, 'portraying the drama of the 1974 invasion and the agony of those who are still missing'.[7] The illustration indicates the state's sponsorship of reveries/nostalgias of loss, inhabited by inherited images. The picture is almost over-determined in its symbolism that has been refracted through countless reproduced images. Its theme is orphanage, or denied filiation. The Greek coup was not just a betrayal by *Mitera Ellada*, and the deposition of the legitimate government, but the deposing of filiation. The picture illustrates a mother and a young boy/girl each holding a photograph.[8] The pose adopted is similar to the black and white photographs from the 1974 period reproduced countless times, showing mothers and children holding up pictures of missing loved ones. The mother is actually a widow, not a grieving mother (the bottom photograph shown in the picture depicts her and her husband as a young couple), and she holds up a photograph of her lost (missing or dead) husband as a young soldier, frozen in time. The contrast between the aged widow/wife and the young husband could not be stronger: the wife becomes the mother holding up a picture of her dead son. So emblematic have these images become that the imagery of women holding up photographs is immediately interpretable in Cyprus as depicting relatives of the *agnoumeni*.

The State has also reconfigured memory as a series of collective representations. Here the indeterminate referentiality of the concept of *The Sacrifices of '74* is critical. It includes three categories: the Refugees in the south, the 1619 Missing Persons after the invasion, and the Enclaved in the north. These three constitute a power field, articulated by the state and the media out of individual experiences of

Figure 5 'Navigated Representations'. *Dhen Ksehno*
(I won't forget). Example of Children's Art.

loss and interrupted mourning, for the production, consumption, and circulation of memories as (i) political signifiers of ethnic/religious oppression, (ii) political imperatives for territorial recovery , and (iii) signifieds of pain. Each of these three categories has become a vehicle for collective ethnic imagining, both in the past and in the future, 'meta-narratives' between history and individual experiences. Taken together these categories enable individuals as members of an ethnic group to experience their pain and their loss through collective symbols (or to appreciate the pain of others if they were not directly affected), and to navigate the resolution, or mourning of this loss, along the axis of time through collectively shared values.

Refugees (*prosfighes*) and the Missing must be treated as metaphors for return, unity through recovery of self/past, and the utopian discovery of the past in the future. Through them discourses are elaborated around key themes of displacement, return, unity/separation. The Missing are a significant and painful plank in the Greek Cypriot campaign to retain world opinion focussed on Cyprus, and embarrass the Turkish Cypriots and Turkey. For the Turkish Cypriots it would be deeply embarrassing if the 'Peace Operation' (as they call the Turkish invasion) which established their State were publicly demonstrated as having been founded upon a prototypical act of massacre. For the Greek Cypriots the dilemma runs deeper. The campaign to keep the issue, and hence the *agnoumeni*, alive risks preventing healing and therapy, and channels aggression outwards towards the Turks. Such a sustained, almost schismogenic, campaign may be due to the risk that a public acceptance of the probabilities of their deaths could symbolically represent an acknowledgement that the North has been lost forever.

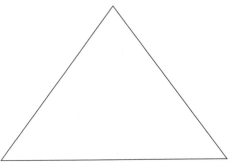

THE MISSING/ *Agnoumeni*
Marginality through liminality

REFUGEES/ *Prosfighes*
Marginality through displacement

ENCLAVED/ *Enclovismeni*
Marginality through oppression

The Enclaved (in Turkish occupied north)
Signifies: Ethnic/religious oppression of Greeks as enslaved.
Tense: Recurrent re-run of the past when Cyprus was under Turkish (ottoman) oppression.
Emotive associations: Represents both the fear that Hellenism will be extinguished in the North and unspeakable apprehension that this will be a portent of the future if the rest of the island were to be overrun by the Turks.

The Refugees (In 'Free areas'/*eleftheres peryohes*)
Signifies: Occupation of Cyprus by a foreign power; political oppression of Cypriot citizens by the denial of their human rights to return to (i.e., regain) their homes. International illegality of Turkish occupation, and the illegal occupation of Greek homes/land by settlers from Turkey, citizens of another country.
Tense: Future: We will return to our homes/recapture our past (*Tha epistrepsoume sta spitia mas*).
Emotive associations: Resistance.

The Missing (Beyond Time and Place)
Signifies: Ethnic limbo for both living and dead.
Interchangeability of 'mourners'/'mourned'
Tense: Liminality/suspension of time
Emotive associations: We can neither mourn a past that is unacceptable, nor accept a future that is unimaginable.

Figure 6 The Symbolic Relationship between the Categories
of the Missing, the Refugees and the Enclaved.

The *agnoumeni* thus function on a double level as both signifier and signified. As *the Missing* they function as a signifier of the invasion. As *the not socially dead/not buried/not socially mourned,* or more precisely as 'the unknown', they function as a displaced symbol of the non-extinguishable hope, both of their own return south, i.e., their recovery by their loved ones (the 'South'/Republic of Cyprus), and their recovery 'as temporarily occupied North' by the South. The *agnoumeni* thus represent the hope of an eventual reunification, not just of split families, but of a split land. They promise the possibility of unification yet symbolise separation. Something similar seems to have occurred in post dirty-war Argentina when mothers refused to accept that their children had been killed stating 'They took them away alive. We want them back alive' (Suarez-Orozco, 1992: 247). Suarez-Orozco notes that mothers are opposed to the state giving them any form of monetary remuneration for the disappearance: 'mothers argue that any such bureaucratic intervention requires them to psychologically become their children's executioners: they would first need to psychologically kill and bury their children before proceeding with the legal route. And this is too costly, too guilt-inducing. It is as if giving up hope is betraying their children' (ibid: 247).

On the national level the state has appropriated an interrupted mourning process, or more precisely inserted itself in the mourning process, and fabricated a simulacrum of mourning into a discourse of resistance to the occupation of the north.[9] It has done so both by a process of double transference (*the missing and refugees* are looking-glass images of each other- the latter move from in front of the mirror to behind it returning to their past selves/homes, whilst the former return from behind the mirror of their past selves/homes to unite with their loved ones), and by an double inversion of identity (the transfiguration of the state as grieving motherhood, and the objectification/alterity of refugees/ *agnoumeni* as signifiers of pain).[10] Refugees and the missing have become strategies of simulation, which dangerously risk becoming simulacra and hence denials of the real. Simulation, as Baudrillard points out, is not simply to feign to have what one has not, to imply an absence (1988). To dissimulate/simulate still leaves the principle of truth and falsity intact, that the-what-is-simulated/dissimulated is nevertheless real or true, and that they are signs for, and of, reality, either in terms of concealment or display. But where one hollows out the signified as progressively unlikely to be made real or pragmatised (e.g. return of the refugees to their homes, or the hope that the missing will be returned), then the sign becomes disembedded/disembodied from its referent: 'the whole system becomes weightless; it is no longer anything but a gigantic simulacrum: not unreal but a simulacrum, never again exchanging for what is real, but exchanging in itself, in an uninterrupted circuit without reference or circumference' (Baudrillard, 1988: 171).

If simulacra symbolically 'murder' the real (i.e. prevent a recognition of one's situation), the dilemma is even more poignant for the Greek Cypriots because 'realism' (i.e. a recognition of the seductive maleficium of simulacra, or recognising that subscribing to this position can prevent one from accepting that such missing may in fact be dead) represents the symbolic 'murder' of their loved ones (as the missing), of their selves and pasts (as refugees), and thus a shattering of the utopic imagined community through the recapture/unification of the north. 'Realism' as 'pragmatism' is equally a murdering of the real, a denial of the past, and an abandonment of the future as constantly imagined – even potentially more dangerous. Of course, everybody recognises that the refugees will probably not return to their homes, or that the missing will never appear. Indeed, the Turkish Cypriot leadership is almost involved in a joint, quasi-perverse 'conspiracy' with the Greek Cypriot government to fabricate a mutually integrating system of signs: either as a signifier with no verifiable signified (for the Turkish Cypriots) (i.e., the absent unrecalled bodies of disappeared Turkish Cypriots indicates that we cannot live together with the Greeks), or as a signified with no signifier (for the Greek Cypriots). But to officially admit the impossibility of return or recovery is to disembowel the struggle, suicidal, uncontemplatable. It is the only strategy we have, Greek Cypriots say – the strategy of simulacra.[11]

In stories, 'rather than being *predictable*, a conclusion must be *acceptable*' (Ricoeur, 1981: 277 emphasis in original). But as these conclusions (i.e., the death of the Missing or the permanent loss of the north) would be unacceptable, so the stories of the refugees or the missing have to be told with different 'endings' that are acceptable, or even told with no endings, which is preferable as it corresponds to desire (of union with the missing), or fear (that they may still be imprisoned). Otherwise, the story would be too horrible to narrate. Or rather, if it were narrated it would require a different morality to render it acceptable, to re-emplot it, which may well imply a reapportioning of agency and culpability. It is therefore almost 'necessary' that it is *imaginable* some of the missing are still possibly alive (even if improbable), not so much for the mourners (whose torture is inevitably reinscribed), but *for the State*. Stories occasionally circulate about how someone was seen in a recent photograph, that he is now in Turkey, that 'he has lost his memory', that he is prevented from returning, or even that he does not want to, or that he has now settled down and (re)married, etc. Many of these stories are further hostages to the seductive illusion of the rumours of simulation, metaphors of 'reality' (photographs) elevated to symbols of hope, or even projections of anxious desire ('even if *they* have lost their memory, i.e., have forgotten us, *we* still remember *them*'). And it is necessary that such stories should circulate as stories, even offered in discourse as *mpellares* (idiocies, illusions) to be refuted, but are nevertheless said just the same; and it is equally necessary that the authorities say they will 'investigate' such stories, because in the back-handed rejection of such stories that are recounted to be dismissed but with a hidden question-mark, the positional relationship between the sign and what it purports to represent is again rhetorically established, even if it is to be denied. The real as concealed is reconjured. It is not veracity (i.e., true or false), that is at issue here, but that 'the sign and the real are equivalent (even if this equivalence is Utopian)' (Baudrillard, 1988: 170).

Such stories plumb historical mythologies. And they tend to circulate on the anniversaries of the coup-invasion. The sister of a murdered pro-Kurdish activist Theophilos Georgiadis gunned down outside his home in March 1994 (by Turkish agents) claimed that he had information on the missing Costakis (see below), and that 13 of the missing were still alive. Another story was that a missing woman was apparently found married to a Turk in a military area but was too afraid to leave. As in the past, women become prizes between the two groups. One of the most well known stories is that of Little Costakis, a five-year-old who disappeared and who is a metaphor for a nationally denied filiation. Some stories say that a Turkish army doctor adopted, raised, and educated him (*to anayose ke to spoudase*), adopted him, and that his mother still occasionally receives telephone calls from him speaking in broken Greek. A common theme is that the missing were taken to become special soldiers, and that they were married off to Turkish girls (*Turkalles*). 'When you cross a Greek and a Turk' a villager said, 'you have the intelligence of the Greek and the coldness (*psychrotita*) of the Turk. That makes them excellent soldiers. They don't have any families and have therefore no obligation', he concluded referring to the Ottoman Janissaries. As yet few dare to state categorically and openly that the *agnoumeni* are dead, and all political parties condemned the Government for recently suggesting that some of the *agnoumeni* were dead. The political costs are too great. It is as if Greek Cypriot society cannot as yet come to terms with the loss not just of the North, but of the Missing, who are a metaphor for the north, for unity, return and wholeness, rather than division and loss. Of course, many of those not affected privately admit that the *agnoumeni* are likely to be dead, but few express such beliefs openly, and the circulation of stories guarantees that the possibility can always exist. In short, investigating the Missing in Cyprus is like investigating witchcraft beliefs in modern society. Of course we know it is not true, but there are some people who believe, and yet there may be some incidents that defy explanation. As even a member of the diplomatic corps pointed out 'we need only one case of an individual having been kept in Turkey in spite of official denials to prove our case, or at least the principle'. She continued by claiming 'you do not kill a prisoner of war – you keep them as a counter', and referred to some examples of individuals who disappeared in 1964 and surfaced years later, having been kidnapped by the Turkish Cypriots.

The State as Scripting Agent

Do you know what 'missing person' means?
A mother of a missing person says:
'A missing person is a human being without a body, a voice which cannot be heard, but is always there, a memory which refuses to go away'
Quotation from leaflet published by the Pancyprian Committee of Relatives of Undeclared Prisoners and Missing Persons, Nicosia, Republic of Cyprus.

If the Missing had become symbolic vehicles for an ethnic recovery both of the North and by their loved ones, the former 'piggy-backed' on the latter, they also soon became legal characters. By 1975 the Missing had become a bureaucratic category recognised by the state and by the international community as requiring relief and representation. A Government Departmental Service for Missing Persons was established to provide relief to the relatives. Dependants of missing persons (wives and fiancées who were pregnant at the time of the disappearances, or parents) received a monthly allowance similar to that received by refugees. In 2000 this amounted to some £240 CYP per month. In 1979 the status of the Missing also became a judicial and legal category through *The Missing Persons (Temporary Provisions) Law No. 77 of 1979.* The law passed by the Republic of Cyprus represented the legal interests of Greek Cypriot Missing Persons, particularly with respect to their property through the establishment of a Statutory Special Committee of State officials.[12] It is important to note that this law was specifically targeted at Greek Cypriots, not all Cypriots, which weakens the claim of the Republic of Cyprus to represent *all* its citizens irrespective of their ethnic identity. The Committee has the right to appoint two administrators of the property of the Missing Person.[13] Dependants are to receive payment from the administrators (section 5.5) who are expected to 'administer the immovable property in a way which is most advantageous to the missing persons' (section 5). The Law specifies that 'No movable or immovable property shall be sold, donated, pawned or in any other way transferred or encumbered, except subject to such terms and conditions as the Committee may approve' (section 8). The Law does not deal directly with the declaration of death, except to say that it is 'subject to the relevant provisions of the Administration of Estates Law' (Cap 189). There are differences in perception of this law. A prominent human rights lawyer suggested this law was to pre-empt the legal presumption of death that would normally follow after a seven-year disappearance. If this legal presumption were to have been followed, the Missing would therefore have been considered dead, a situation the authorities were keen to prevent. By contrast, Justice Ministry officials claim it was implemented to protect the legal interests of the missing themselves, and still has a valid function. However, not surprisingly, representatives of missing persons have a different view as the law restricts the disposal of property. According to the President of the Relatives of the Missing Committee it was designed to protect the rights of under-age children of whom there were then some 1000, and should now be scrapped.[14]

The Law does not indicate the terms and conditions that the Committee may apply to the disposal of property, nor does it specify any rights or means of appeal.[15] The Committee meets approximately once a month. Previously, it appointed administrators. Now, it deals with cases where the administrators themselves have needs as heirs, or as potential donors (e.g., wives of missing men whose children are now of marriageable age). Increasingly, administrators may have conflicting roles: as representatives of the missing person or potential heirs.

In both cases, especially when there is a desire to have access to the property of the missing person, they have to have recourse to the (Ministry of Justice) Committee. Formally, therefore, the Committee has immense power, and the economic stakes have increased. Government employees who are Missing have continued receiving their salaries as if they were still alive. Usually only about a half of the salaries has been paid to dependants, the rest remaining in bank accounts. After 22 years the sums involved can be substantial. The committee is liberal in allowing heirs access to the bank accounts of the Missing especially for health and education reasons, but does not consider that the law gives it the right to authorise sales of property. The Attorney General's representative was adamant: 'the law speaks about the benefit of the missing persons, not dependants'. Immovable property is more problematic. There are no problems when heirs wish to exploit the property, coming to some informal agreement among themselves on the division, although the missing person remains the legal owner. The situation is more fraught when the heirs cannot agree, or if they wish or need to sell the property. Agreements and consensus may be easy to forge in one generation but more difficult to sustain in subsequent ones. The Attorney General's representative claimed that there was a legal solution through *afania* (non-appearance) when individuals ask the courts to declare a person dead.[16] In practice it is almost impossible to have that person declared dead. The Attorney-General's representative claimed that 'relatives say that they don't want to do so for sentimental reasons', and that she 'could not understand why they don't use such a recourse'. Quite apart from the emotional and social traumas involved in such recourse, such statements beg the question of the state's management of the issue since 1974 until roughly 1996 as a national issue that the missing are not dead but recoverable.

The situation is more complex and less mystifying than is presented by the legal representatives and the bureaucracy. A previous Attorney General, Criton Tornaritis, expressed a 'Legal Opinion' that the law did not give the relatives the right to transfer property. His argument was that it was impossible to ascertain whether such people were dead or alive, and that there was still a *de facto* state of war between the Republic of Cyprus and Turkey as Turkey was still occupying the Republic's territory. Furthermore, legal officers lacked access to the North to investigate such cases. As a 'Legal Opinion' it was taken as a guiding principle by the Committee members as an indication of the line Government would take if contested in the courts. Consequently there has only been one case contesting the Committee's decision and the appellant lost, further discouraging any other appeals. Few individuals would wish to openly take on the state, no civil rights group has taken up the issue, and there is no legal aid.

It would be naive not to recognise that the committee does not have political implications, on the micro and macro level. Some committee members appear to view their role as imposing some degree of moral control over relatives of the missing. One committee member mentioned a mother cohabiting with a lover as an example of those cases they would disapprove of in terms of support. The committee's decisions and role give it an overwhelming legal importance in the lives of the relatives of the missing. Relatives are enmeshed in a complex articulation of overlapping institutions for civil representation, political representation, and access to Government resources. They are dependent upon the Justice Ministry's Committee for legal access to their relatives' property, upon the Service for Missing Persons for Government financial assistance, and upon their pressure group (Committee of Relatives of Missing Persons) for political representation. These three bodies are far from distinct, with the consequent dangers of re-enforcing the dependency and clientage of relatives upon the state, and becoming hostage to national and political considerations. For example, at one time the head of the Government Service for Missing Persons and the President of the Committee of the Relatives of Missing Persons were brothers. This could have made it difficult for the latter body to represent the interests of the relatives to the state as individuals meriting individual consideration. At the very least such overlapping relationships can make it difficult for this committee to openly contest the decisions of a Government Department, quite apart from the fact that it receives Government financial support. As one sympathetic centrally-placed official noted 'officials manipulate the chances these people get to exploit these laws'. The Committee of the Relatives of the Missing acts more as a political pressure group to remind the society about the national problem of the Missing and primarily to direct pressure against Turkey, rather than to represent the interests and resolve the problems of individual relatives in negotiating and dealing with the legal and other problems that relatives, as relatives of the Missing, inevitably experience in organising their lives. This does not mean that members of the Committee of the Relatives of the Missing do not act on their behalf to resolve problems, but they do so more on an informal patronage basis, rather than orienting their committee as a body to these ends. This further re-enforces the dependency of the relatives on the state and its various agencies. They are in a relationship of clientage to it and its representatives.

On a macro-political level the ramifications of the Committee agreeing to declare a missing person dead are far from singular, or even just a matter of assertion of rights to property disposal. To declare a missing person dead through the courts could open the floodgates to similar claims, and focus judicial interest on the evidence collected by the state and its agencies in declaring individuals missing rather than dead. The files are secret, but judicial interest would focus on the process whereby individuals were legally assumed to be missing rather than dead.[17] But by far the most important disincentive is posed by the workings of the CMP and the official position of the Turkish Cypriots, which is that the Greek Cypriot missing have long been dead and that this has been known to the government. Indeed the Turkish Cypriots made a claim that the missing husbands of women who subsequently remarried should be considered dead. The Greek Cypriots countered that these remarriages were permitted through divorces granted under

Canon Law in cases of disappearance (*afania*). Women had to ask for a divorce based upon *afania* to remarry; their husbands were not assumed to be dead but rather should be considered as unable to perform their matrimonial roles due to their disappearance.[18] Acknowledgement of death through the civil courts for inheritance purposes would therefore be tantamount to acknowledgement of the Turkish Cypriot claim and a puncturing of the fabric of certainty that has been built up. It would question the whole monolithic statist edifice of The Missing.

A number of processes are occurring concurrently. First, the state has legally reinforced the individual uncertainty of relatives regarding the fate of their missing and institutionally maintained that uncertainty. Second, it has done so by ensuring the continuing presence of the Missing as legal individuals, through salaries, pensions, and representation of their legal rights as property-holding individuals. The Missing are therefore *legally constituted characters* by the state, rather than socially active individuals as characters: legally present but familially absent. This generates a tension, an aporia, which I explore in a subsequent chapter. Their facticity as legal characters is both countered and sustained by the uncertainty of their physical fate. As legally constituted characters they have an existential validity that can only be negotiated and apprehended through those officials who legally represent them. Relatives of the missing are thus inevitably implicated in, and conniving with, the statist representation of the Missing as legally present actors. Third, by collectivising and nationalising the very natural feelings of individual loss, the state has cast a resolution of the emotional and social problem of mourning, and the legal problems of heirs, in the hands of the workings of the CMP, and the Turkish Cypriots and Turkey who are assumed to hold the key to the issue. It is not just that the Missing have to be 'put to rest', for their bones to be returned, to be reburied, etc. It is also that the Missing as legally constituted and represented characters have to be similarly dealt with. This may seem like a trivial point, but the 'naturalness' of the emotions of the relatives, is accompanied and sustained by their legal fabulation as persons. The legal fiction that there is no legal fiction, in short that they cannot be pronounced dead until the due process of law runs its course, is the scaffolding over which emotions are progressively elaborated.

To a certain extent, this officially abetted- fabulation of certainty conjured out of uncertainty, as well as the official presentation of uncertainty as to the fate of the missing to the outside world, is partly a function of the poverty of information available to the authorities. Many witnesses' statements appear unreliable, or are uncorroborated. The authorities only permit relatives' lawyers to see the files, not the relatives themselves, further reinforcing the climate of secrecy (as well as of suspicion). The unreliability of witness statements, or even their subsequent retraction, can reinforce the Government position that until the bones are returned and identified, such men cannot be presumed to be dead. Yet the same information also appears in the files of the UN Committee for Missing Persons (CMP), some of which I examined. Here, matters look far less certain. The files indicate disappointment, which contrast with people's expectations.

It is difficult to discover detailed quotable evidence demonstrating the statist construction of reality. One woman confided that officials told her that her husband would remain a missing person, as there was no evidence he was dead. Yet there is a witness's statement on file that her husband was killed. According to her, a Greek official gave her an official death certificate in order to help her receive a widow's pension, 'but he told me not to believe it – your husband is missing, he said'. She later confronted the witness who denied ever having made that statement, and that he did not remember the event. She now has two official documents: one that her husband is dead, another that her husband is missing. She asked me which is one to believe: the man's original statement or his more recent denial? Taken aback, I said that I thought I would prefer to believe the earlier version because memory plays tricks. 'I went to everyone, but there were no other witnesses. Why didn't they tell me then that they had witness statements that he was dead? These officials are not trustworthy', she concluded. I felt that it would have been indiscreet to ask her whether she thus received two pensions – as a widow and as a wife of a missing person (the amounts are identical). One would expect the bureaucracy to have based its modus operandi on one official definition of her status, as either widow or wife. This is an extreme but good example of how officials sometimes believe one set of witness statements (e.g., that a prisoner was last seen in a Turkish jail), and at others disbelieve them when they appear to be retracted. In the concluding chapter I discuss the political implications of public secrets, including the role of the anthropologist in inadvertently and unavoidably contributing to the potency of such fabulations.

Another example of the statist construction of reality is a (confidential) case that involved a Limassol woman previously married to a missing person. In 1983 she remarried and the Social Services stopped her pension. She wrote to the Minister accepting this for herself, but pointing out that it was unfair that her children would as a consequence also not receive their grant, and hoped that similar cases would not be treated in the same way. She added that she had information that her husband had been killed. The letter was then passed on to the Service for Missing Persons who wrote back saying they conducted their own investigation and had found some witnesses who testified that her ex-husband was not dead but missing, and was therefore presumed to have last been seen alive. This was one case (I have been told there are others) where the state appears to have officially created an *agnoumenos* where the closest relative accepted death. It is clear therefore that the state has an interest in the official maintenance of collective suffering and remembering.

The statist representation of the missing as legally present actors cannot be seen as a complete fiction, for it is anchored in stories that circulate independently in society. Such stories circulate doubt, which thus necessitate a statist recognition. Take the following story. A young soldier was killed in Kyrenia during the invasion, and his friends saw him dead. The news was conveyed to his family who conducted a memorial service (*mnimosino*) although his body was never returned.

Some time later two young soldiers stop by the house as their jeep suffered a flat tyre. They see the young man's photograph on the wall and ask who he is. The grandfather tells them the story. They then tell him that he was next to them in a Turkish army hospital ward as he was wounded. They were then released but he remained in hospital. To them he was alive. The family ceased conducting the *mnimosina*. 'So who are you to believe?', the woman who told the story, asked me. The point about this story, which can be seen as part of the mythology surrounding the issue, is that by being told it circulates doubt and uncertainty. It is not so much the content of uncertainty that is important. It is rather *the very act of being told as a marker of uncertainty* that is important. There are often many common features to these stories: a stranger, a chance encounter, an accident (a flat tyre), and the photograph. The hospital also figures prominently in the cultural iconography of fear. I explore this later. Here too the hegemonic seduction of the photograph as the ultimate verifier of 'reality' is reinforced. It is not the recognition of the soldier through the photograph that is questioned. It is rather the experience of an event by others. What is distinctive however is that through the weaving of these stories with the orthodoxy of officially imposed uncertainty, the state can thus appear to justify its stance on popular notions of evidence, on the synapses between experience and expectation which are far from Weberian bureaucratic-rational. In short, officials themselves rely on such uncertainties and rumours to justify what they would undoubtedly see as their adoption of a caring attitude required of political representatives. One could see this as an attempt to resist the social production of indifference that Herzfeld (1992) identifies as the heritage of the modern state. This could be attributed to the smallness of Cyprus, and the social origins and experiences of officials who may themselves have kin of missing persons and thus inhibited from adopting criteria which could seem hard and bureaucratically indifferent.

The situation is thus much more complex than that presented by Turkish Cypriot propaganda which interprets the Greek Cypriot Government's position in 'Anouilhian' terms, of cynically using the (missing) bodies of Greek Cypriots to blame the Turkish Cypriots for their disappearance, whereas they knew all along where they are. In this more contemporary *mise en scene* that I have described, Creon does not quite know whether Eteocles, the defender of the city, is alive or dead. Or at least he seems to foster this doubt, not by commemorating a tomb of the unknown soldier (*agnostos*) the modern way of creating an imagined community through sacrifice (Anderson 1991), nor through the 'Sophokelean' Durkheimian way by identifying the guilty betrayer through the shame of non-burial (*atapsia*), but rather through the legalisation of *agnorimia*: the inability to know. The woman who told me the story was resourceful enough to question whether these two men had been planted by the Government to sow doubt. She was uncertain and the question was too serpentine to pursue. Perhaps the only difference between her interpretation and the anthropologist's is that her world was full of conscious calculating actors, whereas the anthropologist may be more ready to give some autonomy to the unintended effects of social forces and actions. One has to interpret the situation as a fabrication, perhaps much like religious beliefs, and not as a fiction.

The authorities' fabrication began to take a definitive shape around 1981 when for the first time the number of 1,619 was mentioned. Drousiotis (2000) notes the Service for Missing Persons has stuck to that number since 1981, but the various (unofficial) lists had differing names, even if the number remained the same. A situation was thus created whereby individuals and officials pointed to 'lists' (*katalogi*) as 'official' statements and legitimations of reality, but which were inscrutable, unavailable to relatives or journalists and, it gradually emerged, inconsistent with one another or even with evidence that was increasingly dredged up. The number 1,619 became what Bourdieu calls an 'officializing strategy'.

In November 1995 the journalist Andreas Paraskos discovered that some twenty-seven persons who were buried in the cemetery of Lakatameia were on the Missing List. Of these seventeen reappeared also on the list of the Fallen which was issued by the General Office of the National Guard. Nevertheless, the authorities did not remove the names. There was much resistance initially by the authorities (both Government and the Committee of the Relatives of the Missing) to puncture the façade of certainty they had constructed. In 1998 the Service for Missing Persons and the Committee of Relatives of Missing Persons (CRM) in 1998 removed five names from their list but the latter added five others in their place. Four of these had been born between 1895 and 1918. This meant that these people would have been aged between 56 and 81 in 1974 and in 1998 they would have been between 80 and 103 years old – clearly an absurd situation (Drusiotis, ibid: 25) According to the reply by the new Head of the Committee, Nikos Sergides, and by the government spokesman, the excision of names could only be effected after exhaustive inquiries were made that these people were dead, but the government refused to divulge the criteria it adopted to excise the names (Drusiotis, ibid: 24). In the face of increasing journalistic skepticism and pressure by the UN to complete the submission of names, a rift began to appear between the government and the CRM. The latter stuck to the official line that only with the recognition and recovery of their remains could it be recognized that these people are dead. In 1996, when the government decided to make over to the CMP the files on all the missing persons, both the Service for the Missing and the Representatives of the Relatives (CRM) 'fought tooth and nail to prevent this happening' (Drusiotis, ibid: 26) because they feared that the case would be closed. The Presidential Commissioner for Humanitarian Affairs, Leandros Zahariadis, admitted that there were not many files with trustworthy or credible information, and the majority of files only contained the names of the missing, which were often mistaken (ibid: 26). He noted that witness statements regarding the situations in which they disappeared were not available for all cases, and in the case of soldiers there were no statements or depositions by their officers or their colleagues. This was an amazing admission and set the leaders of the Committee of the Relatives of Missing Persons (CRM) on a collision course with the government. The effort of bringing the files up to date took three years and by March 1998 the work of presenting the names was completed. There were 1,493 files.

With this presentation of these 1,493 files to the UN CMP, the government adopted an official position, which could not be changed. There were many calls for the list to be published but the Services for Missing Persons considered this a secret. The Parliamentary Committee of Missing and the Fallen also refused to publish it. Drousiotis observes dryly:

> From whom was this a secret? From the UN, or from the Turks who themselves had the list? Except for these, the details of the list interested only Cypriot society and particularly the relatives of the missing. The preservation of secrecy, therefore, affected those immediately concerned, by those whose job it was to inform responsibly as to whether the government considered their relatives to be missing or not. (ibid: 26–27)

One can thus appreciate how the situation in Cyprus is more complex, and perhaps generates more cynicism, than is encountered in places where individuals disappeared as a result of state-abetted violence, such as in Guatemala. There, Zur notes, 'the entire history of *la violencia* can be read as a war against memory, an Orwellian falsification of memory, a falsification of reality' (ibid: 159). In Cyprus a simulation of reality became progressively a partial falsification of reality, although this was not a falsification of memory. Rather it was the state's cunning sponsorship of certain narrative themes, embedded in a culture, scaffolded on an entire legal framework that bureaucratized uncertainty. If in Guatemala it was Creon's henchmen who secretly made people disappear, in Cyprus it was Creon's bureaucrats and politicians who represented the disappeared as Eteocles, even if in many cases they held empty files. Rather than being a war on memory, this could be seen as a war on the acquiescence of 'common sense' to retain certain ethnic memories, such as the recovery of the North, even at the cost of sustaining many Antigones searching for hidden bodies.

Conclusion

The demand for the return of refugees, or for information on the fate of the *agnoumeni*, is therefore more than a surface political struggle between Greek and Turkish Cypriots. Nor is it just a struggle over the definition of reality, or even over territory. It is rather a struggle to shore up simulation through simulacra. 'Behind the baroque of images hides the grey eminence of politics' (Baudrillard, 1988: 70). The 'politics' here is how the state harnesses, collectivises, and fetishises the pain of mourning, transforming individual real experiences into a collective wound to produce discourses on symbolic separation, unity, return. By harnessing individual pain to collective political programmes ('All the refugees must return to their homes', etc.), the state manufactures the imaginability of a society having healed itself outside time, characterised by the return of refugees or by information on the missing. By collectivising private pain, appropriating it into a simulacrum of signs about return and unity, the state fabricates a double through the mirror, an imaginary/spectral society, fetishising the refugees/missing into an imaginable alterity of free-floating self-referential signs. In so doing, however, it fetishises pain, reinscribing it back into the lives of individuals, symbolically representing that pain on to, and condensing it into, the image of Cyprus as grieving mother, *i mana mas*. Refugees/*agnoumeni* become the orphaned (because they exist outside real time) children of a suffering mother (an image often used to represent Cyprus after the invasion), homologies of the Panayia holding up her dead son, Christ, whose ultimate sacrifice is *afto-thiseia* (self-sacrifice). If the refugees/*agnoumeni* are signified as sacrifice, the signifier is *pain,* personified by the mother as a double symbol (as reflective sign: all the refugees/*agnoumeni* have mothers, and as symbol: Cyprus as grieving mother). As Feldman has observed 'The production of bodies is the mechanism by which the state apparatus detaches ideological parts of itself, reassembles itself in alterity, and then recuperates itself in this alterity through the extraction of narratives and artefacts of power. *The state (m)others bodies in order to engender itself. The production of bodies-political subjects-is the self-production of the state'* (1992: 115, emphasis in original). In Cyprus, through the narratives of return, unity and wholeness, the state (m)others its own subjects to transfigure itself as an expression of its own subjects' pain. Inevitably, its subjects connive in maintaining such illusions to shore up the only reality they know, to stave off deeper realities which may be more threatening.

NOTES

1. There are two additional categories: the Coupists, and the Fallen, but I leave these temporarily aside.
2. In contrast to other observers (e.g., Constantinou, 1995), who has written a legitimately elegiac interpretation of the Dead and Missing through an analysis of Efthymiou's poetry, I do not see the Dead and the Missing in isolation, but rather as part of a triangulation of memories incorporating The Missing, the Refugees, the Enclaved. All three are mourned and mourners, signifiers and signified.
3. In particular through its book (AKEL: 1975) which was subsequently withdrawn from circulation.
4. Indeed in July 1996 Kate Clerides a DiSy MP and daughter of Glavkos Clerides, the then President, suggested that the twenty-two National Guard soldiers killed in the assault on the Presidential Palace were only obeying orders. This was criticised by D. Christofias, the Communist Party leader who criticised a commemoration service and asked sarcastically whether 'the next step is to tell us that they were defending the motherland?' *(Cyprus Weekly* 29 July 1996).

5. The Republic of Cyprus maintains a boycott on the Turkish-occupied north and tourists are only permitted by the Greek Cypriots to visit for day trips and not to return with any purchases.

6. Freud himself suggested 'It may indeed be questioned whether we have any memories at all from our childhood: memories relating to our childhood may be all that we possess' (3:322).

7. *The Cyprus Weekly, Lifestyle* supplement (9–15 February 1996, p.1).

8. If it is a girl, then the symbolism may even be more powerful.

9. A socially recognised mourning would imply recognition of the death of the missing and, symbolically, an abandonment of any idea of the reunification of the island.

10. Freud called a 'screen memory', a 'memory' of unity, plenitude manufactured and mapped on to the past in order to disguise a present anxiety.

11. The Graeco-Turkish Cypriot complicity in mutually constructing a system of memories that reciprocally remember that which each side wishes to be forgotten is brought out even further by recent developments. In the 12 October 1995 issue of *Fileleftheros* (p.3) it was admitted that the missing might very well be dead: 'something everyone knew but no one dared say'. In February 1996 Denktash admitted that such men were 'probably dead', though he disingenuously abstained from allocating responsibility. By March 1996 Greek Euro MPs had taken the issue to the European Parliament. The European Parliament condemned the statements by Denktash. According to the Republic of Cyprus official *Cyprus Bulletin* the European Parliament condemnation stated that these men 'were killed by Turkish Cypriot paramilitaries' (1 April 1996. Vol. XXXIV, No 7), and linked this up with the enclaved. It is believed that some were killed by Turkish Cypriot paramilitaries between 14–20 August 1974 in Mesaoria.

12. Consisting of the Attorney General, Director of the Welfare Services Department, and the Head of Services for the Missing Persons, and the Chief Registrar of the Courts.

13. Usually relatives of the Missing: spouses, parents, children.

14. The number has of course decreased, and there are no children of *agnoumeni* younger than twenty-four in 1998. Yet children also qualify for grants on attaining adulthood. Daughters received a grant for a dowry house (in 2000 it stood at CYP £7,000), but have no rights to loans at low rate similar to the refugees unless they are refugees themselves.

15. There does not appear to be a Manual for dealing with cases, or any specific guidelines.

16. The Wills and Succession Act allows someone to be declared dead by an order of the court 10 years after the disappearance (Art. 14). It even applies in the case of the armed forces. Declaration can be made three years after peace has been declared. Section 14.5 also allows for those cases where a person has been in peril of his life, he may be declared dead if three years have elapsed. The law therefore permits such declarations to be made. However, in terms of international law, Cyprus is under illegal partial occupation, and this legal problem would have to be resolved.

17. A court ruling in favour of declaring a person dead could encourage other relatives to take the government to court if it emerged that the state suppressed evidence (such as testimonials) even subsequently after the disappearance, to maintain the semblance of certainty that it perceived its political struggle required. The government would then be open to prosecution from its own citizens for mental hardship. Although this is an unlikely possibility, citizens have increasing tended to take the government to the European Court of Human Rights (over discrimination against homosexuals or over police brutality).

18. This claim was accepted by the Turkish Cypriots. Maria Roussou (1986) has written very thoughtfully about how the wives of missing persons were obliged by society and the state to become Penelopes of Cyprus and enter a state of unending waiting.

5

THE MARTYRDOM OF THE MISSING

❧❧❧

There is danger in unnatural silence
No less than in excess of lamentation

Chorus, in Sophocles' Antigone (1947: 174)

Introduction

In this chapter I examine how both groups have turned their missing into martyrs, though with significant differences. These differences are as much due to cultural symbolism as to the different political agendas of the Greek and Turkish Cypriot political leaderships. Briefly put, the Greek Cypriot missing have become metaphors or signifiers for the recapture of a past and a lost territory. As they possess an ambiguous liminal identity, being neither legally dead nor experientially alive, they share certain characteristics with saints or even with Christ. Turkish Cypriot missing persons are signifiers for a future for which they sacrificed their lives. They are therefore associated with the spilling of blood for land and security. There are political differences between the two groups in their attitudes towards the recovery of the bodies of the missing. This can be attributed to their different political agendas, as well as formal differences between Christianity and Islam in the theological significance of the body in the economy of salvation. Nevertheless I show that despite these differences between the political exploitation of the missing by their leaders, at the grassroots there are many similarities between Greek and Turkish Cypriot relatives towards the recovery of the bodies of their loved ones.

The Somatisation of Recovery and the Specularisation of the Self

The role and significance of mortuary rituals in Greek culture has received much attention from anthropologists in recent years (Caraveli, 1986; Danforth, 1982; Sarris 1995; Seremetakis, 1991). In this case we are faced with social responses to death from a political, symbolic and ethnic perspective where there have been no bodies to attend to. I begin by exploring how an extended mourning for the relatives, in particular 'the mothers' (itself a transfiguration of Cyprus as grieving mother), has been cast in terms that seems to permit a resolution of their trauma only through the recovery of the bodies of the Missing.

I then show that whilst relatives may be in a state of mourning, the missing are in a state that is more than just 'liminal'. In contrast to Bloch and Parry (1982), and other anthropological theorists, I argue that missing persons are existentially very dissimilar to those individuals who are in a state between their biological death and its social recognition. Rather, they have an existential ambiguity that transcends the normal social expectations of 'liminality', and thus exacerbates the grief experienced by the relatives. In the case of the Greek Cypriot missing, the fact that the demands of the relatives have not been resolved cannot be explained away by the suggestion that the relatives are not being 'realistic' and thus refusing to accept 'reality', or that the State has 'exploited' the issue. Although there are elements of both, the resilience of the issue suggests that far more complex factors are involved. Finally, I show that the demand for the return of the remains turns the missing into *ethnomartyres* (national martyrs). History, sedimented memories, symbolism, and gender identity coalesce in a potent mixture.

Since the mid-1980s the issue of the missing in the Greek part of Cyprus has become progressively expressed in terms of the rights of their relatives to recover their remains, and rights to (re)burial according to Orthodox rites. In 2001, according to a member of the Greek Cypriot team of the CMP, the return of the bones 'has now become the most important and the most symbolic theme in the talks between the two communities in the (UN sponsored) Committee on Missing Persons (CMP)'. In Chapter 3, I dealt with the political background and implications for such requests. We now need to concentrate on the more symbolic aspects.

The demand for the return of the remains of the missing can be seen as a coded set of statements about ethnicity, gender identity, and emotion. Let us begin with the terms used. When relatives demand the recovery of the *leipsana* of the missing they are using a word possessing religious and alimentary significance. *Leipsana* means relics, usually the remains of a saint. This also applies to those remains of martyred saints discovered buried without proper rituals. Significantly, relatives do not use the term *ptoma* (corpse), or the words for bones (*kokkala*, or *osta*, the latter being more formal, and used to refer to the bones of saints). A *leipsanothiki* is a place used to store the remains of monks, or a storage of relics usually of a sacred miracle-performing person (such as a saint). They can also be items associated with, or intimate to, that person, or have miraculous powers. A *leipsanothiki* is different from an *osteophilakeion* – an ossuary where the bones are collectively buried or grouped after the decomposition of the flesh. A *leipsanothiki* is singular; an *osteophilakeion* is communal. A *leipsanothiki* displays stratification, status, and individuation. It can also be a source of power and grace. *Leipsanothikes* (pl.) are usually found in monasteries.[1] By contrast, an *osteophilakeion* is a collective ossuary, within a cemetery, of lay members of society where differences between individuals in terms of status, gender, and age are dissolved. In Bloch and Parry's terms it represents a depersonalisation of the dead. An *osteophilakeion* is not a source of power in the way a *leipsanothiki* is, which can become a site of pilgrimage. *Leipsana* represent signs of a good exemplary life, or of martyrdom. They are the signs that are left by a soul that has gone to paradise for the living as exhortations to lead a good life. They exert a powerful influence on the living as examples to follow, and exhortations to emulate. They are a source for the regeneration of the spirit and of the group. They are witnesses of truth – the truth of spiritual resurrection and of the eternity of the soul. By contrast, the collectivisation of bones *(kokkala)* in an *osteophilakeion* is a sign of the irreversibility of death, of its lack of discrimination, and of the temporality of the individual. They are, in effect, signs of the truth of the illusory nature of earthly life as a 'lie' *(imaste psemata)*, of its temporality, and its deceivability.

Leipsana are metaphors of liminality. In this respect the language used to describe saints and sinners can overlap. *Leipsana* suggest a state of partial decomposition. *Leipsana* are used to designate remains that belong to individuals in the first stage after burial and during the period they are actively mourned through *mnimosina* (memorial services), prior to their final dispatch. A body, which has remained partially decomposed, cannot be finally dispatched. It is still linked to this world and to the living. This could be because that person was a sinner. Sins *(amarties)* are manifested through partial decomposition, in and through *leipsana*. But partial decomposition could also be a sign that that person was a martyr, who was sinned against. In 1999 the monks of the Galactoforousa monastery opened the tomb of the founder abbot and discovered his intact body. They immediately demanded the archbishop begin sanctification proceedings. The partial decomposition of the body is a demand for recognition from the living that the deceased was a witness *(martyras)* to God through his/her martyrdom. To assist the deceased to leave this world the body needs to be cut loose. It has to lose its link *(desmos)* with this world. Danforth suggests that 'the process of decomposition is metaphorically linked to the untying or "loosing" of portions of bodies of the deceased' (1982: 152). The notion of being 'bound' or 'tied' is linked with being under a spell or a priest's anathema (Blum and Blum, 1970: 75). Bodies that are tied, like those of massacred prisoners, need to be 'untied', 'loosened', or 'released' to assist the decomposition of the body and thus the movement of the soul to the other world. As long as the remains of the dead remain un-commemorated through proper ritual, then they are *leipsana*. Blum and Blum notes that 'for the soul to depart this world the body must not only be returned to earth, but must be accepted by earth as evidenced by the "melting" (decay) [*leiosima*-PSC] as the flesh' (1970: 70–1). Just as memorial services include prayers for forgiveness and for the decomposition of the body, partially decomposed bodies as *leipsana* are like curses of the dead upon the living, requiring proper burial for forgiveness to reign amongst men. *Leipsana* are thus also the somatization of liminality.

The term *leipsana* suggests liminality in another sense. *Leipsano* is used colloquially to designate somebody who is thin, undernourished and looks ghoulish or cadaverous. It thus suggests that even if we do find the missing alive they will look like dead people, because they have been treated badly, even tortured. It is the horror of every Greek mother that her son could look like a *leipsano*, thin and undernourished.

In modern, as well as ancient Greek culture, it is considered one of the worst fates possible for an individual's body not to be buried without the proper religious rites. The remains of the missing thus need to be recovered because they were not buried properly by their loved ones, and are believed to be still roaming the earth. There are two reasons for this. The first is the fear of desecration of the corpse. This provides an entry into the reasoning whereby the Greek Cypriot missing have been increasingly turned into *ethnomartyres* (ethnic martyrs). There is always a fear that the bodies of the missing were either left unburied to be attacked and eaten by dogs, or else buried hurriedly in mass graves. The former has echoes with the gruesome state of Polynices' 'dog-worried body' (*kypnosparakton soma*) as punishment for his crime in Sophocles' *Antigone*. Leaving a body without burial is an outrage to the lower gods. In modern Greek Cypriot culture there is a double connection of dogs and carrion. Extreme right-wing Greek nationalists in Cyprus referred to Turkish Cypriots whom they killed as *shillii* (dogs) – the implication being that, like dogs, they could be killed with impunity. Communists received a similar charming appellation. In such situations there is a real risk of the transformation of analogy into metaphor. It is well known that taxonomic violence defined in ethnic terms (or what is now called ethnic cleansing) is accompanied, indeed justified, by attempts to render the other as an outsider and a source of pollution. However repellent such sentiments are, we must try to understand the cultural symbolism and structural logic that accompanies and 'legitimates' such actions. Paradoxically, an analysis can help explain the transfiguration of the missing/dead (Greek Cypriots) into sacrificial victims or martyrs. Let us begin by noting the Greek alternation of Turks with 'dogs' (*shillii*). At one time it is Turks, who are killed as 'dogs' (*shillii*) and their bodies disposed of; at another time it is dogs that worry Greek bodies. Girard suggests 'in tragedy everything alternates' (1988: 149); 'alternation is a fundamental fact of the tragic relationship' (ibid: 150). Thus dog-worried bodies can also metaphorically mean that the missing were tortured and beaten (*vasanistikan*) by the Turks. In 1974 there were eyewitness accounts that the Turks beat captured Greek Cypriot soldiers very badly before killing them. This has been corroborated by subsequent skeletal examinations during the 1999–2000 exhumations. Zur encountered a similar situation in Guatemala during *la violencia:*

> *It was terrible … there were dead all around. Since we could not bury them, the dogs ate them. They carried bits of them around in their mouths … the dogs were fat in those days* (1998: 80)

Although there are indubitable differences between the Guatemalan and Cypriot cases, there is the common powerful theme of the defilement of corpses as carrion by dogs. Two things are distinctive in the Cypriot case: first there is a movement from metaphorical to analogical likeness and an eventual collapse of distinctions not just between humans and animals, and the reduction of the former to the latter, but also the collapse into animality, by both sides. Second, there is an alternation and symmetry between what happens to the Turks and what happens to the Greeks:

TURKS = shillii/polluting, therefore legitimated killing: metaphorical likeness.
Act of killing performs the transformation of Turks into *shillii*: analogical likeness.
Implications: Removal of distinctions between human and animal. Girard's 'mimetic desire'.

GREEKS: killed by Turks (*shillii*): metaphorical likeness.
Act of leaving bodies unburied performs the transformation of Greeks into *shillii*: analogical likeness.
Corpses of Greeks left improperly buried (worried by dogs): metaphorical and analogical likeness.
Implications: Reciprocal removal of distinctions between humans and animals
Removal of distinctions between Greeks and Turks
Alternation between Greeks and Turks.
Greeks and Turks become 'monstrous doubles' (Girard) of each other.

It could be argued that the disappearances of Greek and Turkish Cypriots were not only separated in time, but were quite distinct. This is correct, but if one were to approach them as a system not necessarily of 'exchanges' but as somehow causally related, and even bearing some structural similarities, then it is certainly worthwhile to examine them together because in popular consciousness as well on the level of political resolution they are linked together. According to Girard 'while acknowledging the differences, both functional and mythical, between vengeance, sacrifice and legal punishment, it is important to recognise their fundamental identity' (ibid: 25). This is an interesting handle on the issue. Contemporary political consciousness may be more comfortable with reciprocal disappearances as an example of 'reciprocal vengeance', even as 'legal punishment' (at least at the level of popular consciousness), because contemporary social science views nationalist sentiments *in extremis* as somehow 'irrational'. Contemporary political consciousness is less comfortable in perceiving such disappearances as a 'sacrifice'. Yet it could be argued that the inexorable logic of the situation, as well as the meanings attached to such disappearances by political authorities (i.e. 'Creon'), finds such associations not just very easy to make, but essential for politics – both for the nation state and the Greek Polis. From this perspective, nationalism is not irrational, but it harnesses the seemingly 'irrational', and it does so by the recasting of deaths/killings as (ethnic) sacrifices made by martyrs.

Girard has suggested that 'wherever differences are lacking, violence threatens' (ibid: 57). Although his theory about violence and the sacred is perhaps too embedded in the logic and symmetry of tragedy, it helps explain the underlying logic of what can be called the unspeakable logic of sacrifice away from more 'romantic' interpretations involving structuralist substitutions. One could take his observation to mean that violence threatens not so much because of reciprocal killing (as indeed happened occasionally between Greeks and Turks in Cyprus during past ethnic disturbances), but because the violence in the new State achieved a new significance. It could be argued that the reciprocal disappearances of Turkish and Greek Cypriots *established a new means of signification of violence*. This introduced the removal of distinctions between humans (as members of ethnic groups) and animals through the treatment, disassembly, and rendering (including concealment) of the human body, and was displayed through accompanying discourses. These discourses included elliptical narratives: 'we should have cleaned them out' (*eprepe na tous katharisoume*), and verbal-iconic representations: graffiti that remain as residues and as distillations of anticipated somatic desecration or subjugation, usually on burnt-out or destroyed buildings that witness the marks of presumed past aggression of the other (e.g, *Kalos Turkos, Nekros Turkos*: 'The only good Turk is a dead Turk'; *Turkos=Varvaros*: 'Turk=Barbarian'; 'Turk, suck my dick', the latter as performative utterance in English designed to be read, and thus witnessed, by everybody). Ethnic intolerance thrives as much as on the iconoclasm performed by the opposing group, as well as on the mournfully cherishing display of that iconoclasm by the iconophiles. At Galactoforousa monastery, a few miles from the Green Line in Cyprus, monks show visitors a room containing anti-Christian graffiti left by Turkish Cypriots who had forcefully taken over the monastery between 1963 and 1974, after the latter killed some monks and a twelve-year old novice. The cause for these killings was probably as much related to local conflicts over water rights, as to the then prevailing widespread reciprocal violence. The monks then fled to the safety of a nearby nunnery. On their return in 1974, they restored the monastery, but retained one room precisely as they found it, containing its distasteful graffiti. This they regularly show to visitors, exhibiting an ambiguous reverence towards a now-protected, intimate, pollution. Ethnic intolerance and cleansing generates an instant archaeology of destruction, as well as its solicitous conservation. One should suspend cynical scepticism towards such processes of folk-museology. They underlie many similar processes that emerged in post-1945 Europe with the preservation and restoration of ghettoes and concentration camps.

The Green Line separating the two communities is another display area of ethnic intolerance. Here, gutted buildings with graffiti provide the area of interface with the monstrous double, and become totems of ethnic intolerance in a literal Levi-Straussian sense: good to think with, and especially subliminally as a simulated witness of ethnic incompatibility. Taken together, they perpetuate(d) an extreme nationalist discourse of insiders and polluting others who needed to be removed, and consciously reduce the (foreign) body to carrion. We thus have to appreciate that violence is not just the application of physical force. Each social system and each pattern of interaction has its own forms of violence, which include the production, distribution, consumption and exchange of violence as a system of signs. Girard further notes the ambiguity and arbitrariness of this type of violence 'the difference between sacrificial and non-sacrificial violence is anything but exact; it is even arbitrary' (ibid: 40), and that 'the sacrificial act appears as both sinful and saintly, an illegal as well as a legitimate exercise of violence' (ibid: 20). One could thus appreciate how the underlying logic of the disappearances orients towards an interpretation that suggests martyrdom.

A second reason for the necessity for the recovery of the remains of the missing is that by not being buried properly those murdered were turned into revenents The term used is *vrykolakiasan*: they are/were turned into revenants. In Greek culture it is believed that those who have been murdered are turned into revenants.[2] As one informant said to the Blums in Greece, 'One of the worst curses you can put on a man is to say, "May you never decay." One who is cursed that way can become a *vrikolax* (i.e. revenant)' (1970: 75). The term *vrykolakas* can thus suggest either that the missing were murdered by the Turks, or that when they were killed (in battle) they were not buried (and thus mourned) according to proper rites. Revenants are believed to remain in exchange with the living (Danforth, ibid: 126). It is not just that the living have an obligation to lay the souls of the dead to rest. It is also that these individuals are *separated* from their souls, which are not laid to rest by the living: *I psyche tous dhen ksekourazete* (lit. , their souls are not laid to rest). As revenants they are symbols of liminality, distinct from their souls. This expression is also used of saints who were tortured. It is believed that their soul went straight to heaven. A secretary of the Greek Cypriot CMP team, after some hesitation, told me of a story she had heard from her neighbour. This woman used to visit the cemetery where her husband was buried. Some time ago she had certain dreams which troubled her greatly. As Danforth points out, dreams 'constitute a channel through which the dead are believed to be able to communicate with the living' (ibid: 135). She dreamt of men 'dressed in white like angels'. They told her that nobody mourned them and asked her for a *mnimosino*. 'She then realised that these were *agnoumeni* in unmarked graves nearby', she told me. She then held a service for them and they ceased to trouble her in her dreams.[3]

The recovery of the relatives and the missing is thus mutual and causal. Just as the missing have to be reunited with their souls and/to recover their identity, their relatives recover themselves *as selves* through their reuniting of the missing with their souls. This has clear linkages with Lacan's notion of the Other, which will be explored later. But it raises an important issue about the nature of the *continuity of the self* in such situations of radical rupture. Writing on Guatemalan widows, Zur notes, 'Violence and terror dismantle established categories which are reassembled in new ways, causing confusion and hindering people's attempts to integrate the "self" of the past with the "self" of the present. Memories connected with disassociated aspects of the "self" frozen in the chaos of "that time", become inaccessible or unspeakable. And, in the end, they can neither be remembered nor truly forgotten' (forthcoming: 10).

Danforth has suggested that a purpose of mortuary rituals is to gradually bring about a common-sense perspective and awareness of the finality of death (ibid: 148–9). This is very similar to Freud's thesis on mourning and melancholia.[4] In the case of The Missing, however, there is a double inversion. First, a common-sense acceptance that the missing are dead is precisely that which is rejected emphatically by the relatives, and implicitly by the state. Indeed, a common-sense acceptance is rejected as politically defeatist, while rejection of the status quo *is* justified as political realism. Such a climate of interpretation helps sustain a symbolic fabulation of the issue of the missing at the grassroots. While the missing are formally quantified and collectively mourned but not considered dead, the dead (casualties) are formally not quantified, but individually remembered. Secondly, the retrieval of the *leipsana* of the missing can be seen as a burial in reverse, just as the mourning of the relatives is mourning before the burial. Because the missing have not been buried properly, the retrieval of their *leipsana* is an exhumation of the bones, a simulation of the final (second) burial, in order to hold a proper (ritualised) first burial. The *leipsana* are to be exhumed to be buried as *bones*. It emphasises Bloch and Parry's point that it is the burial-ritual that creates the death rather than the reverse. Except that this has political and deeply emotional implications. One has to ask whether the relatives should have to travel along such symbolic journeys to recover themselves through the material recovery of their loved ones' remains to finally reach a common-sense acceptance of their non-reversibility (i.e., death)? Although I deal with this issue in greater detail in Chapter 7, I would argue here that the answer would seem to be yes if we examine the role of mourning through demonstrating. I discuss this below.

Much of the symbolism surrounding the missing is a complex mixture of Christianity and Hellenism. Many Greek Cypriots claim that the Turks may not give that much importance to burials 'because they are Muslims, but we as Christians do'. From fieldwork conducted among Turkish Cypriots I show below that this is far from the case. Turkish Cypriot relatives also wish to have bodies to mourn. The difference lies in the political attitudes towards mourning and the cultural constitution of sacrifice. The Greek Cypriots perceive a homology between what they fear was inflicted on the missing by the Turks and what the Ottomans inflicted on the bodies of Saints. In both cases the *leipsana* are hidden, but discoverable. The *leipsana* have to be recovered, both to empower those who recover them, and because it is believed that such remains possess power. One could see these as very distinctive Lacanian symbols of alterity. As Bloch observed 'without the corpse the women can mourn but the regeneration cannot occur' (ibid: 43). Their bodies are also witnesses to their suffering and to the 'barbarism' of the Ottomans/Turks whom they indict. The mutilated body becomes for both groups an icon of the barbarism of the Other. Hence the suggestion on both sides that it is 'the other Creon' (i.e. the political leaders on the 'other side') who have prevented the proper burial of the dead. For the Greek Cypriots, obtaining the remains also represents a moral victory and a transcendence of the defeats of 1974. Like the saints they are *ethnomartyres* (ethnic martyrs). 'I see my parents as Christian martyrs. They died the death of martyrs for their religion and for their native land' was the comment of the priest Papa Loizos to Loizos on his missing parents (1981: 44). Obtaining the sacred relics of the missing, the *ethnomartyres*, means freeing *(yia na eleftherosoun)* their souls, like freeing the occupied territory. It is not difficult to view these relics as national objects of desire: 'they are both necessary for self-identity and a threat insofar as they reflect a disorder too unacceptable to be recognised as part of one's own order' (Shapiro 1997: 59)

Such individuals therefore are martyrs not because they died, but because interpretation subsequently suggests that there *was a sacrifice*. Ritual sacrifice, as Girard notes, has a dual aspect, 'the legitimate and the illegitimate' (ibid: 1). Significantly, he cautions that it resembles criminal violence. The victim is sacred only because 'he is to be killed' (ibid: 1). Such interpretations, such as that of the priest Papa Loizou, were applied retroactively in much the same way witchcraft interpretations are applied retroactively and selectively to extract, or even conjure, necessity out of chance. Otherwise the event would just be a criminal act, which it may well be from the perspective of international law. But modern politics from within the polity clearly understands and requires it to be both: a criminal act, absurd, irrational, ugly, illegitimate and prosecutable in international fora and courts of law, and 'legitimate', a sacrifice, noble, and necessitating further struggles. In the next chapter we shall examine how this duality is represented.

Finally, land and bones are intimately linked in Greek culture. This is different to the Turkish attitude where the *shedding of blood* that is important. The Greek national anthem by Dionysios Solomos contains the verses '*Ap'ta kokkala vgalmeni/ ton Ellinon ta Iera/ kai san prota andriomeni/ haire/ o haire, Eleftheria*', linking exhumed bones, ethnicity, sacrality, and freedom. Novels such *Aeoliki Ge* (1943) (Aeolian Land) of Ilia Vanezis deal precisely with the recovery of ancestral bones. In this novel, villagers from Asia Minor are forced to abandon the land they have resided in for centuries, but they carry the bones of their ancestors and patron saint with them. President Clerides in his speeches often repeats 'We will never give up our land in Kyrenia where the bones of our forefathers are buried'.

There is however a difference between the relatives and the state authorities in the linkages they make between land (or the earth), and bones. For the state authorities, bones establish a claim *to land*. As it is for Creon, land is a territory 'to be fought over, protected and ruled' (Segal 1981: 172). For the relatives, as for Antigone, it is the earth as *patrigoniki ye* (paternal land) that is important, and it is the continuing Turkish occupation of the north and refusal to return their remains that prevents them from properly burying their kin. For the authorities, by contrast, it is because our ancestors were buried in the north that we should not abandon our territory. Although relatives and state authorities might appear to be talking about the same thing, slight differences in nuances can sometimes be concealed from the participants themselves. There is a similar slippage in the employment of related key words such as the house/home (*spiti*), and properties (*peryiousiyes*). Officials present such demands for the return of bones in terms of an old, ethnic tradition, even drawing upon Homer's story of King Priam asking Achilles for the body of his son Hector back, a powerful and morally compelling image: 'We consider it our *klironomia* (inheritance, heritage). We consider it a betrayal that we left our dead behind. The Greeks have always honoured their dead'. Ancient Greek tragedy becomes a pre-run and a projection of the contemporary tragedy of Cyprus. In spring 1994 the Cyprus Theatre Group presented 'The Suppliant Women' (*Troades*) by Euripides in New York. 'The Archbishop, at the end of the performance said that seeing the widows in Euripides' tragedy pleading with the enemy for the return of the bodies of their loved ones for decent burial was as if many in the audience were witnessing the same scene enacted today in real life by the wives and children of the missing in Cyprus' (Biggs and Smith 1995: 193).

Liminality is a term that has often been used in anthropology in a metaphoric sense, as well as indicating a movement from one state to another. This applies particularly to mourning rituals, both for the mourned and the mourner. Yet to use the term liminal for the missing is to cast them facilely according to pre-existing anthropological categories, bypassing their existential ambiguity. The missing are not so much liminal. Rather they are neither formally considered dead, nor informally believed to be alive. On a definitional level this may seem to be a liminal state. But liminality is not usually a temporally prolonged state with no end in sight, and it has direction. Its nature is understood by all as it is set by custom. Its significance emerges out of bridging the gap and tension between two definite and socially recognisable states. In this respect the missing are existentially dissimilar to those individuals who are biologically dead but have not been fully despatched through rituals to the other world, even although the predicament of the relatives is presented as one of mourners who cannot terminate their mourning. The position of the relatives may formally resemble mourners, but the missing as existential characters to be recovered by their relatives have a different valency. Because they are neither formally considered dead, nor informally believed to be alive, they have an existential ambiguity, which can help explain the particular emotional tensions relatives have experienced. Let us examine this in greater detail.

Existential Ambiguity and the Aporia of Mourning

No friend to weep at my banishment
to a rock-hewn chamber of endless durance,
In a strange cold tomb alone to linger
Lost between life and death for ever

Sophocles' *Antigone* (1947: 163)

Relatives of the missing are in a state of symbolic impurity. They are 'set apart' socially and nationally, and set themselves apart, in terms of their own emotions through mourning, and in terms of societal views on mourning. Agni, the (Greek-born) wife of a missing Judge from Kyrenia told me: 'I could never open up my house gladly (*haroumenos*)'. The metaphor of the house as reflecting a psychological condition also occurs in the short story *The Mother of the Missing Person*, (1989) by Angeliki Smyrli, who makes the linkage between an 'Open heart, open house' *(Anikti kardia, anikto spiti,* ibid: 6) This is apparently based on Agni, the narrators' mother-in-law.[5] An open house is a symbol of gladness (*hara*), generosity, communion with others, and growth. People are known to be open (*aniktos*), i.e. approachable or 'closed' (*klistos*), i.e. unapproachable. Agni was saying that she had withdrawn from society, and could not bring herself to fully open herself up. A closed house/ home is a symbol of withdrawal from society, of an incomplete household not in communion with the rest of society, and in its final stage before abandonment and decay. 'I thought nobody lived there', is a comment often heard when the last inhabitant of a closed house is buried, when dust finally covers all things. 'I could never open up my house gladly' thus means 'I could never open myself up. I am imprisoned by my unending mourning'. Mourning, confinement, and darkness are linked. Being in an (en)closed space is also an emotional state. In Greek it literally means to be worried: *stenohoria* (literally, a narrow space). Unending mourning, itself a travesty of mourning which should have an end, a mourning which searches for its own end, being closed in a restricted space, and pain, are related. One could argue that there is interchangeability between the missing and their mourners. The relatives of the missing are themselves the missing in search of their missing symbolically united with them. One newspaper photograph shows a group of relatives holding up placards. A young boy is standing with a placard hanging from his chest with the words: *Ime agnoumenos* – 'I am missing', or 'I am a missing person'. The child of a missing person has assumed the missing identity of his father. If the father cannot be mourned and dispatched, the boy himself has no ancestors, no identity. He is not an orphan, he is an *agnoumenos*- literally someone who is not known, lacking a social recognition and thus an identity. One can thus see how the recovery of the missing to be mourned is also a recovery of the self. There is something fundamentally at play here that recalls Lacan's notion of desire as a means to achieve identity coherence.

Because the missing are formally not considered to be dead, relatives have not been given the social license to individually interpret their situation and to familially negotiate any meanings they wish to give it. Up till 1999, there had been no institutionally sanctioned or licensed opportunity to perform the burial services for the missing. According to Orthodox and Christian theology generally, it is possible to hold mourning and ritual services for missing people who are presumed to be dead. This applies to sailors lost at sea, for example. This has not occurred in Cyprus in the sense of having become a widely contemplateable course of action. Quite apart from the natural resistance of the relatives to accept such a fact, there has also been an institutionally abetted rigidity to contemplate giving such perspectives much social currency. A compromise is usually reached by holding special prayers for their 'safe return' (Crowther, 2002: 27). The few memorial services for the missing that are held tend to be negotiated individually with the village *papas*, and are considered exceptional, and justified on individual 'psychological' (i.e., therapeutic) grounds, thus marginalise the mourner. But they are neither socially nor politically sanctioned. It was only with the slow retrieval of bones in 2000, through the exhumations and their identification that families began conducting mortuary rituals (*mnimosina*) (see below). This applied only to a few families whose relatives' bones were identified. Individuals are thus dissuaded from expressing their grief through rituals (*khideia, mnimonisino*) whose suitability is socially questioned for them. In most cases they do not have the bones to rebury which are behind Turkish lines. The Church's 'solution' to the dilemma between holding the normal memorial service (which would accept the missing as dead), or not holding services at all (which would imply not fulfilling a duty to the missing if they are dead), is through special prayers for their 'safe return' (Crowther, 2000: 27). This further insinuates doubt.

In such a context, suffering and the means to resolve the aporia of mourning, is expressed in three ways. The first is the concealment of suffering, and expressed in what can be called the 'Closed Home' syndrome, although the word syndrome is unpleasantly distancing. This is a grief hidden among close kin not provided with the social frameworks to express their grief, but nevertheless still isolated socially because the missing are presumed informally by many others not to be alive and yet considered legally and officially not to be dead. One could call this introjection. This affects the majority of relatives, and to a certain extent is also found among the Turkish Cypriots, though with some significant differences. A second form is through what can be called public ritual activism. This is a route followed by a relatively small number of women who participate regularly in demonstrations. A final third, which is rare, is expressed through active opposition to the authorities for abetting the concealment of the missing and their non-burial. In line with the theme of this book, one can call this the 'Antigone syndrome'. The three are not separate. Individuals pass through different stages and experience all three at times. I discuss the first two in turn. I leave the third for a later chapter.

The Closed Home

In discussing Argentine mothers of *desaparecidos,* Robben noted that mothers dealt with the dilemma of not having a body to mourn in various ways: 'pathological grief, reconciliation and acceptance of the inevitable, even a refusal to accept the human remains of the disappeared, and political activism' (2000: 87). I am concerned here with might be called 'pathological grief', although there may be difficulties in using such terms except in their etymological sense (*Pathos:* something which befalls one, that which one suffers, subject to suffering, a passive condition). One could therefore define 'pathological grief' as a passive grief. However, as I hope to show the nature and imagery of passive grief can be culturally specific and particularly powerful. An exploration of the metaphors employed may even be useful in devising therapies. Let us begin with Thalia's testimony (a mainland Greek woman). Of note here is her withdrawal from society, and the feeling that society could not understand her predicament.

> For the first year (after the disappearances) I cried continuously. I couldn't bear to look at my children without thinking of my husband and all the plans we had made for when we got back to Greece. I lived there for a year with my mother and brother in the village where I had been born, as I could not have coped on my own. After one year I decided that I wanted to be on my own, to cry and be with my children. I bought a small house with the money that my brother gave me. It was very difficult to manage as I only received a small 'Hunger Pension'. It was really small because due to some legislation the amount we received was only equivalent to what women in the Second World War would have received. I could not even buy my poor little children some sweets. Even now, all these years later, things have not improved very much financially. I get about 350 Cyprus pounds a month to pay for everything, including my children's studies. It is very cold in northern Greece in the winter and I can't afford much heating. It was so difficult. I felt like a social outcast. I couldn't even go to weddings, as I couldn't afford to take a gift. I received no compensation and no extra money. Not only do I miss my husband, but I also have to suffer economically and socially. People did not really understand what I was experiencing but due to my moral standing, refusing to remarry, I gained some self respect as a woman alone. Inside myself I had stopped being a woman. I had to sacrifice everything: clothes, jewellery, and a social life for my family. It was a big drama for my children. I was always crying and sad although I loved them very much. My little boys' first sentence was 'Are you crying for papa?' The children realised that this was a big problem in our family. When I heard about the message my husband sent [see below, PSC], I told my sister in law. I didn't realise that my children had come back from school and they heard what the lorry driver had told me. After this they became very withdrawn and never expressed themselves. When they came home from school they would often lie on the sofa and cry. They only really found comfort in each other. Even now the children hope that their father will come back. I remember when my son was small and I took him to the house of my brother. He ran to him and called him *patera.* I took him in my arms and explained that he wasn't his father. After that he would never go to my brother's house again.

106

In her short story on the Mother of the Missing Person, Angeliki Smyrli employs a metaphor that has particular resonance in Greek culture: that of an empty tunic. This has parallels to other art forms (including some powerful public sculptures) I discuss in Chapter 6. Their common feature is a void that needs to be filled- an absence (such a body) shaped by a presence (clothes to be filled). Smyrli talks about the mother's search for her missing son:

> Whenever she heard that prisoners/hostages (*aehmaloti*), whatever hour of the day she rushed with a suit of Alexander, with the hope that she would find him and clothe him. However every time she returned with an empty tunic and a heart filled with despair (*koustumi adeiio kai tin kardia gemati apelpisia*) (1989: 15–16)

Let us begin by noting that her missing son is called Alexander. In Greek culture, the folktale of Alexander the Great is well known. Alexander's sister, metamorphosed into a mermaid, is condemned to roam the oceans in search of her brother. When she meets ships, she asks sailors for news of her missing brother. Sailors have to respond: '*O Megaalexandros zii ke wasilevi*' (Alexander the Great lives and rules). They dare not inform her he is dead; otherwise, she would drown the ship. The name of the missing soldier thus could not be more poignant, and more bitter (*pikri*).

There is a hint in Smyrli's book that the mother's anxiety for her son is expressed and projected in her repetitive tending of his clothes: 'She kept his clothes clean and in lavender, airs them, and she re-irons the clothes of her son, dusts his books (ibid: 39). Clothes would thus be 'linking objects' in Volkan's terminology (1972): an attachment that could be called pathological to objects that stand for the lost person, a clinging to an object as a metonym, that relate them to the dead person (1981: 101–6). However, Smyrli then introduces a gnawing element of doubt through the theme of an empty tunic, a powerful one in ancient Greek literature: 'However every time she returned with an empty tunic and a heart filled with despair' (ibid: 40). This refers to a long tradition in Greek literature (dating from the sixth-century BC poet Stesichorus, taken up by Euripides) that the Gods deceived men during the Trojan War. The counter (subversive) tradition holds that Helen was never taken to Troy but was spirited to Egypt. The implication is that men fought, and died, for a phantom. A similar theme of deceit by politicians surfaces in Smyrli's book. Their identity is not revealed. They could be the Turks, the Greek Cypriot politicians, and even the superpowers. In colloquial Greek usage the U.S. president is known as *O Planetarchis*, the ruler of the planet. Many Greeks and Greek Cypriots emphasise that the coup was a deceit (*mas koroydevan*), engineered by the U.S. State Department (particularly Kissinger, a *persona non molto amata* in Cyprus), and the CIA in association with the Greek Junta, to precipitate the Turkish invasion and divide the island. If one were to follow this suggestion, there is a double deceit: an intended one on the Greek Cypriots and the whole series of unintended ones that individuals like mothers are constrained to act out, searching vainly to fill an empty tunic. With this in mind we can now approach George Seferis' poem:

Tearful bird
On sea-kissed Cyprus
consecrated to remind me of my country,
I moored alone with this fable,
if it's true that it is a fable,
if it's true that mortals will not again take up
the old deceit of the gods;
                if it's true
that in future years some other Teucer,
or some Ajax or Priam or Hecuba,
or someone unknown and nameless who nevertheless saw
a Scamander overflow with corpses,
isn't fated to hear
newsbearers coming to tell him
that so much suffering, so much life,
went into the abyss
all for an empty tunic, all for a Helen
(Yia ena poukamiso adeiano, yi mian Eleni)[6]

There are two themes here I want to point out. The first is the reference to the bird. As Nicole Loraux reminds us, the nightingale is evoked only in Classical tragedy as a figure emblematic of feminine lament (1998: 60). In Sophocles, Antigone appears the second time by Polynices' corpse, emitting moans, like a bird that has just lost its young. A second theme is that Smyrli also uses the word *adeio*: free, unused, empty, unfilled, an unusual word in this context. This is not fortuitous.

A common theme in the women's testimonies was that they ceased to view themselves as women. They had to be both father and mother to their children, and they aged as neither women nor men but as neutered individuals. They could not fully perform their female roles as transformers of nature into culture (Dubisch, 1986). Smyrli refers to the metaphor of dryness (a symbol of barrenness), and leaving flowerpots unwatered. An important role for Cypriot women is the tending of domestic space, including keeping the courtyard cool in the summer and full of flowers. Later, Smyrli revisits her mother in law and discovers a partial recovery: 'It is true I found her aged, creased by this unending waiting but she is standing straight with an open heart and open house' (*orthia me anoikti kardia kai anoikto spiti*) (ibid: 38). However there is a curious coda which should draw our attention. It again echoes a presence to suggest an absence, as well as Antigone's marriage to death:

She brought her *sentouki*, her chest, with her from Yialousa when she moved to refugee housing. She refused to sell it for anything and said: For me that *sentouki* is all Yialousa. (ibid: 38)

The *sentouki* is a dowry chest, which traditionally doubled as a coffin. They were also used to contain the *leipsana* of saints. Let us recall Antigone's lament, 'So to my grave, My bridal-bower, my everlasting prison, I go, to dwell in the mansions of Persephone' (Sophocles 1974: 164). The open house becomes the tomb. The association of tomb and womb is also found in literature. As Segal reminds us 'Antigone's cave is a place of contact between the worlds: between life and death, between Olympian and chthonic divinity, between gods and men' (1981: 180). He also notes the mutual interchangeability of the mourner and the mourned: 'the deserted (*eremos*) quality of this cave parallels the remote and exposed place of Polynices' exposure' (1981: 167). Agni's room is also dark, unopened, like a cave. The theme reappears in Dorfman's *Maiden* where Paulina, whom I have suggested is a contemporary Antigone, is stuck in a dark house with no electricity and raging storm outside – clearly a metaphor for her own psychic and physical state, and echoing her previous incarceration by the Junta. The association of tomb and womb is clear here: she is entombed in her past and is (perhaps consequently) infertile.

Clearly these images are not just very powerful, but are anchored in culture. They are both symptoms and metaphorical manifestations of internal states. Individuals use them as cultural resources. There is an element of self-awareness. This is a politically sensitive culture. We are not seeing raw Freud. We are witnessing a crafting of metaphors and imagery out of people's experiences and their shaping in a language and symbolism drawn from both literary sources and everyday life.

Public Ritual Activism

The second form for the expression of grief among Greek Cypriots is through public vigils. Vigils assume a highly expressive and cathartic significance for certain individuals, enabling their pain to be externalised and supported by public expressions of familial and national solidarity. In turn, demands for social recognition by the relatives are pursued through vigils.

The exteriorisation, management, and expression of emotions connected with the missing are critical for an understanding of the phenomenon. Relatives of the missing are a highly vocal and visible group on the national political stage. Vigils enable relatives to establish relations of solidarity. Agni said, 'Here, I meet people who have the same problem. Here I feel this is my place. I attend all the meetings. Here, I belong *(edho anigho)*. I want to come here for Christmas'. (She spoke to me in early December 1996 having travelled from her home in Lefkada, Greece). Similar sentiments of solidarity and belonging were expressed by the mothers of the *desaparecidos* of the Plaza de Mayo in Buenos Aires: '(F)or the Mothers the square signifies the best of our lives because the square is the place of our children ... On Thursdays at half past three this square belongs to us'(Guest 1990: 108). Demonstrations by relatives are very different from others connected with the Cyprus problem. They are small and discrete, involving just the close relatives of the missing (usually mothers, wives-widows), in contrast to the mass demonstrations of the refugees or political parties. They all know each other and call each other 'sister'. They have created a symbolic family. Whereas it is possible for any Cypriot, including a non-refugee, to join a refugee demonstration, it is much more difficult to participate in a demonstration by the relatives of the missing. It is too highly charged, and would be intrusive to participate. One can only be a bystander. Indeed, the potency of such demonstrations depends on the exteriorisation of private grief and the presence of an audience. Demonstrations resemble vigils, and employ religious symbolism: lighting candles, holding all-night vigils resembling wakes with the corpse at home, etc. They also employ what psychologists call worry-work, such as writing the names of the missing on yellow slips of cloth and tying them to trees (resembling *tamata* or votive offerings) (Figure 7). Finally, they suggest waiting, not movement. Other demonstrations emphasise movement usually to occupied/banned areas: Marches (e.g. *Poreia Makarios*, the journey of Makarios, *Poreia Agapis,* the journey of love), the return of the refugees to their homes, attempted crossings of the Green Line, etc. This is consistent with refugee status as *xenitia* (outsiders, away from home, but attempting to *return* home). As Seremetakis notes 'the road is one of the central signs of *xenitia* ... the road is the signifier of the non-sedentary, the unsettled, and the nomadic' (1991: 197). By contrast, relatives *wait*: at thresholds, at liminal places: embassies, the Green Line, etc., (see below), not just because they themselves appear to be liminal, but because their condition is non-reversible.

Psychologists who have studied bereavement have noted that in the early stages after loss 'the bereaved continue to act as if the person were still recoverable and to worry about the loss by going over it in their mind' (Parkes, 1991: 93). This has been called worry-work when 'bereaved people find themselves repeatedly reviewing events leading up to the death, as if by so doing they could undo or alter the events that had occurred' (ibid: 93). In the case of the missing this worry-work may have been more acute and pronounced than in more anticipateable deaths (e.g. of older people in times of peace). The majority of missing Cypriot persons were young, and in many cases their disappearances were literally a matter of chance – happening to be in the wrong place at the wrong time as a result of a series of actions and decisions. This was bound to intensify the feelings of anger and blame that inevitably accompany bereavement. A second activity, which becomes more important with the passage of time, is grief-work, based on memory. Eventually worry-work is (or should be) progressively replaced by grief-work. In the case of the missing, however, there has been less social pressure to encourage relatives to move from one stage to the other stage. Or more precisely,

Figure 7 'Worry Work'. Writing Names of The Missing
to a Christmas Tree. An anxious mimesis of state bureaucratic
procedures of filing, naming, and representing, on which the relatives
depend. These procedures were later shown to be inexact.

there has been an implicit political encouragement of worry-work. I explore this
in more detail in Chapter 8. Vigils can be seen socially as worry-work: public
demonstrations of concern for the fate of their relatives who have not yet been
formally or ritually declared dead. On the other hand demonstrations are also
grief-work – public statements of a grief that has not been allowed to terminate
naturally. It is the combination of the two activities that has invested demonstrations with such over-determined potency (such as the apparent readiness of the
women to break into tears after so many years), and helps explain why there
seems to be such a natural readiness on the part of some relatives to demonstrate
publicly.

Parkes has suggested that grief-work has three components: (i) preoccupation with the thoughts of the lost person; (ii) painful repetitious recollection of the loss experience, and (iii) attempts to make sense of the loss, to fit it into one's set of assumptions about the world, or to modify these assumptions if need be (ibid: 93). Demonstrations over the missing perform the last two functions. Public recounting of the last times their relatives were seen performs the second component of grief-work. Identification of Turkey as the culturally acceptable culprit performs the third component. Parkes also suggests that 'a major bereavement shakes confidence in (one's) sense of security. The tendency to go over the events leading up to the loss and to find someone to blame even if it means accepting blame oneself is a less disturbing alternative than accepting that life is uncertain. If we can find someone to blame or some explanation that will enable death to be evaded, then we have a chance of controlling things' (ibid: 103). Allocating blame and anger often go together, and Bowlby (1961) has identified anger as a normal component of grief. Perhaps nothing reflects the complex concatenation of these sentiments more economically than three words used as newspaper heading for a photograph of the mothers of the missing: O *Ponos, i Orgi, ke to Dakri* (The Pain, the Rage, and the Tears). Black-Michaud (1977) has also suggested that throughout the Mediterranean, women keep memories of wrongs alive in the context of feuding.

We still need to locate such expressions of grief socially. Many relatives who demonstrate come from marginal sectors and from modest families. They are bussed in from other towns by their association. The majority are women. Different classes seem to respond to the status of the missing in different ways. For the socially marginal, it is a sign of social recognition and a claim to a nationally elaborated and recognised identity, like the mothers of EOKA fighters, to be a relative of a missing person. The same applies to the widows of the Turkish Cypriot *shehitler*. Agni proudly told me 'there is a book about me', and wanted to present me with a copy.[7] Their class and political marginality is compensated by their symbolic centrality on the national political stage. Their demands cannot be openly denied or trivialised by political parties and the elite. The persistence of the issue of the missing is thus a means by the socially marginal to claim some degree of influence and centrality in a system that gives them little power. The persistence of the relatives' demands, and the transformation of the demands from an insistence on the return of captured relatives to the symbolic return of their mortal remains, is also related to the degree of marginalization of the socioeconomic groups from which the demonstrators are drawn. In the immediate post-1974 period Cypriot society was in a state of shock, and social differences were overshadowed. Over the past ten years, a booming economy has accentuated social differentiation. Relatives claim they hold demonstrations 'because unfortunately our society (meaning the political elite) has got used to the situation'. Demonstrations, and thus demonstrators, become politically central every time relations between the two communities enter a difficult phase. But demonstrating relatives are also much more dependent on the state and the pensions they receive.[8]

Emotions and belief vary between socio-economic groups. It is hardly surprising that the women who demonstrate are highly vocal. They refuse to accept the disappearances. 'It is the only thing I can do for my son', a woman said. The number of women who demonstrate is small and their identities well known. The same women turn up for vigils. They often cry when recounting their experiences to a new person. Writing in about 1975 Peter Loizos noted the 'readiness with which (refugee) women wept when talking about their home' (1981: 176–7). At the time of my initial fieldwork in 1996, the demonstrating women of the missing were similarly emotionally expressive, some twenty-two years after the events. It soon became clear that notions of 'fabrication' or 'genuineness', although important (and even necessary) for the anthropologist to pose (if hubristic and impossible to answer), had to be replaced by other notions. Some women represented extreme cases. One woman had lost five members of her family. But it was clear that such emotion was not just an expression of loss, nor just a mourning that could not be assuaged. It was more than that. Loizos noted that for refugee women 'the process of mourning increasingly impressed itself on me *as a metaphor* for understanding what the refugees were feeling. They were like people bereaved but they could not obtain from custom or religion the conventional assistance to assuage their grief' (ibid: 131). He further noted that 'if the refugees were something like bereaved people, they nevertheless lacked crucial supports that the bereaved normally have expected' (ibid: 131). This is a very perceptive insight, but we need to do more with it. It is the refugees who have been forcibly displaced, and it is not so much loss of possessions but their previous selves in a previous time and different place that they are mourning, and therefore an image of wholeness that they have lost. Mourning is more than a metaphor to understand their predicament. The refugees were 'metaphorized' ('transported', from *metaphora*, to transport) from their previous self/place. They have had to adjust to the notion of themselves as 'the other', and mourn the loss of their previous selves embedded in a place they are prevented from returning to. Recovery of place is thus a metaphor for, and an actual means to, recovery of identity: the recovery of the lost self.

Various anthropologists have pointed to the homology between emigration and mourning. Caraveli has noted 'widowhood and emigration are regarded in the Greek folk tradition as metaphorical extensions of death' (1986: 181). Seremetakis has suggested that 'travel, journey, passage to a foreign land, and exile are central metaphors of death in rural Greece. They are perceived as *xenitia*, which *encompasses the conditions of estrangement, the outside, the movement from the inside to the outside ... Xenitia* is a basic cognitive structure within which life and death are thought. [It] is reversible and situationally contingent' (1991: 85, emphasis in original). Yet the notions contained within the word itself are interesting and provide further clues. *Xenitia* is not just being in a strange place, away from home. It is to be a stranger, an other to oneself, estranged from oneself. This is the 'basic cognitive structure' of *xenitia* – an other *to* oneself (whereas oneself as the other is a completely different process, almost of possession). Nonreversible *xenitia*, forcible expulsion, as with the refugees, is tantamount to death, to being on the other side of the river Styx – itself a symbolic representation of the *nekri zoni* (dead zone).[9] Hence the passion with which many of the first-generation refugees wish to return. And if lamentation is metaphorically similar to possession, it is a 'possession' to repossess oneself not as the other, but as oneself (Crapanzano, 1977; Caraveli, ibid: 171–72). As Holst-Warhaft notes for *Antigone*, 'mourning and possession by the gods are linked' (1995: 164). One has to become the other, to be fully 'possessed', to finally recapture oneself.

I make the above points to highlight the contrast between refugees and the relatives of the missing. The situation of the relatives of the missing is almost an inverse to that of the refugees. Relatives of missing persons are, by contrast, not presented with an institutional framework to express their grief. But they appear to be mourning a bereavement that cannot be assuaged, partly because they have not participated in the customary mortuary rituals, and partly because they are faced with the existential uncertainty as to whether their missing relatives are alive or dead. The vigils of the relatives cannot thus be seen as a metaphor of mourning. They are performances of bereavement and experiences of unterminated mourning. As performances of bereavement they are gendered laments as national protest. Women are given the opportunity to express their loss in socially sanctioned ways. A demonstration against the Turks over the *agnoumeni* is a situation where emotions can be nationally directed by a body of customary expectations and experiences (about the 'barbarism of the Turks', etc.), and socially accepted. As performances of bereavement they are nationally ratified expressions of griefwork. As experiences of unterminated mourning, they are expressions of worrywork. Through these vigils four different processes occur. First, national suffering is authenticated through (and anchored in) individual pain. Second, the individual role of women as mourners is ratified. Third, individual pain is expressed through the performance of women as mourners, and finally, the representation of the nation is gendered through women. The state's subjects thus filially identify with the nation as a gendered representation of suffering. In the words of a social-psychological team 'paraphrasing' responses by interviewed refugees after the invasion: 'Cyprus is my country and I love her more after all she has suffered' (Evdokas, 1976: 49)

Caraveli has suggested that lamentation is a 'process defined not by its setting but instead symbolically demarcates space as mediating ground between the living and the dead, the ordinary and extraordinary experience' (ibid: 191). In some crucial respects lamentation is genderization. It is not just that women use laments to express their gender identities. It is also that lamentation is critically, constitutively, female. Paraphrasing Herzfeld, women have to be 'good at being women' through performances at vigils. Female relatives are known as *i manades tis Kyprou* (the mothers of Cyprus/the Cypriot Mothers). Such expectations help explain the opprobrium attached to women of the missing who remarried. For some time the Church refused them the right to remarry. It was believed that they were betraying not just their husbands, but their role expected of them as grieving mothers/wives, and thus betraying Cyprus. Clearly, they signified Cyprus as sacrificial i.e., scapegoat or surrogate victim, within a context of geopolitics. Yet in another sense like Antigones these vigils can also be seen as a social protest by women against the social lack of provisions for mortuary rituals. Having become obliged to perform as the state's signifiers of the nation's pain, they have turned their suffering into a regenerative act in the absence of a body to mourn: 'I had only one son. Who shall I marry off to give me grandchildren *(pyon na pandrepso na mou kanei angonia)?* I cry all day *(kleo ulli mera).*'

Let us re-examine Figure 5: *Dhen Ksehno* (I won't forget). As noted in Chapter 4, this painting displays a slippage from a wife searching for her husband, to one of a mother holding up a picture of her dead/missing son. Logically one cannot be both wife and mother *(except Jocasta, Oedipus' wife, and Antigone's mother)*. Structurally, this image replicates Antigone's associations. As Segal notes 'Antigone herself doubles with the grieving figure of the Great Mother ... She projects an image of herself as the *mater dolorosa* as well as the maiden wedded to Hades. Logically, Antigone cannot be Kore and Demeter at the same time. Yet mythic imagery often operates with exactly this fruitfully illogical union of opposites. Here a mythic archetype is split into two contradictory and yet simultaneously coexisting aspects of self. The kore is also the mother at an earlier stage. So here Antigone, who takes on herself the task of burying and mourning the dead son, often the task of mother or wife, is the Earth Mother who grieves over her children. The maiden claimed by death, who ought to be resurrected with the new life of the year, will instead remain in the Underworld with her dead' (1981: 180). We will have a chance to further explore this connection in the concluding chapter.

Clearly, I am not suggesting that the mothers consciously model themselves on Antigone, although some may know the Sophoclean version. My interest here is to draw structural parallels as an aid towards understanding a complex situation. Whilst the political and ecclesiastical authorities and elites draw upon such parallels with ancient literature, this is hardly surprising. Indeed, as I show, they use them in sometimes perplexing ways. Many of the elite have been brought up on this staple cultural diet, and they have complex and sophisticated cultural and politico-ethnic agendas, not least being the continual drawing of cultural boundaries between themselves as Greeks and the Turks, as well to appeal to western public opinion. Classical literature may well be last strategy of the weak and powerless. But to see the drawings of such parallels purely as an ideological weapon, or even as a cynical political ploy, would be to evacuate the predicament of relatives of the missing of its content, as well as to empty classical literary themes of much of their force and their relevance to the world we live in. It would treat the predicament of the missing *sui generis*, and as unrelated to art and literature, which it patently is. It would also be to see the play of Sophocles and its subsequent versions, including by Anouilh and Dorfman, both politically engaged writers, as irrelevant to the world we as anthropologists set ourselves to describe. Greek tragedy may be particularly fruitful as a distinct point of departure because, as Lacan pointed out, there is no ideal exaltation in any Greek tragedy, unlike European classical tragedies (1992: 98). As 'social scientists', we ought to be open to the role of literature and art because they too influence people's lives and self-perceptions and presentations in a literate world. What I hope to show is not that literature models life, or vice versa (for things are always more complex), but rather that the polyvalence of literary texts (and their re-working by various authors) provides us with a handle into understanding the situations people face. Correspondingly, the traumas people experience enable us to approach literature with new eyes.

On a political level, demonstrating mothers and wives represent tradition in two ways: first, they keep alive national traditions alive, such as sacrifice and loss, in spite of the pressures of modernity. In that respect they hark back to a pre-lapsarian, pre-1974 unity. Second, they implicitly represent gender traditions: the traditions of mourning and faithfulness that women embody. Demonstrating mothers thus re-enforce the associated notions of patriotism and sacrifice, even if there is always a tension between them and the authorities. However, as Caraveli (ibid: 70) and Sarris (1995: 24) have noted, younger, more educated and urbanised Greek and Cypriot women are much more reluctant to express their grief in such excessive modes of mourning. Men also criticise such expressions of emotion, sometimes for different reasons. However, it is extremely difficult for anyone to openly describe such displays of emotion as excessive because such criticism is viewed negatively as a betrayal of the national interest, and a lack of sensitivity to these women's sufferings. Most middle-class people thus try to bypass the issue and interpret such expressions of emotion as an indication of the *strength* of the women's feelings and the depth of their *ponos* (pain), and thus a *reflection* of the enormity of national suffering. With relatively few exceptions, the westernised middle classes do not demonstrate much, and having a missing son or father appears more as something not to be spoken about, rather than displayed. They also appear more resigned to their death, although it has to be said many found ways of escaping front-line duties. It is these people that the UN and other diplomats meet on the Nicosia cocktail circuit. It is easy for outsiders to conclude that the issue is a cynical political ploy and divest it of its internal political dynamics and cultural resonance. But for the ordinary and marginalised, as I have shown, things are different. In the concluding chapter I discuss how the inability to openly address such issues is not a by-product of the situation but a constitutive element of the public secret.

The emotional and social marginality of the relatives of the missing is reflected in the location of their vigils: at boundaries, or close to liminal spaces, such as outside the UN Headquarters at the Ledra Palace. Relatives suspect the UN of want-

Figure 8 'The Monstrous Double'. Greek Cypriot poster display at the Green Line, showing the 1996 Derynia killings by Turkish officials of Greek Cypriots when they staged an attempt to walk across the 'Dead Zone' *(Nekri Zoni)* and haul down a Turkish flag. Note that there is no reference to Turkish Cypriots.

Figure 9 'The Monstrous Double'. Turkish Cypriot display on the other side of the Green Line, showing photographs of 1974 Mass Graves. The text reads: 'NO MASSACRES, NO MASS GRAVES'.

ing to close the issue. The philosopher Gillian Rose has suggested that in literature the state's power is most clearly questioned in such areas: 'just outside the
boundary we find mourning women: Antigone, burying the body of her fratricidal brother in defiance of Creon's decree, witnessed by her reluctant sister Ismene,
who urges her to desist; and the wife of Phocion, gathering the ashes of her dis-
graced husband, with her trusted woman companion …' (1996: 35)

The boundaries of the city (or the political unit) are also where there is the
greatest need for the rhetorical definition of the self and the other, where identities have to be the most rigidly expressed. This is the area where Polynices' body
is displayed as carrion. This is the area where Greek and Turkish Cypriots put on
poster displays highlighting the monstrosity of the other (Figures 8 and 9).
Beyond, lies the monstrous double. On the other side of the Green Line everything is literally *entre parenthese*. The TRNC is a *pseudokratos* (pseudo-state) where
nothing is true except that all official statements are lies (*psemata*). All references
to the Other in written texts are signalled by inverted commas. As the neutral
UN-speak Green Line, it is an interface of ritual transgressions such as women
attempting to cross the line to return to their homes. Beyond that is the *Nekri
Zoni* (Dead Zone). As I show in Chapter 6 the *Nekri Zoni* is a place of death, a
place where transgressions are staged and managed for the means of representation. Here, order, lawlessness, and violence are choreographed by both sides and
represented in photographs, posters, and the media.

Official Turkish Cypriot Perceptions of Missing Persons:
a Dead Issue?

In 1997 when I conducted fieldwork in the TRNC there was resentment and suspicion among officials regarding discussion of the issue of missing people. They
considered the Greek Cypriots had fabricated the issue as a propaganda issue and
a 'political problem'. The Greek Cypriots considered it a 'humanitarian problem'.
They could not talk about 'the-Missing-as-Missing' except as 'the Greek Cypriot-
"Missing"' – clearly an uncomfortable acknowledgement to the effectiveness of
the Greek Cypriot campaign. Nor was it just a question of differences between the
Turkish Cypriot perception of the disappeared-as-dead-or-lost (forever) (*kayipler*) and the Greek Cypriot perception of their disappeared as *agnoumeni* as missing, of-unknown-fate-but-potentially recoverable either materially or in terms of
knowledge. It was also a difference about the degree of almost permitted politicisation. The head of the Turkish Cypriot CMP delegation, Rustem Tatar, claimed
that 'if the Greek Cypriots had not politicised the issue so much we would have
resolved it by now. They frightened the Turkish Cypriots because of their propaganda. They have not been consistent'. Clearly there is something in this. Ironically as I shall show, the attempt to separate the issue in terms of either 'realism'

(pragmatism) or 'politics' (expediency) is itself a subtly political act. Nor can the Turkish Cypriot position itself be considered 'consistent'.

There were other reasons why Turkish Cypriots officials seemed uncomfortable with the issue. Many seemed initially frightened even to talk about the matter.[10] Whilst on the Greek side I had been encouraged to view the Missing as metaphors of return and recovery, on the Turkish side I was expected to look at them as 'the dead', and therefore not even as a suitable problem, anthropological or otherwise, unless it was designed to embarrass them. Consequently, I became particularly interested in why the Turkish Cypriot authorities seemed so officially uninterested in their dead as objects of grief or mourning whilst being keen to appropriate their sacrifice. 'They're dead; that's it' many said, including ordinary people. It soon transpired that the officially-sponsored silence may have actually insulated the relatives from the rest of society, and they were thus not provided with a space to realise their grief and mourning. By contrast, the Greek authorities gave the relatives a central theatrical space to enact their suffering for the whole society. In both cases tensions arose, and I would argue that the officially-sponsored Greek Cypriot concern for the relatives and the appropriation of their suffering for nationalist-state agendas, is as distorting and as exploitative as the indifference generated by the 'realism' of the Turkish Cypriot authorities. As the Chorus in Sophocles' *Antigone* notes:

There is danger in unnatural silence
No less than in excess of lamentation

The silence of Turkish Cypriot relatives may well be subversive of official presentation, just as the vocality of the relatives of Greek Cypriots whilst appearing to echo official positions, may be subversive of them.

The Turkish Cypriot official position is that all missing persons, Greek and Turkish Cypriot, are dead. According to them, it is important that the people put the matter behind them to look to the future. Whereas the Greeks have turned the issue into a deeply political and symbolic one, politicising the symbol (the return of the bodies) in order to symbolise the political (the return home of the refugees, etc.), the Turkish Cypriots have attempted to pragmatise it, to literally turn into a thing, not a symbol. They accuse the Greek Cypriot authorities of prolonging the agony of the relatives, and suggest that the silence of the Turkish Cypriot relatives is a self-imposed one, rather than, as I suggest a state-discouragement of individual mourning-grief. Many officials told me 'the relatives don't like talking about their experiences'. This was partly true, but it was also perhaps to discourage the observer-investigator from getting behind the officially-encouraged silence about the past as ended and closed, and questioning the space between private emotions and their collective-statist representation. The Turkish Cypriot Association of Relatives of Missing Persons maintains a low profile, and the Greek Cypriot Association of Relatives claims that although they asked them in 1982 through the offices of UN for a meeting, they replied they were not interested. Turkish Cypriot authorities were very reluctant to allow me and my assistants to interview relatives independently of the minders they provided. I discovered that many wanted to talk, suggesting that the 'natural reticence' of the relatives may have been encouraged by the authorities. By contrast, the Greek Cypriot authorities used the symbolism of marginality that the women-relatives represented to place them at the centre of the officially dressed political stage, perhaps to symbolise the marginality of Cyprus, as deserving more attention.

In explaining their differences to Greek Cypriots, Turkish Cypriot officials usually begin by drawing upon ethnic-cultural differences between Greeks and Turks: 'we are realistic; we are secular', meaning, we have accepted the deaths/disappearances of the missing, in contrast to the 'un-realism' and 'religiosity' of the Greek Cypriots. There is a double irony here. First, Greek Cypriots view Turkish Cypriots as more 'fatalistic', suggesting that the term is used to create a distinction between the modern self and the pre-modern, 'backward' other. Second, Turkish Cypriots also use religious symbolism, but in a distinctive way. The same official suggested that the Turkish Cypriots are more realistic because they are predisposed by religion to accept reality: 'the Turks being Muslims are great believers in fate. It is easier for a Turkish Cypriot to bow to the Grace of God and say it is fate. It is what is written on your forehead (*kader*)'. Here, 'fate' meant recognising 'facts', being realistic. By contrast, he suggested, the Greek Cypriots are predisposed to fight against reality because they are religious. There is an element of truth to this in the sense, as I shall show, that Greek Cypriots are more predisposed to employ religious symbolism to represent their missing, whose recovery could symbolise the recovery of the North. Yet what is meant by 'realism' may mean different things to the two sides. The 'realism' the Turkish Cypriots would like to encourage among Greek Cypriots is the acceptance of the division of the island and the establishment of the TRNC, something the Greek Cypriots do not accept.

We need to go beyond such explanations and examine the conditions under which Turkish Cypriots disappeared, and how their leadership dealt with the problem according to their own political agendas. This can help explain a central point I want to develop: that the Turkish Cypriot leadership may well have needed, according to their own agendas, to turn their missing persons into casualties; in short, to declare them dead to show that between Greek and Turk there could be no cohabitation. Yet in so doing they did not harness the phase of mourning collectively, nor addressed the complex feelings that were raised individually for families. Part of this is due to the circumstances of 1963–64. But there were other reasons.

Turkish Cypriot *kayipler* almost became non-people from the start, first by the Greek Cypriot authorities and then by the Turkish Cypriot leadership. Briefly put, the *kayipler* were scripted out of the stage, whilst the *agnoumeni* were scripted in. Officially, Greek Cypriot authorities did not accept in 1963 that there were missing persons in its territory and strenuously refused to admit this in international fora. Until 1997 they did not even advance to the UN CMP the names of those Greeks who disappeared in 1963–64, as this would have indicated that they did not control the whole territory of the Republic of Cyprus, and would have recognised the existence of a Turkish Cypriot political entity limiting the sovereignty of the Republic of Cyprus. To the Greek Cypriot leadership the problem of missing persons is still a problem imposed by the 1974 invasion and occupation of Cyprus by a foreign country (i.e. Turkey). In 1963–64 the Republic of Cyprus treated Turkish Cypriot government employees who had disappeared or did not report to work as if they had left their jobs and resigned. In a climate of Greek Cypriot-induced disappearances, and of intimidation by TMT, reporting for work was threatening, isolating, and demeaning. Some Turkish Cypriot relatives of disappeared public sector employees did however receive compensation. During this period (December 1963) the State could not control irregulars, many of whom attached themselves to armed groups of men (Loizos, 1975; Sant Cassia, 1983). The Greek Cypriot police under the ex-EOKA fighter and Minister of the Interior, P. Yorgadjis, were involved in some heavy fighting. Within a month some 20–25 Greek Cypriots and 200 Turkish Cypriots were reported as missing, and the Red Cross became involved. But because individuals were being abducted and then released, the unfolding reality always included the possibility that the missing were hostages. This led many to believe that their missing relatives would probably be released at some later stage when relations became more peaceful. There were few situations where bodies were dumped to be picked up. Missing people just disappeared.

For the relatives, things were very uncertain. The Republic of Cyprus officially refused to accept that there were disappearances, and treated this either as an insurrection or as a fabrication by Turkish Cypriot leaders. Turkish Cypriots did not report disappearances to the now completely Greek Cypriot-dominated police, the Turkish Cypriot police having ceased collaborating with their Greek colleagues. Turkish Cypriots began withdrawing into enclaves encouraged by their leaders and their paramilitary group, TMT who insisted they could not guarantee their safety unless they moved. Many relatives of the disappeared were poor villagers, of low social standing, not accustomed to the language of human or civil rights. This was then an unsophisticated society, and the language of human rights had little currency. So they turned inevitably to their local representatives, who had limited means of intervention: 'in those days people weren't taken seriously. The authorities were helpless. They didn't do much'. The Turkish Cypriot Communal Chamber began collecting lists of missing persons. Widows were given a salary for life or until remarriage. Initially they were given some relief in the form of food parcels. Some Turkish Cypriot leftists have claimed that the leadership then were not keen to pursue the matter with the Greek Cypriot authorities: 'the leadership didn't want to recognise the Greek administration. Perhaps they feared that if the Greek Cypriot government were to compensate the relatives then that would imply recognition and dependency on the Greek Cypriot state' (CTP politician).

There is evidence to suggest that the disappearance of many Turkish Cypriots was effected by small groups of men who knew their victims. Greek paramilitaries tended to pick on identifiable people, who generated suspicion because they were mobile and travelled, such as vegetable sellers, drivers, butchers, travelling salesmen, etc., whom they might have suspected of belonging to the TMT. These were men whose jobs also required them to carry large sums of money. Although difficult to prove, it seems that private banditry masquerading as bravado nationalism, and aiming at theft, was often the primary reason for the disappearances. Their victims were neither leaders, nor of a readily definable intellectual group (such as students in Argentina seen by paranoid policemen as threats to the public order). They were selected because they were weak, and their bodies hidden rather than displayed. In short, the situation bred general uncertainty even for the people who seemed to be dominating the situation themselves.

The Disappeared: from Missing Hostages to Disposed Missing to Honorary Martyrs

Disappeared Turkish Cypriots soon moved from being missing/returnable hostages to becoming the disposed missing and eventually honorary martyrs (*shehitler*). According to officials who naturally have an investment in a monitorable and controllable social reality, this emerges from a specific date (4 June 1968) when Rauf Denktash, the Turkish Cypriot leader, asked Glavkos Clerides, then delegated to represent the Greek Cypriots, at their Beirut meeting for information on the fate of the Missing. They claim Clerides told Denktash to consider these missing as dead. Denktash then conveyed the bitter truth to the relatives. As a result Turkish Cypriots began accepting this fact.[11] Denktash at the time decided to formally declare the matter closed, and declare that the Greek Cypriot leadership had admitted that the disappeared Turks were dead. In pointing to this incident, which has to be treated as a Durkheimian social fact, we should be sensitive to the ironies of the situation. First, although the Turkish Cypriot leadership now claim that when they withdrew to the armed enclaves they had withdrawn recognition of the Republic of Cyprus, which according to them officially ceased to exist, Turkish Cypriot political leaders nevertheless in practice relied on the legitimising attribution of responsibility from the officialising statements issuing from a representative of the Republic (Clerides). According to the Turkish Cypriots, the Greek Cypriots admit that they cold-bloodedly killed the missing, a point the Turks had long been making. Second, this admission helped orient the Turkish Cypriot leaderships' insistence that Greek and Turk could not live together peacefully, but needed to live separately. At that time, in the inter-communal talks, Denktash was insisting on the need for the two communities to establish separate geographical zones for security reasons. Such disclosures certainly strengthened his position.

It is from this period that the Turkish Cypriot missing became officially classified as *kayipler*, and also included within the general category of *shehitler*, the martyrs or witnesses who had given up their lives fighting for the nation. This further shut the door both on reconciliation, and on a possible compromise joint interpretation that could have turned both the Turkish missing and the much smaller number of Greeks, into national victims or symbols of a bitter, but lamented and transcendable feud. Instead they became *ethnic* victims, selected taxonomically, witnesses of a 'chronic inability' of Greek and Turk to live together. In short, by electing to render evident what probably many people feared ('they have *admitted* they killed our people in cold blood'), in the name of 'realism' and 'compassion' for the suffering of the relatives, the process of ethnic separation was enhanced further. There is no reason to question the sincerity of these sentiments, but they also had certain political and collective implications that require reflection. Finally, the continuous reference by Turkish Cypriot officials to Clerides' imputed admission not only officialized their losses and Greek Cypriot 'admitted culpability', but also has to be seen as a ritualised statement with important implications for Turkish Cypriot political dialogue. To question its veracity, or to impute that it may have been given a certain spin by Denktash, not only flies in the face of the 'evidence' ('but they must be dead'), but can also seem perversely 'cruel' to the relatives, by 'prolonging their suffering'. An imputed 'admission of ethnic culpability' turns into a compassionate 'cruel to be kind', in the workings of the ethnic leaders. By repeatedly evoking this incident, Government employees officialise their role as disseminators of 'realism', whilst further entrenching a definition of the state of affairs 'mediated' (but equally asserted) by political leaders, such as Denktash. Such assertions become rituals of support for political leaders. By appearing to harness politics to 'realism', defining what is 'realistic' and occupying it, the Turkish nationalist right wing monopolised the issue. The Turkish Cypriot left, that had strong contacts with their Greek counterparts and supported peaceful interethnic co-operation, was left with little ideological space to contest and offer alternative interpretations. Indeed the left was so frightened of Denktash's monopoly of rightist ethnic nationalism, that they steered clear of raising the issue of the *kayipler*. A further reason for the reluctance to talk about the Turkish Cypriot Missing is the strong suspicion that some were actually killed by TMT, rather than Greek Cypriots.

Although the disappeared Turkish Cypriots were proclaimed to be dead by their political leadership in 1968, matters changed in 1974. When the Greek Cypriots raised the issue of their own missing persons in 1974 and internationalised it, the Turkish Cypriots countered, not unnaturally, by presenting their disappeared as missing. During fieldwork (in 1997), I discovered that in 1975 the original Turkish Cypriot records of lists of missing persons, collected in the post-1964 period had disappeared, and were untraceable. They thus had to restart collecting information that was some 10 years old to present to the UN sponsored CMP. According to the Turkish Cypriot CMP representative, some watchmen had burned the records to keep warm! The irony of disappeared records for dead people, who are officially re-presented and re-processed as disappeared people, should not detain us here. But the official indifference to official records suggests that between 1968–74 the Turkish Cypriot leadership genuinely did consider the matter as closed and had no plans to make long-term political capital out of it. It is therefore ironic that in order to counter what they claim to be Greek Cypriot cynical propaganda they have been obliged to retie the Gordian knot that Dentktash's 1968 disclosure had been designed to cut through.

The Relatives: Resistance through Silence

The official line that whilst the Turkish leadership has been compassionate in not exploiting the issue, the Greeks have made cynical use of the relatives' grief and uncertainty is problematical. Denktash's sudden disclosure in 1968 did not address the grief of the relatives, nor their mourning. The *kayipler* are grouped together with the *shehitler*, the martyrs (literally witnesses) who had fallen defending the Turkish community against Greek aggression during what they call the wars of 1963 and 1974. Yet paradoxically, whilst there are many monuments to the *shehitler* fighters, there is not one specifically dedicated to the missing persons as a generic group. Nor indeed has any public building or street been named after any missing or disappeared person. For a society that has a voracious need for symbols of suffering and resistance, this is puzzling especially, as one Turkish Cypriot leftist cynically noted, 'if even one of the fighters cut his little finger fighting for the nation, they build a monument'. Perhaps monuments to civilian missing persons goes against the militaristic nature of Turkish nationalism, and could also raise embarrassing questions in Turkey where mothers of disappeared persons regularly demonstrate in Istanbul. In contrast to Greek Cypriot monuments, the only identifiable figure in Turkish Cypriot nationalism is Ataturk, the father of modern Turkey. Monuments to the Turkish Cypriot fighters are represented by abstract or highly stylised sculptures (see Figure 10). Yet the *kayipler* are important as photographic representations of suffering. These are the photographs that until recently greeted the visitor crossing the Green Line. I examine these in Chapter 6.

Many *kayipler* relatives were not pleased with this grouping. They appear to be scripted into a public role that they have performed with such apparent compliance, silence, and submission that, in the apt words of Herzfeld (1985), may well have been subversive. Whilst it may have given the relatives of the *kayipler* some prestige to be grouped with the *shehitler*, they do not have such a strong claim to social prestige as the latter. The *shehitler* families have a strong organisation, the *kayipler* have no representation. They are names, not faces. Furthermore, the

Figure 10 Turkish Cypriot Monument to the *Shehitler* (Martyrs), Nicosia.

grouping of *kayipler* with *shehitler* may have been useful politically but it did not address the key issues of mourning and graves: 'It was very difficult for the families to accept their death. Many people could not accept the *mevlide* (mortuary recitation)for their death. Sometimes they got news of the relatives in Greece. So they kept on hoping'. In 1974 at the height of the invasion, all the male inhabitants of the mixed village of Tochni in the southern part of Cyprus were taken away in two buses by EOKA-VITA men and murdered. Their graves have never found (although in a small place like Cyprus it would be relatively easy to do so). A survivor from one of the buses managed to escape. Many relatives continued to hope that their loved ones may have been in the other bus and may still be hostages. After the population swap-over in 1976, the women and children from Tochni were resettled in the north, in a village named after the old one (Tashkent). In 1987 the authorities erected a monument to all the disappeared men from the village. Relatives objected because according to them this meant they were all considered officially dead and therefore the authorities would neither continue to try to find them, nor ask for their remains. Nor did they appear to get much advice or support from their authorities:

> For years I could not pray even if he is dead. How can you imagine someone is dead if there is no trace? I don't even know if he is alive or dead. I do pray for him but not as if he were dead. He might sort of just come. My friends had dads, you have no home, no furniture, you have lost everything. If you had a grave, you could go there and talk to him. Take a bottle of water and pray for him.

This type of grief has been called unelaborated grief, or impaired mourning (Robben, 2000). Let us note the parallelism between the above quote and one provided by an Argentine mother of a *desaparecido:* 'For those who are religious or who have a place on earth where they have their dead to take flowers to, to say a prayer, whatever, this is denied to them' (Robben, 2000: 90).

For many years, stories abounded of hostages being forced into hard work on road-building, a classical imagery of the fear of a small group being used merci-lessly by a larger oppressing group. This type of work was traditionally resorted to by the poorest members of Cypriot society. In some cases, the return of the loved ones is also linked to a solution: 'I believe he will come back when there is a solu-tion', or, 'I cannot believe he is dead. At the end of the *mevlide* [a prayer said at the mortuary ritual-PSC] there is a section for the dead. I cannot bring myself to say that because I cannot believe he is dead. The Greeks told me that he will be released when there is a solution. I believe he will come back when there is a solu-tion'. Such statements are also implicit criticisms of their leadership: negotiate for a solution and allow us to get our relatives back. There were also strong criticisms of how the Turkish Cypriot leadership used the *kayipler* for political purposes: 'We also find it very hard to accept that the shehitler were and are treated as heroes but the kayipler are not' (40-year-old teacher, son of a *kayip*). 'Many fam-ilies of fighters got the best houses after 1974. The *kayipler* relatives got less. We don't even have a death certificate. We have nothing ... No-one took any notice of the relatives." (42-year-old daughter of a *kayip*). 'The politicians used us for their own purposes. To show that they suffered, especially at elections, to cry, etc.'(33-year-old daughter of a kayip). These are quotations I obtained when interviewing independently of the minders provided by the authorities.

What the relatives are objecting to most is that their loved ones, and by impli-cation they too, are erased by the official concentration on the missing as repre-sentations of death and as signs of an ineradicable past of ethnic intolerance. As a result the missing have no existentiality, no real identity, as beings, but rather become collapsed to the 'essence' of death as a nothingness. Turkish Cypriot miss-ing/ *kayipler* are held up as signifiers (of 'ethnic incompatibility') with no verifiable signified (because there are no bodies). Indeed it is paradoxical not just that the records of missing-persons-as-missing were lost (a supreme sign of official indif-ference to them after their death, indeed not even of them as deceased persons), but also that for many relatives the existential verifiability of their parents (many of whom they may not even remember) comes from documents that confirm an absence. For a number of individuals, the only documents that confirm an exis-tence are paradoxically not even Turkish Cypriot records but foreign ones. To some, their fathers exist as 'photographs in an English book (*sic.*)' with a name and some biographical details: signifiers but no signified. For the son or daugh-ter, a father's reality is constructed precisely through his disappearance as a miss-ing character, as an absence.

This tension between signifier and signified is further reinforced and realised through the co-evalness of the lack of graves and their official status as dead people, an inversion of the normal demonstrability of death. As one man from Tashkent said 'the *shehitler* have the graves and can go there to pray. For us it is not like this. There is nowhere you can go and put flowers'. Visiting graves is important on the eve of Bayram. But relatives do not have graves to do this nor any meaningful symbolic focus. Lacking any organisation or official sponsorship except for the *shehitler* fighters (who have graves), they tend to mourn individually. The same Tashkent man said of his wife's father: 'We made a museum of her Father's photograph. Every family here enlarged the photos of their dead and hung them on their walls and kept everything they had as it was'. Here a formal difference should be noted with Greek Orthodox culture. According to Delaney, Turks attach less symbolism to the body as a post-death artefact. Death is a second birth, 'the second and higher-order birth' (1991: 319). This second birth is imagined as 'spiritual, not physical; the physical body is left behind' (ibid: 314), the dead body being the symbolic equivalent of 'seeds planted in the earth to be born in the other world' (ibid: 313). As a result the recovery of the body does not seem to have the same resonance in Turkish Cypriot culture as in Greek culture. This is also re-enforced by the Muslim idea that it is wrong to make a monument of the grave. The Shehitler cemetery in Nicosia is extremely sparse and undecorated. Paradoxically, although Turkish Cypriots claim that they are not very religious, they justify the lack of decoration of the graves by reference to religious imperatives. This reinforces the suggestion that for the state it is not the graves as such that are important but the *representation* of their death as martyrs through monuments. It is therefore much easier for the state to appropriate this domain of representation and elaboration, bypassing individual sentiments. Thus ideologically for the Turkish Cypriots it appears that the recovery of bodies may have less culturally embedded imperatives as amongst the Greeks.

Another reason why the Turkish Cypriot leadership appears officially uninterested in the return of the Turkish Cypriot bones may well be due to a fear that they would thus have to permit exhumation of Greek bodies which may prove Greek Cypriot claims about the latter's disappearances. The following transcript of an attempted interview by my research assistant, Kate Tripp, highlights the political nature of the issue:

On my first visit to Fatna, an informant living in a village near Kyrenia, the Turkish Cypriot member of the Committee of Missing Persons had arranged for his assistant to act as my translator. Initially he was helpful, relating the story of how my informant's husband, brother and four sons disappeared after being taken from the town of Tokhni by Greek Cypriot soldiers. However, when I wanted to ask her about her views on the fate of her family and on the issue of remains he refused to translate my questions. Instead he informed me, speaking on the behalf of all Turkish Cypriots, that they believe that persons reported missing are in fact dead and that the return of remains is unnecessary. I discovered, just as Robben (1995) discovered during his fieldwork in Argentina that like many ethnographers and journalists researching violent and political conflict I had become a victim of a bad attempt at 'political seduction'. Perceived by my 'translator' and the Turkish Cypriot leadership as someone who in the future might write something of relevance about their regime, they had designed a itinerary of interviews that they believed would convince me to adopt their interpretation of past events.

I asked if she wanted the remains of her family returned to her? But she was not given the opportunity to answer as the assistant continued to speak on her behalf. Without even translating the question, he said that she is very happy with what the Turkish Cypriot government has provided her with. He says that she doesn't want the remains because she knows that they are dead.

My sudden realization did little to resolve the situation and I found it impossible to obtain any information from my informant's perspective. Frustrated, I felt I had gained very little insight into the opinions and problems experienced by the Turkish Cypriot wives of Missing Persons. Although discussions with English-speaking Turkish Cypriots revealed similar sentiments to Greek Cypriots, the formal view is that the issue of the Missing is tragic but irrelevant.

Just as we were about to leave Fatna's house, her grandson who had been studying in England returned home. He spoke English well and I took the opportunity to ask him to translate my questions to his grandmother, despite the presence of my translator. Once again, I asked her whether she was concerned with the issue of remains?

'I am not satisfied at all. I believe they have been killed, but I would like to have the remains returned to me. Like all women I want to be able to mourn them properly. I want information about what has happened. We were never formally told what had happened, it is as if everybody wanted to forget about our tragedy, and us. '

I asked if she wants officials to actively search for the bodies?

'Yes, I do. I want to be able to bury them.'

At this point the assistant wants us to leave. He is evidently displeased that the woman has been able to communicate effectively through her grandson. Before we leave, the grandson tells us that he believes that one day he hopes that Greek and Turk will be able to live together [this is also somewhat subversive of the official line – PSC].

The Greek Cypriot insistence on the return of the bodies may have strengthened the hand of the Turkish Cypriot relatives *vis-a-vis* their own representatives. In 1996 Denktash secretly asked the Republic of Cyprus for his mother's bones in Paphos to be transferred to the North. This was interpreted as a sign of further separation between the two communities. But as a leftist politician observed, until very recently to request from the Turkish Cypriot authorities that they ask for the bones of the missing, or to ascertain their exact fate, was tantamount to questioning the authorities: 'It didn't even enter their minds to question both what the authorities said or to want to take things further. That was really it. They couldn't think otherwise' (CTP leader). Recently, however, relatives have been insisting more openly that they wanted the bones returned, 'so that we can also bury them according to our rites', even though as honorary *shehitler* the *kayipler* are all considered to have gone to Heaven, and *not* to have required the traditional cleansing of the body prior to burial.

In short, it was not so much a matter that the Turkish Cypriots were more 'realist' and their authorities more 'compassionate' than the Greeks. The picture is more complex. Indeed the greatest expressions of pain, or at least the ones that affected me particularly deeply, were Turkish Cypriot ones because they have been told that their relatives are dead but have no tomb, no grave, nor even symbolic graves. 'I have never spoke to anyone like I have spoken to you', a man confided. The openness of that statement is humbling to anyone practising anthropology, and certainly creates a sense of responsibility. C.S. Lewis observed 'sorrow .... turns out to be not a state but a process. It needs not a map but a history' (1966: 10). Turkish Cypriot authorities gave it a topography, just as they were busily changing every name of every village, Turkifying them in order to create a new state, but they left no space for process, for a history, for individuals. As in *The Suppliants* the State has attempted to take the funerary laments away from the women: 'praise, not lament, is what the young must learn if they are to emulate the champions in glory' (Holst 1992: 168). By contrast, the Greek Cypriots appear to have transformed sorrow into an unending process but whose map is elsewhere. Certainly the *kayipler* are martyrs, *shehitler*, but they are martyrs because they provided a whole victimology for the authorities in their project of constructing a state. It is as if the new state had to consume its own subjects to project the sacrifices the nation, like Medea, had to experience to symbolise its suffering.

Conclusion

Here, some of the reflections of Richard Werbner might be useful. Talking about the tensions over the past in Zimbabwe he notes: 'Increasingly, new moral uncertainties confront people in what might be called postwars of the dead- the intense peacetime struggles over the appropriation of the heroism, martyrdom or even last remains of the dead' (1998: 7). He employs the metaphors of buried and unburied memory. 'Buried memory' he takes to include the use of monuments to the dead and heroes and the tensions that it raises: 'If buried memory attempts to contain and even silence popular commemoration ... it does so at very real, lingering cost. Buried memory produces what ... I call unfinished narratives: popular history in which the past is perceived to be unfinished, festering in the present- these are narratives which motivate people to call again and again for a public resolution to their predicament ' (ibid: 9). Such observations could certainly be applied to Turkish Cypriots. As Werbner noted: 'Subjected to buried memory, people do not so much forget as recognise – and ever more forcefully – that they have not been allowed to remember' (ibid: 9). By contrast the Greek Cypriots appear to have followed the metaphor of unburied memory. Where I differ with Werbner is over what he believes to be the contemporary nature of the post wars of the dead. As I have suggested, such moral uncertainties are far from new. They are also found in ancient Greek tragedy and doubtless in other areas, and they can provide us with a model to understand contemporary predicaments. As anthropologists we ought to be open to the possibilities contained in history, classics, drama, and literature, because they too deal with human and social predicaments.

NOTES

1. Sarris (1995); Abbot (1969).
2. Danforth (ibid: 53); see also Stewart (1991).
3. What is one to make of such story, almost designed for an anthropologist? Its significance only emerges out of its banality, because it was presented apologetically, prefaced by her hesitant statement 'I am a believer (like the woman I am going to talk about). I believe in God'. In other words, I will only tell you such fantastic stories if you can accept (and expect) such fantastic stories from me as a believer – a secular perspective. In indicating that she did not expect people to give them credulity, least of all an *epistemonas* (scientist) from abroad, she indicated that such beliefs operate on the margin of modern consciousness, and therefore are worthy of scrutiny.
4. Cf. Freud's thesis on mourning and melancholia (1959).
5. In the book Agni (which means Pure) is given the name *Avgi* (Dawn).
6. *Helen*, Seferis (1973: 353–4).
7. Angeliki Smyrli (1989).
8. For example, the Council of Ministers gave some £900,000 Cypriot to the families of the 162 Greek nationals who either died or are missing since the Turkish invasion (*Cyprus Weekly*, 5–11 July 1996, p.14.)
9. Especially in children's art where this unbridgeable gap between the Greek/free area and the land of the underworld is separated from the living by the river.
10. Soon after I arrived, a friend whom I was visiting, received a call from the Kyrenia Police Chief asking what I was doing asking questions about The Missing. Somebody had reported me. He then asked my friend: 'I suppose he will want to speak to all these leftists', and reeled off a list of names not enamoured of, and by, the Denktash regime – precisely the people I had just mentioned to my friend that I wanted to interview! The prescience was ominously amusing and also an indication how transparent and naïve my questioning was. I am happy to state however that I received the greatest courtesy from Turkish Cypriot officials and immense kindness and generosity from the Turkish Cypriots.
11. Not surprisingly there is no mention of this in Clerides's memoirs and I have found no reference to it in the Greek Cypriot press. Perhaps this may have been a confidential acknowledgement by Clerides, which was then used by Denktash to genuinely address the relatives' grief and concerns, and embarrass the Greek Cypriots.

6
L'IMAGE JUSTE,
OR *JUSTE UNE IMAGE?*

❦

It is the action of society on the body that gives full reality to he imagined drama of the soul
(Hertz, 1960: 83)

Introduction: Re-presenting Polynices

This chapter examines the use of photography, both still and moving, as an instrument of power. The image, and more specifically photography, has been used extensively in Cyprus to convince, facticize, demonise, and evoke. I examine photography with reference to the body. The problem is essentially similar to that posed by Sophocles' Creon. How does one re-present the human corpse for statist purposes? By preventing the burial of Polynices, Creon destroys the distinction which human civilisation draws between the deaths of men and the deaths of beasts. As Segal notes, he negates the division between men and animals in an especially offensive way for 'he reduces the human corpse to the status of carrion' (1981: 157). We have to ask how photography in the contemporary world in the hands of political authorities represents a reworking of the Sophoclean dilemmas. The first concerns the desecration of a human being through its re-presentation as a corpse left unburied, or as a series of photographs (i.e., representations) which symbolically retain the dead permanently as desecrated corpses, and thus as unburied memories. The second is the paradox that to uphold the law the ruler performs an outrage. As with Creon, Greek and Turkish Cypriot political authorities also stage re-presentations of the past through the use of photographs in public places as instruments of power. Although there have been some excellent studies of differences between Greek and Turkish Cypriot Museums (Papadakis, 1994) which includes references to the political use of photographs in museums, the specific role of photography in Cyprus deserves special

131

attention. In this chapter I examine photography from two perspectives: first, its use as a representation of suffering, and second, as an activity closely implicated in the state's search for legitimacy. In the next chapter I then examine the role of popular art as a therapeutic device.

The first thing to note about public photographs in Cyprus is that they are used to depict the aggression of the other and thus constitute the self and one's group as a victim. In Cyprus, as in Northern Ireland, 'victimage is the generic institution shared by all sides of the conflict as their common material denominator and as the operator of all political exchange' (Feldman, 1991: 263). For both Greek and Turkish Cypriots, photographs both authenticate and facticize claims of victimage – the Greek Cypriots in the face of the Turkish aggression and occupation, the Turkish Cypriots in the face of Greek Cypriot 'ethnic cleansing'. As Susan Sontag noted 'the camera record justifies. A photograph passes for incontrovertible proof that a given thing happened' (1978: 5).

Victimage is evoked differently by Greek and Turkish Cypriots. This is not a case of mere inversions. An examination of how photographic representations of the issue of missing persons are used provides valuable insights into the iconography of suffering and the constitution of victimage. Here, I explore a paradox in the iconographic representation of suffering. This is that whilst published Turkish Cypriot photographic material is effective locally among Turkish Cypriots but, I suggest, less effective internationally, Greek Cypriot published photographic material has the reverse effect, namely whilst it may be less effective locally (or nationally), it may be much more compelling on the international level. The differences are not because Greek Cypriots have greater access to international fora, or that Greek Cypriot claims for their missing persons are 'all propaganda' as (some) Turkish Cypriots claim. Although there is certainly some truth to these claims, some differences can be located in the specific nature of the photographs used. In Cyprus narratives and images are authored, circulated, and consumed with an aim to convince. That does not make them any less 'true' or valid, and we have to ask why certain groups choose to represent their experiences and suffering in different ways. I am interested here in the iconography of suffering, and the phenomenology of its reception. I suggest that the iconographies of suffering by the two groups are not mirror reflections of each other. There are substantial differences in the articulation of photographs as representations of suffering, their accompanying narratives, the structures of the images, and the relationship of photographs as mnemonics or representations. I suggest that the Turkish Cypriots use photographs 'directly' as self-evident representations of truth and of 'what really happened' – much like the standard 'Realist' approaches to photography. Such images are particularly powerful, but also subject to the limitations attendant on their use. They can be seen as direct statements to the viewer along the lines of irrefutable statements of fact and assert an unambiguous political resolution. Generally speaking, they are also referentially incomplete. By contrast, I suggest that Greek Cypriots employ images according to a particular tradition of iconography and narratology, often drawing upon traditions of laments that are literary or mythical. Even more importantly, they employ a triangular relationship between the person depicted in the photograph, the absent person evoked, and the viewer. Such photographs may be less strong but they are haunting, and pose a question.

Susan Sontag wrote, 'A photograph is both a pseudo-presence and a token of absence' (ibid: 16). Sontag was referring to the existential ambiguity of photographs, but her words contain a particular valency when applied to representations of suffering. Does one depict suffering through absence or presence? If one depicts suffering through absences, how does one do so effectively without exhausting the waiting? Conversely, if one depicts suffering through (its) presence, how does one do so without either appearing to be insensitive to those who experienced it, or to do so effectively such that it is not just 'pseudo' in its etymological sense of deceiving the viewer? Other questions are also raised for commentators (like myself) who decide to explore such issues. The love-hate relationship intellectuals have had with the photograph (from Baudelaire through Benjamin to Sontag and Berger) is also a Platonic distaste for the plurality of its representativeness and a jealous fascination with its demiurgic potentialities. We cannot escape such dilemmas, just as Medieval and Byzantine scholars polemicized on the contradictory nature of the image (Goody, 1997). As Rose noted pithily, ' Philosophy would abolish representation' (1996: 55).

In the next section I suggest that Greek Cypriot representations of suffering are through absences that appear (and I use the word advisedly and cautiously) to bear certain parallelisms to Christian iconography. By contrast Turkish Cypriot representations are through presences, although I would hesitate even further to relate these to Islam.

Greek Cypriot Iconographies of Suffering: Absences

Greek Cypriot photographs can be grouped into three types, which I call: 'Penelopes and Vigils', 'Absences and Losses', and 'Death in the Eyes'.

(i) *Penelopes and Vigils*: These are photographs of groups of (often black-clothed) women demonstrating in vigils and holding up photographs of their loved ones (sons/husbands), suggesting an unresolved political-humanitarian issue (very similar to the Argentine mothers) (Figure 11, insets of Figure 13). Other photographs of single individuals usually depict an old woman holding a photograph of her son (or husband? – we have already noted the slippage in time, a vibration between co-evalness and its lack, in Figure 5).

(ii) *Absences*: These consist of a child holding a framed wedding photograph of his mother and father, thus appealing to the third party viewer. Another variant is that of a child holding up a picture of the missing father (Figure 12). I discuss the theme of absence and loss more fully in Chapter 7, but let us observe that this

Figure 11 'Penelopes of Cyprus'. Vigils c.1974.
Official Greek Cypriot publicity material.

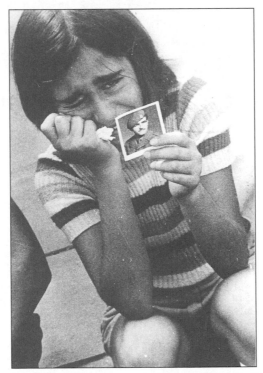

Figure 12 'Absence and Loss'. Child of Missing Greek
Cypriot, c. 1974. Official Greek Cypriot publicity material.

Figure 13 'Death in The Eyes'.
Official Greek Cypriot publicity material.

type of photograph of a relationship between a child and an absent parent, represented by the photograph, contains both absence and loss. More precisely the emotion on the child's face suggests *absence as loss*, rather than loss as absence. The child clearly has not accepted the situation and the photograph suggests that it was taken at a critical, traumatic, unrepeatable point in time. By contrast, the time-frame /tense in the Penelopes at Vigil photographs could be a present continuous, and the emotion conveyed is of denial: denial of the rights of wives to be with their husbands.

(iii) *'Death in the Eyes'*: The most widely used picture was taken by a Turkish war correspondent of five Greek Cypriot soldiers kneeling on the ground with their hands raised behind their heads in evident distress surrounded by armed Turkish troops (Figure 13). These men disappeared after the photograph was taken. Others depict groups of men in captivity in Turkey with some encircled faces of the missing.

Such photographs refer to a continuing drama. But they also employ a specific symbolism. Much Greek Cypriot symbolism surrounding the missing is a complex mixture of Christianity and Hellenism. Many claimed that the Turks 'as Muslims' might not give that much importance to burials, 'but we as Christians do'. There are indeed theological differences in the treatment and significance of bodies between Christianity and Islam, although as indicated in the previous chapter Turkish Cypriot relatives also wished for the return and proper burial of their loved ones. But such differences are nonetheless reflected in the official treatment of the representation of bodies, a point I return to below. Briefly, for the Greek Cypriots, the sacrifice of the person has to be represented as an absent body, the quintessential example being, of course, Christ. By contrast, for the Turkish Cypriots it is the presence of a (dead) body, the body of the dead hero/fighter that signifies a sacrifice and transforms him into a *shehit* (martyr). The differences can be represented schematically:

Greek Cypriots: Sacrifice indicated (hinted) through desomatization (absence of the body).
Signifier: Absence (of body) / *Signified*: Sacrifice.

Turkish Cypriots: Sacrifice demonstrated through somaticization (presence of body as death).
Signifier: (Presence of) Body/ *Signified*: Sacrifice.

The religious associations of the photographs can be pursued further. The photographs of the relatives of the Missing closely follow icons of the Panayia (Mother of God) mourning her son prior to the resurrection. There is much slippage here which strengthens the symbolism rather than weakening it. For whilst the women appear to be mothers holding up photographs of their sons, many are in fact wives holding up photographs of their husbands twenty years ago. Penelope may have aged but the image of the unrecovered Ulysses remains the same. The slippage from (dependent) wife to (assertive, powerful) 'mother', so critical a theme in modern Greek literature (as for example in the works of Alexandros Papadiamantis), is accompanied by the oedipal regression of (dominant, young) husband to (dependent) 'son', as so often occurs in the developmental cycle among Greeks when men in their twilight years become 'genial nonentities' in the apt words of John Campbell (1964).

Finally type (iii) photographs depict absences. The most powerful and widely used one depicts five kneeling soldiers surrounded by Turkish troops and in evident distress. This is to me the most profoundly disturbing photograph that emerged from the 1974 events. The potency of this photograph can be more fully appreciated in conjunction with Paine's analysis of the Hebron Massacre, 1994 (Paine, 1995). The photograph shows individuals in an act of total physical submission both facing, and with their backs to, their captors.[1] It is widely believed that these men were killed soon after in Pavlides' Garage, Nicosia. With this background knowledge the photograph becomes particularly powerful. The mental linkage between physical submission → killing that the photograph evokes then subliminally slips into a prototypical act of religious submission before sacrifice, their sacrifice. Canetti pithily observed that kneeling is 'a form of powerlessness which is active', and kneeling is a 'gesture of supplication' and therefore of sacrifice: 'kneeling is always in some sense a prelude to a last moment' (1973: 457). The bodily semiotics thus evoke the association:

Capture → Murder → Sacrificial Killing/Massacre/Desecration/Sanctification.

In addition there is the look, which I call 'Death in the Eyes'. As Pier Paolo Pasolini noted, 'it is always the victim's look that suggests the violence which will be done to him or her'. We must also not lose sight of the purpose of the dissemination of these photographs. Greek Cypriots use the photograph both as interrogation and as evidence of disappearances, a 'document' that these men were captured and disappeared. But the document is not there. It is the anguish on the first soldier's face to which our gaze is dawn. This is the hidden document; 'The face is the evidence that makes evidence possible' (Taussig, 1999: 221)

Texts also reinforced this association. Here is Angeliki Smyrli's possibly elaborated account of the separation of men and women following the descent of Turkish soldiers into their village: 'It was such a painful scene, that I cannot bear bringing it to mind again, the drawn faces of the women, who left the church's courtyard, leaving their husbands and their children *kneeling* there' (1989: 26–7, my emphasis). The Greeks are also referred to as *Christianous* (Christians) further establishing the sacrificial associations. But for all these to become *representations* of sacrifice we need to know that they are/were powerless at the moment they were sacrificed. Here some insights by Girard may be useful: 'all our sacrificial victims, whether chosen from one of the human categories ... or, *a fortiori*, from the animal realm, are invariably distinguishable from the non-sacrificeable beings by one crucial characteristic: between these victims and the community a crucial social link is missing, so that they can be exposed to violence without fear of reprisal. Their death does not automatically entail an act of vengeance' (1988: 13)

Turkish Cypriot Iconographies of Suffering: Presences

The corpse seen without God and outside of science, is the utmost of abjection
(Kristeva, 1982: 4)

The most striking feature of Turkish Cypriot photographs is that they make heavy use of corpses. This immediately raises some important ethical issues: should one use photographs such as these, what do they hope to achieve? As I hope to show the effects are somewhat ambiguous. The photographer, as Barthes (1984) pointed out, is an agent of death. Here then is a double association with death. Turkish Cypriot photographs can be grouped into five types:
(i) Inventories of the Dead
(ii) Fatal Wounds (Figure 14)
(iii) Wounds of History (Figure 15)

Figure 14 'Fatal Wounds'. Official Turkish Cypriot publicity material.

Figure 15 'Wounds of History'. Official Turkish Cypriot publicity material.

Figure 16 'News on the Face'. This famous photograph was taken by Don McCullin in 1964 at Ghazeviran, although the location and date is never given in the publicity material. Material published by the Public Information Office, TRNC.

Figure 17 'Erasure'. Official Turkish Cypriot publicity material.

(iv) 'News on the Face' or Reaction-shots: Faces as reflecting knowledge of loss (Figure 16)

(v) Erasure (Figure 17)

The most striking common element in these photographs is that whilst they represent two 'spaces', the private and the public, in reality they contain the traces of often violent and sudden public inruptions into private spaces. This makes them different from Greek Cypriot photographs that both unfold and are enacted in public spaces. In addition, Turkish Cypriot publicity material also use simple photographs often of domestic origin depicting the individual person who disappeared. These can be called 'Inventories of the Dead'. Many are not just similar to formal photographs found hanging in Cypriot living rooms or in small stand-up frames for mantelpieces, but actually emerge from these intimate contexts. Their origins lie not in the surveillance, regulating, inventories of the modern state with its Identity Card and Passport records which bestow the subjects of the nation state with some rights wrought through an 'exchange' with the state which in return for its claims to regulate its subjects, also grants them rights to representation. Indeed, these are not official Republic of Cyprus photographs of its citizens, as the Republic did not recognise their disappearances between 1963–74. Due to fear and official indifference, relatives of the missing Turkish Cypriots did not have access to the state's bureaucracy to report disappearances. The ontology of these photographs thus betrays the traces of that struggle and displays the evidence. These photographs were collected by the Turkish Cypriot political leadership initially after 1967, and more intensely after 1974 to document that they too had missing persons, and they were collected from the relatives themselves.

There is a poignant irony here that in countering what the Turkish Cypriots would recognise to have been unofficial state-abetted violence against them, they are also reproducing its forms of control, and indifference. These are private photos that have been appropriated by Turkish Cypriot authorities and official proofs of the irredemability of relations between Greek and Turkish Cypriots. From the perspective of the Turkish Cypriot political authorities such photographs are unambiguous inventories of casualties, of *kayipler*, of lost/dead people. For the relatives themselves, by contrast, such photographs were taken as a rite of commemoration, originally displayed in living rooms as an act of celebration of family membership, and finally retained by the families as an act of defiance and even as a statement that far from being dead, these individuals are still alive in the sentiments of the relatives. There is thus something unsettling and depersonalising about the use of such photographs by authorities and their wrenching away from the private domain. This is rendered even more bizarre by the admission that many records of the missing were themselves found to have been lost in 1975, and the process of data collection had to recommence.

By contrast, the use of personal photographs by Greek Cypriot relatives had a different trajectory. As the majority of Greek Cypriots disappeared over a few weeks during a time of massive dislocation, with nearly a third of the population fleeing their homes and with families split, the private photograph constituted the only link with the lost person and the means to trace his whereabouts. They were handed over to the authorities or to released prisoners as a plea for information. They represented hope, fear, and a link with that person, and they may also have contained the unspoken assumption for many relatives that as long as they were to continue to search, their missing would remain alive. In the weeks between the coup and the post-invasion period there was much uncertainty as to the fate of the missing. Many Greek Cypriots were still in the Turkish-occupied North, in hiding, or displaced as refugees in the government-controlled south, unable to make contact with their kin, including their sons in the National Guard.

For many ordinary Greek Cypriots therefore the facticity of their missing is 'proved' by the photograph. Clearly, with the passage of time they have accreted to themselves other additional meanings- for example of *ethnomartyres*. (National Martyrs). But it is important to recognise that these private photographs began their public life not so much as inventories of lost (dead) people, but as questions.

Type (2) Turkish Cypriot photographs, which I have called 'Fatal Wounds', usually depict bodies that appear to have been photographed in situ after a massacre or a killing. Here the detail is almost forensic (Figure 14), although the neat arrangement of bodies can sometimes raise some doubts. Indeed some of them (such as of the child in Figure 15) were taken during autopsies. Paradoxically the wounds depicted here are those of an autopsy performed by (Greek Cypriot) doctors, although the baby was killed. We are given no details. Let us note with Schwenger that photographs of corpses create a double association with death, where the subject (viewer) cannot fully confront the object (the corpse): 'The corpse is never wholly object, for it is always image – an image of otherness that is also, paradoxically, the image of self, image *as* self' (2000: 400).

The depiction of the spilling of blood indicates sacrifice. Girard has suggested, 'When men are enjoying peace and security, blood is a rare sight. When violence is unloosed, however, blood appears everywhere – on the ground, underfoot, forming great pools. Its very fluidity gives form to the contagious nature of violence' (1988: 34). I suggest that these photographs perform an epiphanic function for Turkish Cypriots – they indicate that now that blood has been spilt, one cannot return to the situation *status quo ante*. Spilt, contaminating, blood separates Greeks and Turks. The Tashkent Monument to the Missing in the North has the following Turkish inscription:

Do not forget this is the Monument of those who made the soil of our country. In every inch of the soil there is their blood and their bones. This Monument is the monument of our brothers who were taken from their homes in Tashkent Terazi on 14 August 1974 and brutally murdered by Greek Cypriots. As long as we live, we are not going to forget that which has been done to them and to us.

Greetings from the Suffering Mothers of Tashkent to the Free World.

The irony here is that during fieldwork I discovered that it was the authorities that planned, designed, built the monument, and composed the dedication. The Mothers and relatives opposed the monument as it indicated that their Government considered their relatives dead (although their bodies have not been recovered).

In the fourth type of photographs ('News on the Face'), the face of the survivor can be seen as a reflection of the terror experienced by the disappeared. These are called 'reaction shots' in the film world, effectively pioneered in Eisenstein's *Battleship Potemkin*. An excellent example is the cover of the 1993 Turkish Cypriot book (Figure 16) which uses a powerful photograph of a highly distraught woman with clasped hands being consoled /held by other women, with the caption underneath: 'PRIZE WINNER: A British photographer, Donald McCullin, won the overall prize in the annual World Press Photo contest in the Hague with this picture showing a Turkish-Cypriot woman after she learned the terrible news about her husband', although no date or location is given (CRTCMP 1993).[2] This is indeed a powerful photograph and enables us to raise some key questions regarding the depiction of violence and suffering.

Representing Suffering: Creon as an Artist

I now explore the problems associated with active depictions of suffering, and raise some questions about their effectiveness. Are such depictions, in the laconic words of Godard, not the precise (i.e. suitable) image, but just an image (*c'est ne pas l'image juste; c'est juste une image*)? Some twenty years ago Susan Sontag noted that the effectiveness of photographs of suffering is limited by repeated exposure: 'Images transfix. Images anaesthetise. An event known through photographs certainly becomes more real than it would have been if one had never seen the photographs' (ibid: 20). But she noted in a somewhat Platonic interpretation that the more one is exposed to an image, the less effective it becomes: 'after repeated exposure to images it becomes less real' (ibid: 20), and suggested that concerned photography 'has done at least as much to deaden conscience as to arouse it' (ibid: 21). Images, in short, come between us and what we intend to comprehend, and photography does so in a very special way.

Sontag suggests that repeated exposure to powerful images generates a desire for more powerful ones: 'To suffer is one thing; another thing is living with the photographed images of suffering, which does not necessarily strengthen conscience and the ability to be compassionate. It can also corrupt them. Once one has seen such images, one has started down the road of seeing more – and more' (ibid: 20). Attractive though Sontag's humanist interpretation is, it suffers from a number of problems. First she maintains that there should be some natural correspondence between the image and sentiments. Second, she implicitly assumes a unidirectional causality between the event and the photograph. But photography does not necessarily just falsify reality, it can also create or stage an event. It can, in other words, be fundamentally implicated in the event it purports to depict. This is what Creon as artist does in Anouilh's *Antigone*. He plants a body outside the city walls suggesting this is Polynices'. Third, Sontag does not fully explore the relationship between photography and the three poles of constructing a field of apprehension: 'reality' (experience), the imaginary, and the symbolic. Rather, she assumes that she is exploring the relationship between 'the event', photography, and the viewer. Photography can cunningly hide itself in both the imaginary and the symbolic. Finally, although she recognises the aestheticising power of photography, she locates it ontologically in the image, rather than phenomenologically in the act experience of seeing: 'the aestheticizing tendency of photography is such that the medium which conveys distress ends by neutralising it' (ibid: 109) … 'As much as they create sympathy, photographs cut sympathy, distance the emotions' (ibid: 110).

To by-pass these problems I propose examining the representation of suffering in two interrelated ways: (i) the relationship between the image and our emotions, and (ii) the relationship between photographs and memory. First, the relationship between the photograph and our emotions should be considered. Here some thoughts of Berger are useful. Although there are similarities between Berger and Sontag whom he acknowledges for her undoubted insights, the two start from the same premise but reach different conclusions. Sontag begins by noting that photography isolates an image from the flow of time and experience: 'the force of a photograph is that it keeps open instants which the normal flow of time immediately replaces. This freezing of time – the insolent, poignant, stasis of each photograph – has produced new and more inclusive canons of beauty' (ibid: 111–12). This is almost like Yeats' concept of beauty through the aesthetics of violence, and echoes Baudelaire.[3] Whereas Sontag is fascinated by the aesthetic power of the image through its commemoration of the instant, she is also disturbed by the aesthetic dislocating effects of the image on emotions/conscience and that it can emotively seduce the rational basis of conscience. She oscillates between a 'Catholic' commemoration of emotion as captured in the image, and a 'Protestant' distrust of such images as seducing us away from a deep Kierkegaardian contemplation of their moral implications.

Berger, by contrast, is interested in the phenomenology of experience of viewing. He begins by noting that 'between the moment recorded and the present moment of looking at the photograph there is an abyss' (1989: 87). The fundamental difference between a photograph and memory is that 'whereas remembered images are the residue of continuous experience, a photograph isolates the appearances of a disconnected instant' (ibid: 89). Nowhere is this difference stronger than in photographs of war or suffering. As Berger points out, McCullin's most typical photographs 'record sudden moments of agony … that are utterly discontinuous with normal time … The image seized by the camera is doubly violent and both violences reinforce the same contrast: the contrast between the photographed moment and all others' (1985: 39).

Such comments assist understanding the underlying themes of Turkish Cypriot photographic material. The framed studio portraits, the bodies photographed from above focussed on the carnage created by bullet-exits in domestic settings that transform homes into morgues through the polluting and desacralizing bodily eruption of matter, the uncontrolled spilling of bodily fluids on to the floor, and the sudden terror on the face of the recipient of the news of the events, have two common interrelated features. One, they indicate a time outside time, an event discontinuous with everyday experience by its very terminality and intensity. Indeed, like rituals to which they can be approximated, they occur outside normal time. After having viewed the photographs, just as after having gone through a ritual, the viewer-participant is left with no doubt that for both the subjects and himself, life cannot /should not be the same again, and one cannot revert to one's mental framework *status quo ante*. The connection with ritual, in particular the employment of photographs by subjects of their agony as redemptive rituals of suffering, is one I want to return to. In particular, I suggest that the employment of such photographs have a direction away from the event as non-repeatable, transforming it from senseless death of subject self /barbarism of the Other to an archetypal sacrifice /lesson. But let us at this stage follow Berger who notes 'as we look at them, the moment of the other's suffering engulfs us. We are filled with either despair or indignation. Despair takes on some of the other's suffering to no purpose. Indignation demands action. We try to emerge from the photograph back into our lives. As we do so, the contrast is such that the resumption of our lives appears to be a hopelessly inadequate response to what we have just seen' (1985: 38).

A second, related, feature is that the photographs, especially of bodies (Figures 14 and 15), anaesthetise the viewer. It is not persons as subjects who are photographed, but wounds. Such wounds transform the body into impossible object, and thus barely recognisable subject. We cannot gaze at these pictures of excessive eruptive suffering without anaesthetising our sensibilities.[4] As Berger notes, 'the reader who has been arrested by the photograph may tend to feel this discontinuity as his own personal moral inadequacy. And as soon as this happens even his sense of shock is dispersed: his now moral inadequacy may now shock him as much as the crimes being committed in the war' (1985: 39–40, emphasis in original). He concludes that such pictures become 'evidence of the general human condition. It accuses nobody and everybody' (1985: 40).

'Nobody and everybody' – but only to a certain extent when scanned in newspapers in the metropolis where, I would suggest, this means: 'not us, but them'. But when such photographs are employed by subjects themselves to depict their suffering to the metropolis using the very images harvested by the international media as emblems of suffering, the situation changes. The flagging of photographic authorship by metropolitan observers is important. Foreign (war) correspondents and photographers confirm and authenticate the claims made. But they do more than this. The verificatory strength of the photograph as a conjurer of facticity authenticates the experiences of subjects as constituted by suffering. To many right-wing nationalist Turkish Cypriots such photographs as representations of suffering *qua* suffering confirm their belief that they are victims of genocide, and authenticate their claims to the wider world. They constitute their subjectivity as suffering objects. Terms like holocaust, genocide and ethnic cleansing, are strong words that have been loosely used, but it is precisely their lability that should interest us here. Such photographs and associated narratives by subjects as representations of their suffering become markers of irreversible time (e.g. 'Never Again'). They become a watershed of 'history' narrated by subjects as a series of events ('These are the facts of Cyprus ....') to which there must be no return ('... and the main reason why Cyprus must stay divided'), and they contain an imperative for a clear unidirectional solution ('Thank You Turkey'). Yet such photographs can come dangerously close to a pornography of violence. They literally confirm Metz's observation that photography can become a 'thanatography' (1985: 83).

The over-determination in the use of images is because 'the ethical status of photographs is fragile. With the possible exception of photographs of those horrors, like the Nazi camps, that have gained the status of ethical reference points, most photographs do not keep their emotional charge' (Sontag, ibid: 21). It is evident that it was the intention of the publishers to retain the emotional charge of such photographs. I suggest that this is why it is important for right-wing Turkish Cypriots to retain that ethical charge by grasping and holding on to the notions of genocide. Just as ethnographic films in former communist countries had voice-overs of the commentators to exclude the possibility of subversive dialogue puncturing official certainties, so too captions serve the purpose of privileging one unambiguous interpretation and excluding all others. As Sontag noted, 'what the moralists are demanding from a photograph is that it does what no photograph can ever do- speak. The caption is the missing voice, and it is expected to speak for truth' (ibid: 108).

These photographs must be placed within a long tradition of atrocity photographs. Zelizer, who has studied the trajectory of holocaust photographs and their subsequent use side by side with contemporary atrocity photographs has noted: 'Many atrocity photos lacked basic identifying attributes, and they were as patterned in the type of information they neglected to provide as in that which they provided. Captions gave very little information about what was being depicted. Horrifying for the visual portrayal they offered about death and suffering, they generally omitted any definitive detail about the victims ... Details about the taking of the photograph itself was also often missing' (1998: 118). This applies to many Turkish Cypriot photographs. As Zelizer wryly observes: 'The image's referentiality was thus undermined even as the image's symbolic force was underscored' (ibid: 118). Indeed, many of the photographs

depicted here appear in serious substantive Turkish Cypriot publications dealing with constitutional issues by lawyers (e.g. Stephen, 1997).

One can see the use of photographs of corpses as an attempt by the modern
state to echo Creon's actions. By displaying such photographs and decontextu-
alising their subjects, political authorities can be seen, like Creon, to be symbolically retaining the exposed, unburied, polluted, and damaged body as a
reminder of the past. Like Creon's 'treasury', they can be seen as the modern
state's photographic harvest of human carrion. Creon, like his modern equivalents, is particularly explicit about the intended visual impact: 'the citizens are
to look upon the body eaten by birds and dogs and (be) outraged' (Segal, 1981:
157). But which sensibilities are outraged? At what men do to each other during their lives, or at what we do to them after their deaths? The ruler does not
seem aware that what we do to them after their deaths may itself be an outrage.

Photography and Memory

At this stage it is worthwhile to explore further the relationship between photography and memory. When we examine photographic representations of suffering we should concentrate on the way photography is used as a prop to, a
substitute for, and a legitimation of memory, both official and personal. In
Cyprus, photography has often been used to legitimate official memories. In
this section I compare differences between Greek and Turkish Cypriot
approaches to the use of photographs as aids to memory.

The Turkish Cypriot community entered the world stage of mass media
during the inter-ethnic disturbances of 1963–64. Soon after the first disappearances Turkish Cypriots began withdrawing into armed enclaves. Following
Anderson (1991), one could say that such experiences of encirclement, violence, and disappearances, crucially affected the way the Turkish Cypriots constituted themselves as an imagined community. They increasingly imagined
their community through these photographs that circulated in the local and,
even more importantly, international media. Sontag wrote 'One's first
encounter with the photographic inventory of ultimate horror is a kind of revelation, the prototypically modern revelation: a negative epiphany. For me, it
was photographs of Bergen-Belsen' (ibid: 19). Sontag chanced upon such
images at the age of twelve whilst browsing through a bookstore in Santa Mon-
ica. The element of chance discovery with its consequent unpreparedness, the
young age, and the disarming serendipitousness of the bookstore must have
contributed to the intensity of the effect, but for Turkish Cypriots such images
were clearly closer to home. It may not be fanciful to suggest that Sontag could
remember the specific incident and the vistas it opened up, precisely because of
the disjuncture between the conditions under which she made such a discovery,
and the ability of such photographs to create such an unimaginably realist

world. The viewing of these photographs was a watershed: 'it seems plausible to divide my life into two parts, before I saw those photographs ... and after, though it was several years before I understood fully what they were about' (ibid: 20). She laments the revelation: 'What good was served by seeing them? They were only photographs – of an event I had scarcely heard of and could do nothing to effect, of suffering I could hardly imagine and could do nothing to relieve' (ibid: 20).

This lament is not just for a lost innocence about the world and the self (although there is a congruence between the innocence of a 12-year-old girl and that of the world encountering such representations of inhumanity when the camps were opened up in 1945). It is not so much a lament for a pre-lapsarian ideal world, although as presented in Sontag's text, it may appear that way. It is also a lament about the role of the photograph in making us aware, in ways unapproachable by painting for example, of the inadequacy of our feelings. The photograph substitutes the event. Events are now approached through the photograph as a means of memorialising it and rendering it more ontologically 'real' and thus closer to us.

Sontag also laments the effects of photography on our emotions: 'When I looked at these photographs, something broke. Some limit had been reached, and not only that of horror; I felt irrevocably grieved, wounded, but a part of my feelings started to tighten; something went dead; something is still crying' (ibid: 21). Coming as she does to photography from a Platonist perspective, Sontag seems to be saying that because of our 'realist expectations' of photography, the very act of seeing a photograph depicting such ultimate horror, prevents us from realising its full implications, and that photography trivialises suffering by depicting it so effortlessly. Because of our expectation that 'the camera cannot lie', we assume that it cannot 'exaggerate' either. Ultimately it sustains a superficial relationship to our emotions both because our awareness that 'it is just a photograph', and also because 'Once one has seen such images, one has started down the road of seeing more – and more. Images transfix. Images anaesthetise' (ibid: 20). It seems clear that Sontag concentrates more on the problematical nature of the photograph as illustration, rather than on the problematic relationship between photography and memory.

Turkish Cypriot photographic material appears unidirectional and unambiguous, in the mould of nineteenth-century realism, although it attempts to retain a high emotional charge. As with this genre, it presumes an 'omniscient observer detached from and external to the scenography being presented' (Feldman, 1994: 90). The conclusions suggested by the photographs are likewise unambiguous: 'this is what happened to us, and the only way we can never experience anything similar again is for us to live separately from the Greek Cypriots'. They are directed at the Turkish Cypriots, used to reinforce collective experiences, as well as to document /prove their experiences for the international media. Such photographs do not depict missing people as absences.

Rather, they are depicted as presences, as dead persons – *kayipler*. Even the McCullin's famous photograph of the distraught woman, whilst triangular, is unambiguous. The subject is the woman's grief and agony, but whilst the face and the body posture refer to an event away from the photograph, we are left in no doubt that that event was not just unambiguous, but also final. It depicts a moment of intense anguish, but the event is irrecoverable.

Yet there is a sense in which what is being evoked is not so much the past (although this is certainly the content and intention of the publishers of these photographs), but the commemoration of the role of photography as the scaffolding of official reality. Sontag has suggested 'What determines the possibility of being affected morally by photographs is the existence of a relevant political consciousness. Without a politics, photographs of the slaughter-bench of history will most likely be experienced as, simply, unreal or as a demoralizing emotional blow' (ibid: 19). I suggest that in the case of these photographs, what is occurring is the reverse: it is not so much the relevant political consciousness that sustains these photographs, but rather these photographs that sustain a relevant political consciousness, including that of photography as an official incontestable approach to the past and as the legitimating medium of official reality. Indeed for outsiders ignorant of Cypriot history, such photographs are experienced as another example of a now long world history of ethnic intolerance, which is precisely the official purpose of using these photographs. The 'relevant political consciousness' is precisely that for the Turkish Cypriots the pre-1974 period was literally 'unreal' (unimaginable). The 'demoralising emotional blow' for the outside observer is that after having viewed these photographs it is impossible to revert back to a prelapsarian belief that these two ethnic groups can live together.

There are severe limits to the use of these types of photographs. Zelizer (1998) who studied the use of holocaust photographs identified three phases: forgetting to remember, remembering to remember, and remembering to forget. We can identify the second type, remembering to remember, as the current phase in the use of atrocity photographs by the Turkish Cypriot leadership. She notes the risk of memorialising the past: 'Not only does visual memory reveal disturbing limits to the resonance of visual images as historical documentation but it casts doubt upon the ability to use photos in bearing witness to the events of the past. It suggests that remembering to remember may have outlived its usefulness' (ibid: 200). *En passant* we should note the irony of the situation. Whilst individual Turkish Cypriot relatives are prevented by their political authorities from asking for the bones of their missing to effect 'closure', these same authorities make liberal use of photographs of corpses to sustain an openness of these wounds. Creon is a jealous artist. He desires to monopolise representation. This highlights an important point. Zelizer's third phase, remembering to forget, does not automatically follow from this second phase. It has to be wrought, often out of the compromised silences of those who have suffered. In the concluding chapter it will be necessary to return to the tension between *amnestia* (ban on recalling misfortunes) and the *mnesikakein* (the recalling of misfortunes) that the Athenians explored long before Renan's famous formulation in *Qu'est que c'est un Nation*. It also underlies the conflict between Creon and Antigone, and Paulina and Gerardo in Dorfman's play.

Let us consider the photographs employed by Greek Cypriots, the most famous one being that of the captured missing soldiers (Figure 13). This is triangular in that it links the soldiers, their captors and the viewer, who is actually the Turkish army correspondent who took the photograph. It is the metaphoric space created by this triangulation that contains the question: 'What has happened to these men?' Similarly the photographs of mothers holding up photographs are triangular in that they link the mothers, the photographs of their loved ones, and the absences that the photographs evoke (Figure 11). Such photographs are questions, not statements, and they take place in real time, in contrast to the Turkish Cypriot photographs that concentrate on an unrepeatable event of horror. Barthes observed that 'the photograph repeats what could never be repeated existentially' (1984: 4). Turkish Cypriot photographs can be seen as *photographs of photographs* – they mechanically repeat an unrepeatable act, and thus imprison historically their subject matter. Greek Cypriot photographs highlight and sustain a continuing drama which may enable the viewer to identify with more effectively than with the Turkish Cypriot photographic material. The photographs of missing persons that their womenfolk hold in their hands, modern equivalents of the *soudarion* (the cloth used by 'Veronica'/ *Veron Icona* to wipe Christ's face on Calvary and receiving his image), are links to the past, and evidence of the past. They evoke a past that is recoverable at least symbolically through answers to the questions posed by the very act of displaying the photographs. There is an absence of such questions in Turkish Cypriot material, which are primarily statements. Because the Turkish Cypriot leadership was particularly concerned to declare their missing as dead in the interests of (what they considered to be) compassion and political realism, and therefore concentrated on presenting the *kayipler* as (dead) *shehitler* (martyrs), they by-passed tackling the existential, but necessary, *aporia* of recollection for the relatives. The Turkish Cypriot political leadership culturally interpreted disappearances as deaths although no 'evidence' was sometimes available. By contrast for the Greek Cypriots, a person's existence is pursued through the act of continually asking for information of his fate. Whereas Greek Cypriots record an absence to conjure up a presence that has to be re-explained as a disappearance, Turkish Cypriots record a disappearance as a death, and hence for the relatives a proof of having lived. It is these differences that help explain that whereas the Turkish Cypriots begin by utilising photographs of dead people as proofs of their disappearances as deaths, the Greek Cypriots record representations of absences as metaphors of a presence that needs to be commemorated, much like an icon. One could say that whilst the Turkish Cypriots exhibit an optimism in the effectiveness of the image, Greek Cypriots betray a pessimism about its fading. Paradoxically, the former may be more idealist than the latter.

Conclusion

I suggest this helps explain differences between Turkish and Greek Cypriots in their approaches to memory and its relation to experience. I am of course referring to their respective Public Information Offices, but they nevertheless interrelate to grassroots sentiments which they also help inform. Underlying this are differences in the political fabulation of the past and its appeal to 'memory' and 'experience'. Because of their pressing political problems especially between 1963–70 when they tended to view their survival at stake, Turkish Cypriots use photographs in a relatively matter of fact way (i.e., 'Realist'), although their aim is highly emotionally charged. Greek Cypriots use photographs as representations of what is in effect an iconic predicament: representation as participating in some fundamental way in that which it represents. Here some of the thoughts of Berger may be useful. The former (i.e. the 'realist' position) is close to what he called a 'unilinear way – they are used to illustrate an argument, or to demonstrate a thought which goes like this: ——➤' (1984: 60). For the Turkish Cypriots, photographs have the function of ensuring that the past is not forgotten, by being documented. This oscillation operates between two incontestable semaphores: 'History repeats itself' (TCNN, July 1996: 4), and 'Never Again'. Documentation through photography creates facticity. The uncertainty of disappearance easily slides into, and becomes the province of the certainty of death. Photographs of the dead /representations of death thus colonise and imbue the representations of the missing in Turkish Cypriot material. When one looks at Turkish Cypriot photographic material there is no doubt that one is looking at photographs of people who died through disappearance, whereas for the Greek Cypriots they are photographs of people who disappeared through dying. The *Fact Note on Missing Persons in Cyprus* published by the Turkish Cypriot Human Rights Committee December 1996 shows a school photograph with the underlying text: 'All these children disappeared in August 1974 and have not yet been accounted for by their known abductors. Primary school pupils at Turkish Cypriot village Murataga on opening day on 1 September 1973. The school did not re-open on 1 September 1974 because all the pupils had disappeared in August 1974 following Greek Cypriot armed attacks on the village' (Figure 14). Such photographs state unambiguous facts. As Berger notes, some photographs are used 'tautologically so that the photograph merely repeats what is being said in words' (ibid: 60). They point to an event so traumatic that it exists outside time, but nevertheless marks an irreducible chasm between the before and the after. It legitimates the genesis of the total and complete separation of the Turkish from the Greek community through a prototypical act of destruction. Such photographs seek to illustrate collective experiences through images where Turkish Cypriots have been encouraged by their nationalist political leadership to objectify themselves as subjects of suffering. Such images do not appeal to individual memory. Rather they illustrate a collectivised ethnic memory empty of individual experiences. This is congruent with the attempt by the Turkish Cypriot leadership to manufacture a collective monophonic past and to provide it with a series of representations. To many readers of this book, many Turkish Cypriot photographs now seem like an 'unbearable replay of a now familiar atrocity exhibition' (Sontag, ibid: 19). This is precisely one of the purposes of these publications. The danger, as film scholar Kaes has suggested, is that at a certain point in time 'the vehicles of memory – films, photographs, narratives – stop energizing and become instead energized by memory itself. In such a scenario, memory breathes life into the photographs rather than the other way round' (1989: 179).

By contrast, the Greek Cypriot approach appears Platonic-recollective. It evokes an absence and potentially anticipates a resurrection. This may well have roots in the Christian tradition, including its iconography. Many photographs, like icons, employ a double image- an image within an image. The most famous photographs of the mothers depict them holding up images/photographs of their loved ones. These photographs suggest a double suffering: of the missing person, but even more importantly of the relatives. The spectator identifies not so much with the objects, the missing persons, but with the subjects, the mothers. Here it is useful to distinguish between the internal and the external signified. The internal signified is the suffering of women. It is not a heroic but a quotidian suffering faced by civilians the world over as a result of war or oppression. The external signified is therefore that of continued oppression through the denial of information of the fate of the missing. It is thus a continuing story. The dominant tense is the continually extending present, the *passato continuo* rather that the *passato remoto*, the tense employed by the Turkish Cypriot photographs. In the western iconographical tradition the theology of women's faces has long been used to signify ecstasy or suffering (Feher, 1989). Yet the hand-held photographs, like the crucifix, commemorate an absence, a body that is not there. It is through the identification of their fate that the living achieve their soteriology, and the missing their resurrection (their *anastasi*) to be buried properly according to Christian rites. Through the equivalent of such second burials (Bloch and Parry, 1982) they are loosened from the earth and this world, and united with both their loved ones and God. They are *martyres*. Whereas the Turkish Cypriot photographs commemorate a black epiphany and move unidirectionally, Greek Cypriot ones anticipate a soteriology through resurrection-reunion, and they move backwards and forwards from the image to real-time experiences and back again. Such photographs are effective because they evoke individual memories and emplot them along various lines of recollection. Some further observations of Berger are useful: 'memory is not unilinear at all. Memory works radially, that is to say with an enormous number of associations all leading to the same event' (ibid: 60). He uses a star image with lines radiating from a single (empty) point as illustration:

Berger suggests that 'if we want to put a photograph back into the context of experience, social experience, social memory, we have to respect the laws of memory. We have to situate the printed photograph so that it acquires something of the surprising conclusiveness of that which *was* and *is*' (ibid: 61 emphasis in original).

I suggest that Greek Cypriot photographs are visually compelling because they are able to move from the *was* to the *is*, and back again. They may be more effective internationally than the more emotively draining Turkish Cypriot photographs employed to sustain the Turkish Republic of Northern Cyprus's line that Greek and Turkish Cypriots cannot live together. Such campaigns may have a decreasing purchasing power in an increasingly integrated western Europe the further back in time such images recede, but they are effective (for the time being) among Turkish Cypriots. Ultimately such an approach is anti-image, and anti-representative, because it only presents one interpretation of the past, rather than re-presenting the past. To effectively respond to suffering we may have to approach it not through the seductive realism of the photograph, but through its means of representing the symbolic and the imaginary. In the next chapter I examine the symbolic and the imaginary in popular art to suggest that such forms of representation may be more effective in evoking suffering.

NOTES

1. The photograph was taken by a Turkish Army official photographer (Ergun Konuksever) from a tank which was captured by the Greek Cypriots (in Sedarli/Chattos village).
2. The date is 1964 and the village is Ghaziveran. The lack of specificity of time and place clearly turns the photograph into a document highlighting a continuous present.
3. Perhaps this is because 'photographs of the last century were nouns (about space, solidity, permanence) … the photograph today is a verb' (Slater, 1997: 102); it is about events, action, movement.
4. In discussing the representation of *Les Disparus*, P. Loraux notes 'L'anesthésie implique, d'abord, la disjonction d'un sentir et d'un ressentir' (2001: 47).

7
PAINTING ABSENCES, DESCRIBING LOSSES

❧❧❧

Take, eat; this is the body of Cyprus ...
Drink ye all of it; for it is the blood of Cyprus ...
Bitter bread, bitter wine, bread-wine of refugee life ... Under the tress and on the mountains,
Our Last Suppers bring us the crucifixion. But Golgotha, only you lead to Resurrection ....

(Pavlides, n.d.)

Introduction

This chapter is about the inadequacy of ritual both in its anthropological and religious senses to sometimes relieve emotions. I would like to begin by pointing to
an enigma in Sophocles' tragedy, and in so doing reflect on a problem in anthropological treatments of ritual. This concerns the force of emotions in what people do, and the relationship between ritual and emotion. Our Durkheimian and
residually structural-functionalist tradition in anthropology often implicitly
assumes that ritual generates and channels emotion. There is a paradox here.
Whilst it is possible to understand the force of emotion in the classics such as a
Homer or Sophocles, it is sometimes difficult to explain in anthropology. We may
understand why Achilles drags the body of Hector around the walls of Troy, or
why Ajax cuts the head of Imbrios from his slender neck and hurls it like a ball to
roll in the dust, but we find it difficult to understand and explain why an Ilongot
man from the Philippines, facing the loss of someone dear, is impelled by his rage
to kill his fellow human being and toss his head away (Rosaldo, 1984). I have
selected two similar situations (revenge at the loss of a loved one and desecration
of the body) to explain why one set of actions may seem understandable or com-
prehensible and another not. The difference is not merely that one culture
(Ancient Greece) may be familiar to us and the other not. This explains nothing,

except the fact of difference. Rather, it may be due to other factors. The classics deal with characters and their emotions. Characters create stories; 'a character is the one who performs the action in the narrative ... characters are themselves plots' (Ricoeur, 1992: 143). Their emotions become more understandable. Their actions sometimes say much more about what they feel than their words. This gives us a handle on the force of emotion. Often because it is tragedy it is an imitation of actions and of life: 'Tragedy is essentially an imitation not of persons but *of actions and life,* of happiness and misery. All human happiness or misery takes the form of action; the end of which we live is a certain kind of activity, not a quality ... a tragedy is impossible without action, but there may be one without Character' (Aristotle, 7.1450a 16–24). In anthropology, by contrast, we concern ourselves with society, with rituals and structures, and emotion has little to do with this unless it is tied down. In addition, as Rosaldo points out, 'Anthropologists do not have the life experiences sometimes to understand or even imagine some of the emotions that people from other cultures do' (ibid: 179).

I believe we can turn to Sophocles' play to understand something about the force of emotions in dealing with death, and this may enrich our anthropology. Sophocles' Antigone is not an easy person to understand, nor is Creon. As the Oxford Classical Dictionary noted, Antigone's role in the play has been the subject of endless dispute (1996: 104). Lacan talks about her 'unbearable splendour': 'she has a quality that both attracts and startles us, in the sense of intimidates us; this terrible self-willed victim disturbs us' (1992: 247). It is precisely this conflict between both characters' concentration on morals and principles, and their difficulty in controlling their own emotions, even their wilfulness, that is of interest. Both Antigone and Creon are willful. Is this just because they believe in what they are doing, or because they are driven by some higher principles, or is it also because emotion was the driving force to deal with the trauma they had experienced? I suggest we can gain an additional understanding if we recognize that both are engaged in a cathartic process in the sense of a psychic purification. Both have suffered a tragedy, and both stick to their positions with a passion. That passion conceals the full recognition of their drama from them, prevents them from seeing themselves, and locks them into their tragedy. Remember, each has just faced a calamity: Antigone in having lost two brothers, aware all along of their father's curse, and Creon in having the disaster of the ship of state that was Thebes thrust into his arms. They face a real collapse of meaning, and this is not just one of heuristics or of theory; it is about the things /persons /principles they hold most dear, it is about their lives, themselves. Both respond with what could appear an almost exaggerated intensity to their drama. There is anger in their actions and in their words. This may be a key. Deep anger is a means for them to express and act out their losses. Their exaggerated actions provide us with a key – not just about what is the right and wrong ways of doings things (the patterned communication of ritual), but of the inability of ritual and rules to fully cater for, absorb, and channel our emotions. Both characters (though in differing ways) try to conceal their traumas, and give vent to their emotions, through a clash of their conflicting conceptions of rights and laws. Antigone's calamity in having lost two brothers at their own hands requires a response from her that is so great, so self-denying that it becomes virtuosic in another sense. It 'balances out' the actions of her brothers. Interestingly, it is the prohibition on Polynices' funerary ritual that generates her intense emotions, rather than the funerary ritual for her other brother, Eteocles. Why this is so has generated intense debate. Here some insights from Rosaldo may be useful. First, he suggests that we ought not to equate death with funerary rituals. Second, he suggests that emotion is prior to, and more dominant than, ritual: 'Just as the intense emotions of bereavement do not explain obligatory ritual acts, so obligatory ritual acts do not explain the intense emotions of bereavement' (1984: 187). Rituals can thus serve as the vehicles for processes that occur both before and after the period of their performance. 'Funeral rituals, for example, do not contain the entire process of mourning. It is a mistake to collapse the two because neither ritual not mourning fully encapsulates or fully explains the other' (Rosaldo, 1984: 192). If we were to follow this suggestion then we could see rituals as an occasionally inadequate means to legitimate and control emotions. Rituals therefore, do not necessarily provide 'closure' to adopt a bland word that has been adopted by therapists in the western world. We therefore need to explore other means of coming to terms with emotions.

I propose to do this by reference to popular art. I suggest that popular art, precisely because it may be seen as 'naïve' or 'simplistic' by political and artistic elites whose tastes are generally oriented towards the European metropolis, can be used to resolve contradictions in the relationship between belief and theoretical knowledge. As these tensions and contradictions cannot be addressed directly by elites, I suggest popular art may be used to express deep contradictions, much like Levi-Strauss suggested for myth in primitive societies. Such contradictions can be seen in terms of *apories* (pl. of *aporia*)- a term used in deconstruction to indicate 'a kind of impasse or insoluble conflict between rhetoric and thought' (Cuddon, 1991: 55). The *aporia* has recently received much attention by philosophers. Derrida (1993), for example, explores the *aporia* involved in a philosophical exploration of death as end (*finis*) and/or border. To him the possibility of impossibility is an aporia. He suggests 'if one must endure the aporia ...[ ]... *the aporia can never simply be endured as such.* The ultimate aporia (death) is the impossibility of the aporia *as such*'(1993: 78). Rose has suggested 'The aporia or gap is the Janus-face of the universal. Together, universal and aporia are irruption and witness to the brokenness in the middle' (1996: 10).

This chapter examines the iconic re-presentations of an *aporia* among Greek Cypriots. This is that until very recently Greek Cypriots refused to accept that their missing were dead. The aporia can therefore be expressed as a riddle: when can an absence not be presented a loss? How can one conceal losses as absences and yet conjure them through presences? This is no mere word play. Greek Cypriot society has been traumatised by the 1974 disappearances following the

Turkish invasion. These disappearances have not been officially accepted as final by the Greek Cypriot authorities and by their relatives. As we have seen, Greek Cypriot missing persons are treated as lost (i.e. potentially recoverable) rather than dead (i.e. absent and non-recoverable). We are therefore in the presence of an aporia – an insoluble conflict between rhetoric or the one hand, and reasonable experience on the other. Aporias emerge out of the disarticulation between experience /knowledge, hope /fear, and belief. In this chapter I show that popular art can be seen as an attempt to resolve these insoluble tensions. I suggest that we can approach popular art as a type of therapy or coping mechanism in dealing with social and personal trauma. We may thus view popular art as a useful halfway house between the discursive strategies favoured by western medicine (such as counseling, PTSD therapies, psychoanalysis, etc.), and non-discursive, ritually based strategies often favoured by other cultures, such as possession, etc.

In contrast to myth, paintings have two distinct advantages in attempting to resolve contradictions, or to express an *aporia*. First, paintings are supremely referential and inter-iconic. 'Popular art' is often engaged in a dialogue with tradition, and can refer to images drawn from cinema, religious iconography, political propaganda, etc. They can thus tap various iconic associations for the viewer. In so doing they can recast an *aporia* in a new form, or suggest a resolution to past predicaments. Second, paintings can be used to represent the imaginary in different time frames that myth rarely can, especially in dealing with and anticipating the future. This temporal flexibility gives them an important role as therapeutic devices.

The Church of The Missing

The Alexandros Papachristophorou Foundation and Church outside Nicosia was founded in 1995 by Pater Christophoros, a priest and leader for many years of the Committee of Relatives of the Missing. It is a major pilgrimage centre, a place of remembrance expressing the continued trauma of relatives of missing persons. It is also a place where relatives of missing persons meet visiting dignitaries and politicians. The complex is used for exhibitions, and documentation.

The church is named after the Papas' missing son, Alexandros, who thus becomes identified with the saint. The west side of the church facing the iconostasis consists of a wall completely covered by little windows each containing a photograph of a missing person. To the right of the Church is *The House of the Missing Persons (Oikos ton Agnoumenon)*. This contains an art gallery of murals representing the story of the Missing and their drama.

An analysis of these murals provides a useful insight not just into the symbolism of the representation (including the visual sources), but also into the narratives of loss and absence. The murals were painted by the Greek artists Kostas and Haras Zouvelou. To refined aesthetic sensibilities these murals could be dismissed as kitsch. Yet the Church receives many visitors and pilgrims, and many commented to me how touched they were by them. As I shall show, their apparent simplicity and directness conceals as much as they display. An analysis of their iconography can help us understand that these pictures are an unsuccessful attempt to resolve a number of contradictions between the political treatment of the Missing (the formal ideology that unless there is documentation of their death the state considers them still alive) and private experience and 'intuitive' knowledge that they are lost forever. I discuss the murals below, giving them titles that best capture their iconography, as well as their time frame.

1. **The Long March** (Figures 18 to 21): The Struggle of the Relatives to obtain information on their missing. This is by far the largest mural. The style is in the tradition of social realism and shows people marching. Some of the poses are clearly taken from Bernardo Bertolucci's film, *1900*, which in turn was based upon the famous painting called *The Fourth Estate*, by Giuseppe Pelizza de Volpedo, painted between 1898–1901 (Milan, Galleria Civica d'Arte Moderna). Time frame: Present.

2. **Saviour Mother Church** (Figure 22). Allegory of the Church. The Panayia reaching out to save a sinking boat. Time Frame: Past-Present-Future.

3. **Early Christian Martyrs** (Figure 23). A scene in a dungeon representing imprisoned Missing Persons. The words KYPROS (Cyprus) AND ELEFTHERIA (Freedom) incised on the walls. Time Frame: Past.

4. **The Cross of the Missing** (Figure 24). Allegory. A Mother and daughter carrying a cross with the number 1619 in place of the INRI sign, with faces of the missing carved out of the rock resembling Mount Rushmore. Time Frame: Past-Present-Future.

5. **The Meeting with the Risen Christ** (Figure 25). A family of a missing person clearly mourning his loss suddenly meeting him. Here the symbolism seems closely modeled on the disciples' meeting the risen Christ. The missing son, bare-chested, and wearing army fatigue trousers, seems as surprised by their mourning him as they are by his appearing to them. Interestingly the two groups (the living relatives on the one hand, and the Risen Christ /*Agnoumenos*) do not touch. A physical gap between the two groups symbolises that the two groups occupy different time zones: the family in the here and now, the risen son, the future. Time Frame: Future.

6. **The Unconsolable Family** (Figure 26). A family consisting of a father, wife and daughter at the dinner table waiting for their son-brother who will never return. Symbolises: Incompleteness. Time Frame: Present.

Figure 18 'The Long March'. Mural at Ayios Alexandros
Church dedicated to Missing Persons.

Figure 19 'The Long March'. Mural at Ayios Alexandros
Church dedicated to Missing Persons.

Figure 20 'The Long March'. Mural at Ayios Alexandros
Church dedicated to Missing Persons.

Figure 21 'The Long March'. Mural at Ayios Alexandros
Church dedicated to Missing Persons.

Figure 22 'Saviour Mother Church'. Mural at Ayios Alexandros Church dedicated to Missing Persons.

Figure 23 'Early Christian Martyrs'. Mural at Ayios Alexandros Church dedicated to Missing Persons.

Figure 24 'The Cross of the Missing'. Mural at Ayios Alexandros Church dedicated to Missing Persons.

Figure 25 'The Meeting with the Risen Christ'. Mural at Ayios Alexandros Church dedicated to Missing Persons.

Figure 26 'The Disconsolable Family'. Mural at Ayios
Alexandros Church dedicated to Missing Persons.

Sophistication Through 'Naivete'?

The symbolism of these murals could not be more unambiguous. Indeed their
very naivete raises questions not so much about their 'propagandistic' purpose,
but rather how such a relatively politically sophisticated culture and society could
sustain such direct, unambiguous, unproblematic messages. There is one immediate striking feature. They do not depict the Turks in any way, negative or positive. This is very different to the representation of the Turks at the Green Line
(Figures 8 and 9). The murals cannot thus be called political in the conventional
sense. The murals are located in a church complex, and popular Christian iconography aspires to simple messages. Yet it is the naivete and directness in messages
that is problematical. We could be amazed by such paintings because they seem
to have been painted 'out of time'. It is as if the Renaissance had not occurred.
There appears to be little personal interpretation by the artists. This is odd
because Cyprus possesses a vibrant and sophisticated artistic community. Let us
compare this art to the secular (and subversive) sculpture *O Agnoumenos* (Figure
28).

This is a life-size free-standing thick metal plate sculpture, with the outline of
a figure cut out of it situated in Nicosia. This is a powerful work designed not for
tourists but for Greek Cypriots because of its monolingual Greek title. One looks
through it, there is nothing to see, except that very fact. The sculpture is literally
a silhouette. It is a subversive work because it plays upon the tension of complete-

Figure 27 Graffitti on Gutted Buildings by the 'Dead Zone'. Text says: 'We want our Missing back'.

Figure 28 'The Missing Person'. Sculpture in downtown Greek Cypriot Nicosia.

incompleteness, of either having had its content removed, or of never having had that content in the first place, and thus representing a category. If it is a category, whose category is it? Is it a category of memory, or of the state? Is it a nationalist work or a profoundly anti-statist one? There is clearly a world of difference between this and the murals. Whilst the former displays a 'kernel of doubt' as empty space, the murals can almost be seen as its direct opposite.

The closest one can get to understanding these pictures is that they appear to resemble social realism, in that no doubts, ambiguity, personal interpretations, or alternative voices are allowed to intrude. There is a 'smoothness' and 'complete-ness' about these images that excludes the personal or even the local. The collec-tion of murals suggests a faith not so much in images *per se,* in their ability to convey an unambiguous message, but rather an absolute confidence in how to view and interpret the problem of the missing persons. The narrative appears to be monophonic rather than antiphonic, or even polyphonic which most religious art can still be. But is that confidence so strongly grounded? I suggest not. Behind the apparent certainty lies a plethora of questions we have to decipher. I suggest that whilst these murals seem to depict unambiguous messages, they conceal a number of contradictions, and an immense uncertainty. In this respect, the fres-coes appear closer to Levi-Strauss' notion of myths, which encode a basic set of contradictions than icons.

According to Levi-Strauss' celebrated definition, through being told, narrated, or in this case depicted, myths attempt (ultimately unsuccessfully) to resolve underlying contradictions. Although these murals appear similar to social realism in their apparent boundless certainty, they are in fact different to the latter form of art. Social realist art operates in an unambiguous, unified, time frame – that of the constructed past and a realiseable future. By contrast, these paintings operate in two irreconcilable time frames: that of the here and now, and that of religious time, in other words beyond time, time out of this world. Here, as in myth, 'any-thing can happen'- the missing can appear as early Christian martyrs, or as shad-owing the risen Christ. The attempt to employ religious iconography to express (and resolve) what is recognizably a political problem on a societal level, and an existential one on the personal level, is thus vitiated.

The main tension the paintings try to resolve is that between political power-lessness and religious certainty, or at least the certainty that religion aims to offer. Put differently, the murals unsuccessfully attempt to resolve the main contradic-tions between the political treatment of the Missing (the formal ideology) which holds that the Missing should be assumed to be alive unless their mode of death is clarified – in short that they are absent – and private experience and 'intuitive' knowledge that they are lost – i.e. it is reasonable to assume they are dead. By dis-playing a monophonic security, the paintings conceal a profound insecurity. They betray a fear that the missing are lost forever, which can only be transcended through a religious soteriology. The contradiction these murals express is the fol-lowing: how can one reclaim these people who have politically been kept alive and whose death has not been faced by the state, nor recognized by society, when all logic and experience suggests that they may well be dead? And the 'resolution' that can only be offered to this predicament is that they are alive outside time. Rather than becoming absent, these missing are still lost. They thus can even represent 'us'. Recovery of the missing is tantamount to the recovery of self. Ultimately, therefore, these pictures address the problem and tension between loss and absence.

Absence and Loss

Here some insights of Dominick LaCapra may be useful. He suggests we should tease out the differences between absence and loss: 'the difference (or non-identity) between absence and loss is often elided, and the two are conflated with confusing and dubious results. This conflation tends to take place so rapidly that it escapes notice and seems natural or necessary' (1999: 700). He relates absence to structural trauma, and loss with historical trauma: 'In an obvious and restricted sense losses may entail absences but the converse need not be the case' (ibid: 700).

LaCapra situates absence on a trans-historical level and loss on a historical level. By trans-historical he means 'that which arises or is asserted in a contingent or particular historical setting but which is postulated as transhistorical' (ibid: 700, note 7). Here one could refer to Figure 23. An event that arose out of a particular historical setting is transformed into a prototypical scene of a trans-historical early Christian martyrdom. Absence and loss can in some senses almost be seen as opposed. They also have different aetiologies, not just in the way the past is interpreted, but also in the way the past is dealt with, and in the means adopted to transcend or recover that loss or absence.

Let us begin by observing that both Greek and Turkish Cypriots faced a problem of the 'absence' of loved ones. How both groups responded to that fact varied. Initially, as with situations of death and trauma to which they certainly approximated, both groups were faced with two sets of experiences: absence and loss. In 'normal' mourning processes, the initial experience of sudden absence (of a loved one) is worked through as a loss, which in turn leads to a fuller acceptance of absence. I wish to suggest that on a societal level Greek Cypriots have never fully worked out the relationship between the two. This could be interpreted as a chronic case of melancholia, and this is indeed what the psychoanalyst Vamik Volkan has suggested (Volkan and Itzkowitz, 2000). I deal with this below.

LaCapra suggests that 'When absence is converted into loss, one increases the likelihood of misplaced nostalgia or utopian politics in quest of a new totality or fully unified community'(ibid: 700). This applies particularly to the Greek Cypriots. The recovery of the missing is viewed as a means to recover not just lost territory but also heralding a type of reunification of the living with their missing loved ones. I suggest that the two groups responded to their loss /absences differently. Simply put, the Greek Cypriot experience of loss was of a sudden, massive, widespread societal dislocation, in a war situation that created a common solidarity and group awareness *qua* group and predisposed the survivors to fear the worst. Their initial experience was that of loss (of loved ones, land, etc.) rather than absence. They transformed those real losses into symbols of absence. By contrast, Turkish Cypriot experiences in the 1963–4 were perhaps much more individual, extended over a longer period, and in a situation of reciprocal hostage-taking where the relatives may well have 'reasonably' expected to get their loved ones back, as indeed did happen to a certain extent. This does not make their suffering any less serious, nor less worthy of our sympathy. Indeed in some senses the very fabrication and simulation of normality by the Greek Cypriot authorities who controlled the state after 1963, renders Turkish Cypriot experiences more horrific and traumatisable. Nevertheless, it is important to note that their experiences and expectations then were more oriented towards the pole of absences. They subsequently transformed their real absences into symbols of losses. The photographs discussed in the previous chapter could be seen as such symbols. The process can be represented in the following diagram:

Greek Cypriots:
On a Public level:
(Experience of) Loss (1) → Absence (structural) /Recapture → Symbols of Absence (2)
On a Private level:
(Experience of) Absence (1) → (Experience of) Loss (2)

Turkish Cypriots:
On a Public level:
(Experience of) Absence (1) → Rupture → Symbols of Loss (2)
On a Private level:
(Experience of) Loss (1) → through refraction of symbols of loss → absent Symbols (private)

The two trajectories are not mirror copies of each other. Here I deal with Greek Cypriot ones. For Greek Cypriots the private experiences of loss were transformed on the societal level into symbols of absence. They became markers of a structural trauma, which can probably never be resolved. As LaCapra notes: 'when loss is converted into (or encrypted in an indiscriminately generalised rhetoric of) absence, one faces the impasses of endless melancholy, impossible mourning, and interminable aporia in which any process of working through the past and its historical losses is foreclosed or prematurely aborted' (ibid: 698). A good example of this is the mural of the Mother and her Daughter carrying the *Cross of the Missing* (Figure 24). The Mother and Daughter are condemned to carry the cross of the missing for the living /society for all time. The switch from Christ to the mother /wife of the Missing Person as the person carrying the cross is a further demonstration of identification of permanently enacted suffering.

LaCapra suggests that 'the anxiety attendant upon absence may never be entirely eliminated or overcome but must be lived with in various ways. Avoidance of this anxiety is one basis for the typical projection of blame for a putative loss onto identifiable others, thereby inviting the generation of scapegoating or sacrificial scenarios' (ibid: 707). We can represent the process in the following way:

Loss → Absence: endless *aporia*: Carrying the Cross (Collective)

Yet on the private, individual, level as the society did not provide the institutional means to resolve the trauma of absence, to provide closure, and because the issue was kept alive on a political level, the private experience of absence has been transformed into an unending experience of loss. I suggest we are witnessing here the beginnings of the creation of sacrality. As Georges Bataille observed 'Sacred things are established through a labour of loss: in particular the success of Christianity must be explained by the significance of the theme of the appalling crucifixion of the Son of God, which takes human anguish to the point of a representation of loss and unlimited decline' (1998: 70).

A good example of how the private experience of absence has been transformed into an unending experience of loss is the mural of *The Unconsolable Family* waiting for their Missing Son to come to the dinner table (Figure 26). Here the overriding sentiment is that of despair. As LaCapra notes 'the conversion of absence into loss gives anxiety an identifiable object – the lost object– and generates the hope that anxiety may be eliminated or overcome' (ibid: 707). The emphasis on the symbols of absence – the empty chair and dinner setting, the substitution of the son by the photograph above, the uneaten bowl of fruit, suggest a self-conscious exploration of the symbols of melancholia. He suggests 'when mourning turns to absence and absence is conflated with loss, then mourning becomes impossible, endless, quasi-transcendental grieving, scarcely distinguishable (if at all) from interminable melancholy' (ibid: 716).

This picture merits further attention. The empty dinner place is clearly a trope of absence. Without having seen this picture, many Greek Cypriots often described this imaginary scene to me as an indication of the pain and suffering experienced by the families and the fact that they still hoped for the return of their loved ones. Interestingly, however, I have never come across such an actual practice among the families of the missing. It is clear that this represents an allegory for describing absence, rather than a literal practice. Relatives adopted other actions (such as retaining items of clothing), but these were closer to *momento mori*. There is certain self-awareness here in the use of the popular symbolism of melancholia that should alert us to the fact that something subtle is taking place. As I shall show, it is precisely because of this self-awareness that certain psychoanalytical attempts to describe the predicament of the Greek Cypriots as a refusal to face reality and to persist in melancholia (e.g. Volkan and Itzkowitz, 2000) seem unsatisfactory.

From a cultural perspective in terms of the representation of Greek dining rooms, something is missing in this picture which gives us a clue as to the relationship between sentiments and faith. There is a total absence of any religious element in the living room, such as icons, etc. I believe this is not fortuitous. Christian theology considers sadness a sin. Of all the paintings, this is the most lacking in hope, and therefore problematic from a Christian perspective. As Kristeva elliptically notes 'The depressed person is a radical, sullen atheist' (1989: 5). These pictures are subversive of formal Orthodox notions of *engarteresis* (the acceptance of suffering through patience and forbearance). Writing on depression and melancholia, Kristeva explores the feelings associated with the word unconsolable (or 'disconsolate') which can apply to this picture. It suggests a 'paradoxical temporality: the one who speaks has not been solaced in the past, and the effect of that frustration leads up to the present ... "Disconsolate" turns the present into the past when the trauma was experienced. The present is beyond repair, without the slightest solace' (1989: 148). This mural, like the photographs to which it approximates in style and origin (for these murals are illustrations of staged photographs, rather than based upon sketches from life), suggests an unresolved absence experienced as a permanent state of loss. How is the tension between loss and recovery anticipated and resolved?

The mural depicted in Figure 25 gives some suggestion of a 'solution'. Yet this is not fully a recovery. The returning soldier appears as a risen figure, almost as a phantasm, even in a manner similar to the period between Christ's Resurrection and Ascension – a transitional period, which accords well with the previous discussion in Chapter 5 of the missing as being located betwixt and between in Turner's felicitous phrase. He is separated from his family. It is almost as if both groups cannot believe whom they are seeing: the son that his family could be mourning, the family that he could (re)appear. There is no joy, just amazement. There is an 'unreality' about this picture that differentiates it from the rest. The closest one could approximate is a Resurrection picture. The recovery anticipated here is not a collective but a familial one. The murals thus represent a collective struggle and problem, but they portray individual, familial loss, and suggest a familially based recovery. The nature, timing, and aetiology of such recovery is left vague. The viewer is not guided to visualise whether this will be an individual real homecoming or a symbolic one. Like the family in *The Returning Soldier*, we are never sure whether the recovered missing person is our phantasm. He is perfect, like a saint, unblemished, handsome, resplendent, a *levendis*.

Clearly, the symbols provided by religion provide a useful way for Greek Cypriots to 'resolve' this predicament. But these murals also indicate that formal orthodoxy and traditional icons cannot offer much relief. Holst-Warhaft (1992) has suggested that in contrast to Catholicism, Orthodoxy cannot offer much consolation to people's feelings as it lacks the rituals which closely follow and replicate the passage of the individual through life to deal with extreme crises. Indeed, these pictures veer more towards popular Catholicism, rather than formal

Orthodoxy. As in myth, the function of repetition is a doomed attempt to resolve such contradictions, and can be likened to acting-out such predicaments. There is no reason to exclude the possibility that Christian symbols could not be used in new ways to give expression to such underlying contradictions. LaCapra has suggested 'in acting-out, the past is performatively regenerated or relived as if it were fully present rather than represented in memory and inscription, and it hauntingly returns as the repressed … to the extent someone is possessed by the past and acting out a repetition compulsion, he or she may be incapable of ethically responsible behaviour' (ibid: 716). He suggests that 'with respect to traumatic losses, acting-out may well be a necessary condition of working-through, at least for victims' (ibid: 717).

Art as a Counter-depressant

There may thus be culturally variable therapies to problems of loss and absence. But why do it in painting? To suggest that Pater Christoforos commissioned these murals to commemorate his son and as a means of self-aggrandizement (as indeed some insinuate more or less openly in Cyprus), is I think too ungenerous, and leaves out the important question of why this particular articulation of iconography was chosen. Indeed from a religious point of view these paintings are problematical. There is no 'kernel of doubt' (Goody, 1997) that normally accompanies the act of religious representation. These pictures are here to do things and in an even more permanent form than political speeches or rhetoric. They convey messages more subtly than words, attempting to pose questions and *apories* that cannot be openly expressed.

Some indication for the reasons comes from the work of Julia Kristeva. She writes:

> Aesthetic and particularly literary creation, and also religious discourse in its imaginary, fictional essence, set forth a device whose prosodic economy, interaction of characters, and implicit symbolism constitute a very faithful semiological representation of the subject's battle with symbolic collapse. Such a literary representation is not an *elaboration* in the sense of 'becoming aware' of the inter- and intra-psychic causes of moral suffering; that is where it diverges from the psychoanalytic course, which aims at dissolving the symptom. Nevertheless, the literary and religious representation possesses a real and imaginary effectiveness that comes closer to catharsis than to elaboration; it is a therapeutic device used in all societies throughout the ages. (1989: 24–25 emphasis in original)

These pictures can be seen as an aesthetic device utilizing the soteriological symbols and discourse provided by religion in an imaginary fictional mode to resolve some of the problems experienced by relatives of the missing. They can be seen as a cathartic device whereby pilgrims can explore their predicament in a situation of symbolic collapse (the object of desire has disappeared and is a cause of pain). The effectiveness of the Ayios Alexandros murals cannot be explained by reference to their aesthetic skill, or even their drama or subtlety of vision. They do not require much previous knowledge of high culture to be grasped. Rather, these murals 'speak' – perhaps too much for some tastes – including through a blatant unashamed plagiarization of other pictures or of films. Although it could be argued they are 'bad' paintings because they are clearly so derivative, they are excellent examples of mythic thought. As in myth, anything can happen.

Psychoanalysis, Mourning, and Melancholia

This discussion enables us to tackle two important issues in the representation of collective grief of other cultures. First, are the tools and insights of psychoanalysis useful when transposed from the individual to the collective level? Second, how applicable are the insights of Freudian analysis to other cultures, especially in respect to mourning and melancholia? This is clearly a huge topic which cannot be dealt with fully or even partially here, and I want to do so purely by reference to the recent extensive writings on mourning by the psychoanalyst Volkan. He has defined what he calls the 'perennial mourner':

> The 'perennial' mourner knows that a death has occurred, but behaves although it has not. The individual is locked in a chronic review of the lost relationship, in an attempt to find some resolution to it. The patient fluctuates between bringing the dead back to life and 'killing' the dead to end this mourning process ... the patient remains in a state of limbo. We can say that a perennial mourner has a closer relationship with the representation of the dead than with the representations of living people (Volkan and Ast, 1997: 134).

Volkan distinguishes the perennial mourner from the depressed mourner: the perennial mourner's identification with the mental representation of the lost object is temporary and unstable, and he is unable to mourn effectively. This does not seem to be the case with the relatives. In other writings (Volkan and Itzkowitz, 2000) however, he suggests that Greek Cypriots have never come to terms with the fact of loss, which he sees in terms of melancholia – even an inability to accept loss. Volkan calls this 'complicated mourning'. According to him, the history of an ethnic group can be seen in similar ways to that of a person, i.e. groups, like individuals, have certain experiences that leave indelible traces in their collective psyche. This is interesting, but problematical. Certainly 'history' or historical experiences can have certain effects on group identities, but the history Volkan concerns himself with is that of de-ethicised *evenements*, rather than on

Braudelian 'structure'. He bypasses economic or political forces in the evolution of polities, and tends to render history in terms of personalities (e.g. Mehmet the Conqueror; Ataturk, etc), their actions (e.g. breaching the walls of Constantinople as a type of rape, Oedipal tensions, violation, etc), and their effects on mass psychology. This is interesting, but scientifically flawed. History is not problematised, but rather seen as a key to current problems. Here, for example, is his treatment of what he calls a 'chosen trauma':

> The tern 'chosen trauma' refers to the mental representation (a cohesive image) of an event that caused a large group of people (i.e. an ethnic group) to feel victimized, humiliated by another group, and to suffer losses, especially that of self-esteem ... . While a group does not choose to be victimized, it does 'choose', consciously as well as unconsciously, to psychologize and mythologize what has occurred and define its ethnicity by referring to this event.
>
> Chosen traumas are linked with the inability or difficulty of the large group in question to mourn; for a trauma to be 'chosen', it must one that cannot be mourned adaptively. Furthermore the humiliation pertaining to it cannot be reversed. (Volkan and Itzkowitz, 2000: 232–3)

The authors identify the 1453 Byzantine loss of Constantinople, the 1922 *Megali Katastrophe* and the 1974 Turkish invasion of Cyprus as the Greeks' chosen traumas that have not been worked through:

> There is resistance to mourn over these losses since it would mean the acceptance of a different identity from that held by modern Greeks. Newer traumas (i.e., the tragedy in Asia Minor in 1922 and the tragedy in Cyprus in 1974) strengthen the Greek feelings of hurt. In this respect, the Greeks seem to have become perennial mourners. This increases the sense of victimization and entitlement. (ibid: 240)

That these events certainly had mass social, political and economic (and even psychological) effects are indubitable, and there is a certain attraction to this approach. But there is opaqueness in its apparent transparency. Volkan's treatment suggests that once these traumas are recognized then they could relatively easily be resolved. His solution is residually individualist rather than collective: it is leaders who can take groups out of their traumas (ibid: 245). Clearly, all societies have their myths that have very definite social effects, but such myths are rarely universally subscribed to, nor isolated from changing political and social interpretations across time. It is their political use that needs to be unmasked, including their use as a rationalisation and legitimation of 'realism'. Most Greeks do not mourn the loss of Constantinople or indeed the 1922 debacle, but many Cypriots feel aggrieved at having lost their homes, properties and loved ones. The latter was not a 'chosen trauma'. It was, and is, an inflicted trauma mainly as a result of *realpolitik* by the machinations of powerful countries on large numbers of ordinary people, admittedly aided by local individuals bent, in the words of Thomas Paine, on 'the mean and interested struggle for place and emolument'. An island of 600,000 people can hardly mourn by 'responding adaptively' to what they consider an invasion by a regional superpower of some 65 million and the forcible ejection of a third of their population from their homes. Clearly, political authorities (like Creon) have their own agendas, but they cunningly craft them, as the art of the possible, out of the very real pain and suffering experienced by individuals as a result of active policies of mass repression (as in Guatemala and Argentina), or geo-political concerns of much more powerful neighbours (such as Turkey's occupation of Cyprus).

Volkan fails to distinguish between popular historical folklore, and personal experiences of loss, and thus risks mass-pathologizing whole ethnic groups. Hence, 'the Greeks seem to have become perennial mourners' (*sic.*). Admittedly my criticism could be faulted, as the theme of this book is about the political, ethical, and existential necessities for mourning, as well as the creativity and artistry involved. But as I hope is rendered clear, this is not an ethnic-cultural issue, it is rather one embedded in social life, and mourning is not necessarily a mere ritual. There is an additional danger in adopting a popular Freudian interpretation treating such traumas as 'illusions', much like Freud's treatment of religion as a social stage mirroring the evolution of an individual's full self-consciousness and maturity – a profoundly anti-anthropological approach. Such approaches also deny events any moral agency and causation, and treat victims of events as a medical category rather than a political and social category. On the contrary, I would suggest a different interpretation. This is that rather than seeing 'the Greeks' as 'perennial mourners', the notion of 'unforgettable grief' (what the Ancients called *penthos alaston*) can be seen as a *cultural resource or strategy to cope with loss*. It is as much a cultural strategy to cope with loss as the Illongot response. We therefore have to work *with* the symbols of that culture rather than risking pathologizing that culture and society.

These observations are important because in the course of this chapter I want to show that unterminated mourning is not necessarily melancholia and that one cannot pathologize the relatives of the missing on a collective basis, and thus de-ethicize our analysis. This is not to deny that individuals did not suffer from traumas and psychological problems. On the contrary, many did suffer deeply. It is rather to show that it would be ethically and analytically disingenuous to follow such suggestions by characterizing a group of individuals as having 'chosen' their traumas, and concurrently being 'unable to mourn adaptively'.

At this stage it is therefore worthwhile to reexamine Freud's thoughts on melancholia in his seminal essay *'Mourning and Melancholia'*. Freud starts with a problem. Why is it that mourning and melancholia (now more commonly known as depression) are so similar in their symptoms, but different in their progression? I did not find that Freud's list of symptoms of melancholia applied to most of the relatives I know, particularly in one symptom: 'cessation of interest in the outside world' (1984: 254). Some may well have been, but the ones I knew were actively engaged with the world, although, not being a clinician, I did not ask specific questions. Freud emphasizes the major differences between mourning and melancholia. Although he recognizes that melancholia can be the reaction to the loss of a loved object, he soon suggests different reasons ('exciting causes'). He terms these ' a *loss of a more ideal kind*. The object has perhaps not actually died, but has been *lost as an object of love* (e.g., in the case of the betrothed girl who has been jilted)' (ibid: 253, my emphasis). In melancholia, 'one cannot see clearly what it is that has been lost, and, it is all the more reasonable to suppose that the patient cannot consciously perceive what he has lost either' (ibid: 254). This certainly does not apply to the relatives of the missing I interviewed. They apprehended clearly what they had lost (loved ones), and additionally in other cases, land, houses, property, etc.

Observers working with refugees in Cyprus have noted the destruction of their life–worlds and the consequent symbolic collapse. It is thus very possible that the tales of exaggerated loss, which stimulated the resentment of the resident Greek Cypriot population in the south, could be seen as a type of melancholia. I have suggested that some sort of state-abetted transference and elaboration is certainly occurring: the loved ones/missing are projected on to the lost, occupied, territory, etc. and become metonyms for the north. Indeed Freud suggests that mourning and melancholia may be triggered not just by the loss of a loved person, but also by 'the loss of some abstraction, which has taken the place of one, such as one's country, liberty, an ideal, and so on' (ibid: 252). It is hard to see the loss of one's own home and land in a small-scale society as merely the loss of some 'abstraction'. For many, much more was involved.

Freud characterizes the melancholic as someone who 'knows *whom* he has lost, but not *what* he has lost in him' (ibid: 254, emphasis in original). This is not applicable to the relatives of missing persons I met. Many were highly articulate and aware that the loss had permanently transformed them. A complex and rich refugee poetry of exile, *xenitia*, is itself a strong tradition in Greek literature, and gave emotional sustenance to more literary individuals. Freud's characterization thus does not apply to the majority of relatives I interviewed.

Freud then draws out an important distinction: 'melancholia is in some way related to an object-loss which is withdrawn from consciousness, in contradistinction to mourning, in which there is nothing about the loss which is unconscious' (ibid: 254). Whilst one can suggest that perhaps the loss of loved ones, homes, land and territory, was an 'object-loss withdrawn from consciousness', this would seriously diminish their whole symbolic and cultural significance. What was 'withdrawn from consciousness', or in Lacanian terms 'foreclosed' (his translation of Freud's *verwerfung*) was an inability to recognize that serious inter-ethnic conflict occurred between 1963–74, and an attempt to recover a completely fictional past of peaceful coexistence between Greek and Turkish Cypriots. Why they do so is interesting, and this will be explored in the last chapter. But the actual losses suffered were not 'withdrawn from consciousness'. They were continuously recalled.

One could surmise that certain women who lost their husbands but were not also refugees were more predisposed to activism, although their actions might have veered towards what Freud termed the manic phase, certainly political activism. This will be discussed later.[1] Individuals who had precise and identifiable losses (a husband), rather than those whose losses were much more extensive (such as also other villagers and relatives, houses, land, village, etc), and therefore involved a total symbolic collapse, may have been relatively 'privileged' in coming to terms with their losses, and in providing a clear focus for their activism. It was my impression that mothers experienced losses differently to wives and fiancées. The former appear to have interiorised their sufferings more than the latter who had to concentrate their energies on raising their children. They derived pride from having raised their children well against many odds. The empirical material from Argentina suggests that the age of the child mattered little for the mothers as they still continued to imagine that their adolescent and adult children to be infants in need of maternal protection (Robben, 2000: 77; see also Gorer, 1965: 121).

Freud further distinguishes between mourning and melancholia: 'In mourning it is the world which has become poor and empty; in melancholia it is the ego itself' (ibid: 254). I did not find the latter description characterized the relatives of missing persons. Rather, it was the former. He then identifies 'the most remarkable characteristic of melancholia' (ibid: 262), that it can turn into mania, ' a state ... the opposite of it in its symptoms' (ibid: 262). Freud is adamant that 'melancholia contains something more than normal mourning.' In melancholia 'the relation to the object is no simple one; it is complicated by the conflict due to ambivalence'. He notes that the ambivalence may either be constitutional or proceed directly from the experiences that involved the threat of losing the object. He shows that 'the exciting causes of melancholia have a *much wider range* that those of mourning, which is for the most part *occasioned only by a real loss of the object, by its death*' (ibid: 266, my emphasis). He sees melancholia as emerging out of much wider situations: 'In melancholia ... countless separate struggles are carried on over the object, in which hate and love contend with each other' (ibid: 266). He notes that two of the three preconditions of melancholia are shared with obsessional self-reproaches arising after a death has occurred. These are loss of object and ambivalence. Anna Freud took this further suggesting that the bereaved always has an ambivalent attitude towards the deceased; corpses become transitional objects (1969: 310–3). They thus become essential for the mourning process. According to S. Freud the third characteristic is 'the regression of libido into the ego' (ibid: 267), which he identifies as melancholia's real cause.

Freud was interested in the parallelism of mourning with melancholia, but he is very clear that whilst some processes may be similar, the 'exciting causes' between the two often differ, and that melancholia is rarely occasioned by deaths of individuals, but by other factors. Many relatives, especially mothers, complained to me about suffering from insomnia, depression, and psychosomatic disorders. However it would be wrong to apply such a reading, which derives from statements by individuals, to a generic collectivity to suggest a collective 'chosen trauma'. Such attempts are pernicious. It is pernicious first because it does not recognize the social and general conditions under which absences became turned into losses. Second, it is pernicious because it medicalises a whole population; and third, because it does not recognize the social construction of that 'reality' and culturally specific way of dealing with losses. Furthermore, many of the relatives wish for nothing more than closure in a culturally acceptable and meaningful way, however painful that may be. This includes the return of the bones for burial. They do not wish to prolong their condition of uncertainty, although relatives have experienced some considerable psychological disturbance, and will in some cases, undergo further psychological disturbance. Similar conditions were noted in Malawi. There, Englund notes, 'It was not simply the loss that constituted refugees' predicament. Traumas often arose from the impossibility to observe, under the conditions of both war and exile, the full range of procedures that enables people to regain their well-being after the loss' (1998: 1168).

Two other factors should be noted. First, the conditions under which individuals disappeared are significant. Freud's analysis is oriented towards individual patients, not whole groups affected by social traumas. This is an essential feature in any study of the effects of bereavement. There are many variables that determine grief. They include relationship to the deceased, age, gender, and mode of death and personal vulnerability (Parkes, 1996). We have to recognise that such deaths were not 'normal', 'routinised', and part of the anticipated pattern of social and individual life. These were not societally and individually 'normal' individual deaths. Rather, they were losses and absences that had to be construed as deaths. These losses were collective, affected hundreds of families, took place within a relatively short and bounded period, and the circumstances were extraordinary for individuals and the whole society. Rosaldo makes a telling point: 'Undoubtedly, certain people do live a full life and suffer so greatly in their decrepitude that they embrace the relief death can bring. Yet the problem with making such an easy death (I use Simone de Beauvoir's [1969] title as she did, with irony) the paradigm case of dying, is that it makes it appear as routine for the survivors as this one apparently was for the deceased' (1984: 185–6). Furthermore the disappeared did not generally affect members of society, such as the elderly, whose loss society is predisposed to routinely expect and accept. They affected the young in the majority. Parents, or young wives, were faced with the task of treating the loss of their children, or their husbands as sudden, unanticipated, absences.[2] Sanua (1974) has shown how deaths by violence show an increased risk to mental health. There is a world of difference between the trauma of an individual who refuses to accept a loss through a death, and that of a whole social group who have collectively experienced an unexpected absence through the organized application of military violence, and whose only point of similarity between them is that they all never would have expected to experience such traumas. Greek Cypriots experienced a historical trauma, i.e. a series of *losses* as a result of historical events that were put into effect by actors, participants, collectivities, and bystanders. They did not experience a structural trauma, i.e. a series of *absences* as a result of the inherent properties of the anticipatory unfolding of social and familial life, or as a result of some collective natural disaster. This parallels the situation of Argentine mothers of *desaparecidos*. Robben notes 'Resignation to death was emotionally and socially less acceptable than postponing grief for years until the fate of the disappeared was entirely clear' (2000: 89). The perniciousness of this perspective is that when we perceive the phenomenon on the individual level from the comfort of our rou-tinised lives, and not taking account into the experiences that people had, the phe-nomenon does appear to be one of 'unrealism' and a refusal to let go. If we do this, we blind ourselves to the social aspects of this loss.

Such experiences primarily affected the poorer and weaker members of society. Quite apart from the complex issue of the political use by the state (i.e. 'Creon') of such families, it is important to recognize that the relatives of the missing were victims of events. They may have an 'investment' in the recollection or preserva-tion of the past, and in the use of certain memories, which the state tried to erase as subversive. One may even view such memories as weapons of the weak. Some indication of the necessity of remembering is suggested by La Capra for whom the distinction between structural trauma and historical trauma is essential for under-standing victimhood: 'with respect to historical trauma and its representation, the distinction among victims, perpetrators, and bystanders is crucial' (ibid: 723). He then makes an important point – one that is often lost in the bland approach of psychoanalytical medicalization: '"Victim" is not a psychological category. It is, in variable ways, a social, political, and ethical category' (ibid: 723).

With these observations in mind we can now reconsider why these pictures are so important and why they must be placed within the historical context of 1974. Let us recall the initial equations:

Greek Cypriots:
On a Public level:
(Experience of) Loss (1Absence (structural) /Recapture) $\longrightarrow$ Symbols of Absence (2)
On a Private level:
(Experience of) Absence (1)) $\longrightarrow$ (Experience of) Loss (2)

Public discourse in the Greek part of Cyprus narrativises the events of 1974 in very specific ways. For Greek Cypriots, the 1974 Turkish invasion and post-1976 absence of the Turkish Cypriots from the south entailed a loss not just of their loved ones (the missing persons) and their properties and homes in the north, but also of what they (wrongly) believe to have been an original pre-lapsarian ideal state. To Greek Cypriots, these absences are identified as losses. Hence they need to be recovered – not just their properties and homes, but also symbolically their loved ones in some form or another. This attitude permeates officialdom. The offi-cial legal position, supported in sentiment by most Greek Cypriots, is that Turkish Cypriot properties still belong to them, to be reclaimed on their return as they are considered full citizens of the Republic. It is the Turkish army's occupation of Cyprus that prevents this unity. (Interestingly, the Turkish Cypriot leadership has appropriated Greek Cypriot properties in the north and refuses to recognize their claims). This results in the projection of a utopian nostalgia in the past, when 'we all got on well like brothers' (let us recall it is the conflict between brothers that underlies the tragedy of *Antigone*). As La Capra has noted: 'When absence is converted into loss, one increases the likelihood of misplaced nostalgia or utopian politics in quest of a new totality or fully unified community' (ibid: 701). But this absence is itself narrativized and necessitates symbols. Greek Cypriot society (in contrast to Turkish Cypriot society) is woven through with symbols of absence expressed as losses that need to be filled: of the missing, in public works of art (such as *O Agnoumenos*), in the perfectly preserved Turkish mosques kept as reminders of a unitary ideal past and evoking a utopic future (these mosques can be seen as trans-historical buildings, signs of continuity, versus the historic gutted buildings, signs of rupture, along the Green Line which become symbols of the barbarism of the other especially the Turkish army), and in the divided maps that inscribe a fragmented unity ('Temporarily Inaccessible due to the Turkish Invasion', written across the northern part, like Ruth Benedict's broken cup). As La Capra perceptively notes, 'When absence itself is narrativized, it is perhaps necessarily identified with loss (for example the loss of innocence, full community, or unity with mother) and even figured as an event or derived from one' (ibid: 701).[3]

Among individuals the main set of experiences has been the progression of absence into loss. Here some comparison with studies of responses to deaths in wars may be instructive. Rubin (1992), who followed families of children killed in the Yom Kippur war, found that parents continued to remember and to relate to vivid memories of the lost child who remained an important part of the family. Rubin calls this a 'two-track model of bereavement' (cf. Parkes, 1996: 132). For Greek Cypriot parents none of the features of death are known; they are only imaginable. Nevertheless, the notion of a two-track, and indeed conflictual, model of bereavement has some relevance to both Greek and Turkish Cypriots. I have suggested that in the case of the Greek Cypriots, loss and recovery is the main theme of the murals, and an immense anxiety lies beneath their apparent certainty. In particular, taken together, the apparent certainty outside time as in *The Resurrected Soldier* (Figure 25) has to be seen in association with the anxiety within time of *The Unconsolable Family* (Figure 26).[4]

By contrast, among the Turkish Cypriots on the official, public level, because of the political project of carving out a separate state, the authorities ('Creon') have been less interested in the production of symbols of loss which are unrecoverable, but as sacrifices. Hence the political use of photographs of the dead bodies discussed in the previous chapter, or the monuments to the dead, as representations of the (absent) body of Eteocles given a state burial for the defense of the city (such as that of Tashkent monument). On the private level by contrast, the *aporia* faced by

Turkish Cypriots is different but inexpressible: how does one express the experience of losses without any symbols except the ones provided by the state. Doka (1989) has coined the notion of 'disenfranchised grief', which refers to losses that cannot be openly acknowledged, socially validated, or publicly mourned. One could refer to Turkish Cypriot relatives of missing persons as disenfranchised mourners who experienced unelaborated grief. Although the authorities recognize their grief, their mourning is not permitted to find its full expression due to the reluctance of the Turkish Cypriot leadership to permit exhumations and the return of their bodies. To revert to the Antigone metaphor, on the Turkish Cypriot side, Creon prefers a coenotaph (an empty honorary tomb), because he fears that exhumations may show that Eteocles, the defender on the city, may well have assisted in an unprovoked assault on Polynices. Political authorities need heroes, but few of them are unblemished. Better to represent them through manipulable symbols of one's own creation, rather than through anything that may become a *corpus delicti*. As C.S Lewis noted enigmatically 'All reality is iconoclastic' (1966: 6).

If we have established that for Greek Cypriots, especially the relatives of the missing, the disappearances cannot therefore be routinized as merely absences but as *losses*, two consequences follow. First, we need to examine how individuals attempt to deal with these losses as losses, and to recover something about their selves from their situation. The means can vary. Second, we need to examine an interrelated issue: how do individuals thus come to accept 'reality'. They can only accept their 'reality' as a loss, not as an absence. So we need to look at some form of attempted recovery (of loss) rather than an acceptance of absence. Acceptance of absence is contingent upon, and pursuant of, symbolic recovery of loss.

Exhumation of the Self

Widows of missing persons in Cyprus were keen to talk about what they assumed to be the last known information of their loved ones, when such information was available. Recounting focuses attempts to recover the loss of the loved one and of the self (see also Klass, 1989: 159). Similar desires were encountered by Zur in Guatemala who noted 'constructing narratives collectively is a means of coming to terms with the events of the past and integrating them into their lives which makes sense in the present' (1998: 170–71). Women, as mothers, sisters, and wives /widows not only were more prominently visible than fathers and brothers in expressing ritual and political activism, but seemed to settle more easily into roles as suspended mourners and appeared more willing to talk about their predicament, their pain, and their health problems. It appeared that men experienced more difficulties in integrating their role as suspended mourners with other aspects of their lives. It seemed more 'natural', even in terms of Cypriot cultural expectations, for women to adopt the role of a waiting spouse or mother. They also felt more 'comfortable' in that role than men. It appeared that the men experienced more difficulties not just in adopting the role of suspended mourners, but also in giving vent to their feelings. In short, Cypriot culture imposes an emotional division of labour whereby women can assume such roles, which men do not have to assume to such an extent. By not being provided with such long-term identities, they did not have access to the cultural repertoire of physical symptoms (such as insomnia, etc) which alert us to a situation of existential and social unease. Indigenous therapeutic strategies may thus have been more accessible to the women than to the men. This should alert us to the possibility that in such a culture, and possibly elsewhere, men may have grieved more silently than the women and have suffered to an equally great extent, but without the cultural legitimisation to express their grief openly. For some women, though not all, expressing one's grief was a performance and it was something they did 'well' as artists – for there is artistry in the social performance of roles. The activists had been doing so for a considerable time. Men could not assume such roles in the drama of their lives and losses. They were the silent bystanders of their own drama and it was more difficult to talk to them than to the women, a telling reversal of roles and of the accessibility of the male anthropologist to other males. It is worthwhile recalling the figure of Haemon in Sophocles' *Antigone*, – perhaps the most constrained and the most silent figure of the play – aware of the tragedy he is witnessing unfold. As the fiancée of Antigone, and Creon' son, he is not just caught between conflicting loyalties of love to Antigone and *pietas* towards Creon, he is the only figure in the play who does not act out his role either out of a combination of hubris, principle, or *moira* (destiny), but out of a sense of compassion for the two.

In many cases however, wives/widows had few details to focus their attempts at the recovery of their men-folk, so they resorted to two demands: clarification of the situations under which their men folk disappeared, and concurrently, the return of their bones. Here it is worthwhile to tackle an important issue. Freud often talks about 'reality testing': 'the capacity to distinguish between mental images and external percepts, between phantasy and external reality, to correct subjective impressions by reference to external facts' (Rycroft, 1972; 138). There are two points here. First there is the tension between mental image (the missing person is lost and not yet dispatched) and external reality (a reasonable expectation that the person is dead). Second, there is possibility that the attempts to bridge mental image and external percepts are culturally variable. From an anthropological perspective it could be argued that if social worlds are culturally constituted, then 'reality testing' occurs differently in various societies. Nevertheless in most societies the return of the bones for ritual processing is usually an important means to come to terms with a death (Bloch and Parry, 1982). Other mechanisms of coping can be victims blaming themselves, or, as in Sri Lanka, possession through avenging ghosts (Perera, 1995). The process of asking for the return of the bones of loved ones is traumatic and ambivalent. On the one hand it is the ultimate demonstration of 'reality testing', a sign that the relatives wish to return to normality and to vacate their liminal condition. But it also validates the depositions of the relatives/mourners that the disappearances were far from ordinary. It further validates their claim that that their victimhood is not 'psychological' and thus marginalisable, but social and political. It thus has ontological reality. This is not to dispute that, perversely, there are many examples of victims blaming themselves (Perera, 1995; Robben, 2000). At the same time the return of the bones confirms the suffering of the missing. It is not hard to see that the demand can become an almost 'obsessive' means of testing the 'reality' of the relatives against the indifference of the state, and the recognition of their suffering. The demand becomes a proof of the existence of the mourner *qua* mourner, that the mourner was 'justified' in claiming and sustaining that condition. It becomes a proof of the existence of the mourner; a validation of Derrida's aphorism 'I mourn, therefore I am '.

The demand for the return of bones becomes a sullen act of defiance that is deeply wounding to the mourner. It generates feelings of guilt that the relatives require the missing person to be proved dead in order for them to be able to rejoin 'normal' life. Of course, what is 'normal' for them is this condition, and they may experience further traumas when the bones are finally retrieved and returned. As LaCapra notes: 'In some disconcertingly ambivalent form, trauma and one's (more or less symbolic) repetition of it may even be valorized, notably when leaving it seems to mean betraying lost loved ones who were consumed by it' (ibid: 717). Similar processes seem to have occurred in post-Dirty War Argentina. Exhumations risk depoliticizing the body as symbol and thus devalorizing the labour of love that mourners have invested in their role as searchers. Robben notes that in Argentina many 'condemned the exhumations considering them as a government scheme to have them accept and psychologically participate in the deaths of all disappeared' (2000: 91–2). One group decided 'to keep their emotional wounds open in order to resist the societal process of forgetting' (ibid: 92) They also began to identify with the ideals that were the reasons for the disappearances of their children.

In spite of its apparent 'naturalness' and its resonances in historical and cultural traditions, the demand for the return of the bones to achieve narrative closure is a complex process. In many cases people may claim that they recognize the bones intuitively, or through recognizing items of clothing which may well be extremely common. This occurred in Sri Lanka when some mass graves were uncovered. Here, 'scientific proof' for positive identification was absent and medical records unavailable (Perera, 1995). As Perera notes 'as far as survivors are concerned what governs events such as these are emotional and social compulsions. Thus the usual "reality" is replaced by a powerful belief and the necessity to believe in *something* that constructs an alternate reality. In this case that something is a symbol that people can identify with their disappeared loved ones – the sarongs, protruding and false teeth and so on' (ibid: 6 emphasis in original). Increasingly, however, identification of loved ones, like claims to paternity, is becoming scientized and routinised through DNA testing. This removes both control over identification from relatives and demotes familiar, intimate, knowledge as the criterion for identification, in favour of scientific knowledge and techniques. Knowledge of identification is arrived at not intuitively through the eye or through feelings or senses, but through procedures delayed and mediated through the giving of intimate bodily fluids, such as blood. No longer can a mother or wife demand 'Show me his socks and I will recognize my son', (as the journalist Robert Fisk observed during the Bosnian exhumations, *The Independent* 9 October 1996). The power to identify and ratify belonging, kinship, and to claim an intimate link with the dead much like Antigone's washing /claiming of her brother's body, is removed from kin and placed in the hands of strangers, individuals whose knowledge, language and demeanour, can link them with the state, and therefore become a source of suspicion.

One can thus appreciate that the process of reality testing is not only culturally variable, but is increasingly routinised and medicalised. Relatives may not wish for, or be accepting of any set of bones. DNA testing subverts the process of symbolism. It detaches the notion of the body/bones as a symbol of belonging grounded in ritual practices and knowledge over which the relatives have some control, and turns it into a manifestation and precipitation of belonging. Prior to DNA testing, it was the relative as *Antigone* who claimed belonging and pursued it through the demand of the bones. Now it is the body as artifact that demands ownership by a specific person. Anouilh's Creon cannot indulge in his artistry by substituting bodies. Bones identified through scientific processing become artifacts: identified and produced by one set of people through determinate reproducible techniques to be claimed by others. DNA testing materialises the symbol and spiritualises matter. Scientific testing and identification may thus in these cases further prolong social traumas, rather than resolve them.

NOTES

1. Most of the women who tended to fit the characterisation of the melancholic were mothers who lost their sons, refugees (particularly from Asha, which experienced collective violence).

2. In the West it has been suggested that the loss of a child showed higher scores on the Texas Inventory of Grief than found in other species of bereavement (Parkes, 1996: 121; Neidig and Dalgas, 1991) But see Scheper Hughes (1992) for an admittedly completely different response that required anthropological *explanation*.

3. An astute reader versed in Lacanian theory might view this overlap of absence and loss as providing the basis for perceiving The Missing as the Lacanian Other with all its attendant contradictions and tensions.

4. 'The conversion of absence into loss gives anxiety an identifiable object – the lost object- and generates the hope that anxiety may be eliminated or overcome (La Capra, ibid:707).

8
ANTIGONE'S DOUBT, CREON'S DILEMMA

Creon: What else could I have done? People had taken sides in the civil war. Both sides couldn't be wrong: that would be too much. I couldn't have made them swallow the truth … Would it have been better to let you die a victim of that obscene story?
Antigone: It might have been. I had my faith.

(Anouilh: *Antigone*, 1960: 54–55)

Introduction

In Anouilh's version of *Antigone*, following the battle for Thebes, the bodies of Polynices and Eteocles are mashed to a pulp and are unrecognizable. Creon has both bodies reassembled; the latter carefully displayed as a 'hero', the former carefully dissembled as a 'traitor'. There is artistry is the project. This can be called the conspiracy theory of politics. Real-life politics is messier. It often starts as a conspiracy that degenerates into a cock-up, but survives as a cock-up interpreted subsequently as a conspiracy. This chapter deals with what I call Antigone's Doubt.

All is not well in Thebes /Cyprus. Remember that in the Greek Cypriot version, the enemy is believed to have killed Eteocles (the defender of the city) and buried him secretly. Relatives want his body for proper burial. After some 20 years it emerges that some bodies believed to have been secreted by the enemy (though not all) were actually hurriedly and secretly buried in the Kingdom of Thebes /the Republic of Cyprus. In order to strengthen their case, and also because of the chaos during the fighting, the political authorities (Creon) buried them hurriedly and forgot about them, telling the relatives that their bodies are 'on the other side'. Increasingly fearful of a scandal, Creon keeps silent. After all, the situation serves an important political purpose. But in response to pressure, Creon secretly permits the exhumation of some corpses and returns them to relatives overseas in

Greece. Except that they turn out to be the wrong bodies ... This is Antigone's doubt. She faces three questions. The first is as kinswoman of the unburied brother. Is the body of my kinsman actually recoverable and bury-able? Perhaps Creon was lying all along? Perhaps I have been demanding his corpse from the wrong people whereas in fact it was already close-by and not identified? The second doubt is as *kinswoman of the buried brother* (Eteocles, the hero). His body was returned and given a full burial. It now turns out it was somebody else's kinsman – which leads us back to the first question. The third doubt is as Antigone the *kinswoman and subject of Creon,* citizen of, and subject to, the rules of the city. Not all bodies are recoverable; some are genuinely inaccessible. For the Antigone whose relatives' body is still unrecoverable, she still has to compromise with Creon to represent her to recover the body. Can she still do so? The political leaders also face a dilemma. Creon's dilemma is that he is both kinsman of Antigone and ruler of Thebes. As kinsman he is finally moved to permit the '(re)burial' of Eteocles and the unification of the relatives with their loved ones, and assumes responsibility for the injustice done to the relatives. As a political ruler he may argue that the polity faced a crisis and that although some mistakes were made, he nevertheless still did his best to represent the concerns of the relatives, as the majority of bodies are still unrecoverable without the cooperation of the authorities in the north. Creon's dilemma thus still revolves around compassion or political expediency. Can he come clean and still retain some legitimacy?

Rumour and the Contestation of Official Realities

Virisque acquirit eundo (Rumour acquires strength as it progresses)

Virgil, *Aeneid,* iv.175

In recent years various accounts have emerged of the coup and invasion period that have profoundly disturbed both versions of events offered by the state and the Missing Persons' Committee. In 1995 an investigative reporter made a number of revelations which profoundly shook the political establishment. In a series of reports in the weekly news periodical *Selides,* Andreas Paraskos published a number of stories with the following headlines: 'Tombs of the Missing at Lakatameia'; 'Revealing Disclosures regarding the Missing'; '27 Missing among us'; 'They buried the case of the Missing'; 'He discovered his name on the List of the Missing', etc. In a society that attributes particular potency to the printed word, such disclosures had far-reaching consequences. Among some of the revelations were the following. First, that there were forty-five graves of unknown soldiers at Lakatameia cemetery (Nicosia) in three collective tombs: for people killed on 22 July, 24 July and 15 August 1974. He claimed that in 1981 under conditions of great secrecy one of the tombs was exhumed as a result of which the identity of at least one of the dead was established, but that the name of this person is still on the list of the Missing.[1] On another tomb the name of an individual has been placed as a smaller slab over the original slab with the name still on the Missing List. He also claimed that according to the 1977 Makarios-Denktash agreement, the Greek Cypriots had to submit a complete list of names of the Missing, but never did so. (Paraskos 1995, 204: 16). As the accounts isolated a number of important cultural themes, I quote from some of them and then provide an analysis. He begins with an interview of a wife of a missing person:

> Around 6pm 16th August 1974 I telephoned my husband Kypros Kyprianidi (an employee of the Ministry of Trade) whose battalion (316TP) was stationed at Aghios Pavlos, Nicosia. The next morning I went to the district to meet him, but there was fighting and I left. When it quietened down I went to the commander of the Battalion, Dimitris Alevromayiero, and I asked him what had become of my husband. At the meeting there was also present a (Greek) Cypriot officer who told me that they did not know anything. I crossed our lines and went towards the UN soldiers whom I asked whether the Turks had taken any prisoners. They replied in the negative. I pleaded with them to ask the Turks who were very close by ahead. The Turks told them that they had not taken any prisoners during the fighting, but that there had been casualties. After several days I went again to my husband's battalion, I asked soldiers and I learnt that there were dead who were taken by men of SMEF [a body of the National Guard – PSC]. I went there and I found the soldiers who collected the dead. I asked them whether they had buried anyone who wore a pair of blue jeans and a military shirt. One said that he remembered a dead person wearing jeans. They had taken them to bury them at Lakatameia. I returned to Alevromayiero, and told him that I wanted to do an exhumation. He replied that I had to have recourse to a judge to obtain a permit. I went immediately to two judges who told me they could not issue me with the necessary exhumation permit, whilst exhorting me to go ahead without one. 'Don't worry', one told me 'if they pick you up we will be the judges of your case'.
>
> It was towards the end of September. I was decided. I couldn't live anymore with my agony. We went by night to Lakatameia cemetery with digging tools and my own people (kin), and we opened the collective tomb that was at the edge of the cemetery. With gloves and masks we descended and started looking at each one. The first person I recognised was a man who worked at ZAKO, but whose name now escapes me. Finally I also found my husband. Trembling, I searched through the pockets of his shirt and I found wrapped up in a plastic bag, his National Guard card, his passport, and 5–6 pounds. They hadn't even taken the trouble to look through their pockets! It was still evident from the way we found the bodies that they had just wrapped up the bodies in blankets and then simply thrown them into the pit. Dawn was breaking when we finished. I went shocked and indignant to Alevromayiero and I gave him my husband's National Guard card. He could not believe that I could have gone to the extent of an exhumation.
>
> However, I did so, and I know that after me others did so too. (Angeliki Kyprianidou, in *Selides* (1995, 210: 46)

Such Dantesque scenes of women scrabbling through collective tombs in search of their loved ones, an inverted version of the Orpheus-Euridice myth, raise immense problems of interpretation. Its matter of fact tone, the presentation of a sequence of events and actions as almost naturally following from each other, the economy of emotive expression as the motor compelling the woman towards a symbolic voyage to the underworld, is problematic to a western European audience expecting more details, or even more self-displayed insights by the narrator into her mental and psychological state when faced with this horrendous predicament. The narrative is unpolished, lacking in artifice, indeed almost dead-pan in spite of the telling amnesia (of the name of the other corpse she recognised – perhaps also an unwillingness to intrude on other people's private grief by identifying their missing as dead?). The absence of disclosed detail that we might expect from our own cultural perspective to authenticate both the narrative, and invest the disclosing and dangerously voyeuristic anthropological moment with aesthetic autonomy, should not be interpreted as amorality or indifference. Rather, it is a reluctance to move easily from a descriptive external account of a situation to the exposure of self through an emphasis on sentiments, which should only be expressed in certain contexts, and certainly not to an investigative journalist who has his own agenda. Yet the willingness of this woman to be quoted, not as an anonymous (or an unknown- literally, *agnosti*) source, but as a named individual, and an active witness and participant to her discovery of her grief, is critical to her constitution of herself, and part of her moral about state amorality. She individuates herself and her husband from being *agnoumeni*, passive victims of official indifference and propaganda, into persons and reclaims both her and her husband's identities: 'however, I did so, and I know that after me others did so too'.

One other was Maroulla Shamishi who, together with Androulla Palma, later broke into the tombs at Lakatameia cemetery in 1998. During the coup and the invasion she was a nurse at the General Hospital:

In all stories there are those who conceal the truth *(Se oles tes iistories iparhoun 'chini na kripsoun tin alitheia)*. During the coup, the Greek officer Alevromayiero was in charge of the hospital. It was chaos. They went around with guns. He ordered the doctors and us: 'This is a dog – don't treat him! This one is ours – treat him!' To save the lives of some individuals we gave them a nurse's uniform. They killed or beat many. They buried them alive. My husband hid at the hospital until the 16 August 1974 when he felt that as a reservist he had to go otherwise he would be sent to prison. I was out of my mind *(Dhen imoun ego o anthropos pou ekana afta ta pragmata)*. Alevromayiero sent them to their slaughter *(sfaghi)*. He knew who was killed and from what day. But he didn't want to tell. On the 16 August 1974 in the evening my husband phoned me up. I didn't hear anything after that. The last battles were on early 17th in the morning. The bodies had been 48 hours out in the sun and they were swelling, so they collected the bodies. They were collected on the 18th or 19th August.

I went to the cemetery at Lakatameia twice to try to find my husband. I took my *cugnados* (brother-in-law) with a bulldozer, six people in all, less than a month after. I see it like a film. I couldn't go there again. I took bottles of cologne, gloves, *zivania* (alcohol), and special clothes to throw them away. You could imagine what a state I was in. They had them in piles like multi-story buildings. I went to a young woman's house and she helped me because she could see that I was yellow with upset … .

The Government didn't solve our problem. I went from office to office. They told me: 'We will give you a paper that he is dead but don't you believe it. But they gave me neither a body nor a tomb. I also have a paper showing him to be an *agnoumenos*. I think he is on the list of the 126 but now I don't believe anything whatever they tell me – until they give me his body [This was a list of 126 Missing Persons that the Government withdrew from the list of 1619 individuals that it had originally said were missing – PSC]. I met with Christakis who was with my husband. He says that my husband was dead when they picked him up at the airport. He signed a deposition that my husband was dead. However sometimes I wonder whether that is really his signature … (because) I have other information that my husband was killed during the cease-fire. All those killed at Ayios Pavlos were killed during the cease-fire of 17th August … *O Theos mou kratise stin zoi.* – God kept me alive, my *timiotita*, and my strong will. For many years I kept his pyjamas, slippers, his plate on the table. To us they said it is a humanitarian issue, but it is a political issue. I could have got married … The government should have given us enough support to raise our children well. No one ever came knocking at our door. They should have built us a house, educated our children and sent us *psychologii* (therapists) … I saw so much, I lived through so much, I don't believe them whatever they say, these *poushtopezzevengies* (lit. passive homosexuals who pimp their wives). All these people are criminals. They knew these men were dead. If they were rich kids, there would be another story … (May) all the curses of the orphans (be upon them) (*ola ta katara ton orfanon*) The mask and the lie come later (*I maska ke I pseftya tha erthei meta*).

I wanted these bones to be freed. Perhaps God required this that we would go to the cemetery to do this exhumation (in 1998). Their soul won't leave. (*Dhen tha vgeni tin psychi tous*). I don't know how I will react when they come to my door with all the bones [interview with PSC].

In early 2001, the remains of Maroulla's husband were found. She received a letter from the (now retired) officer Alevromayiero, addressed to her as 'the wife of the hero Andreas Shamishi'. The letter was full of praise for her husband who had 'given his life for freedom'. She was outraged by his quote from Plato (*sic.*): *phila tin patrida kai adikos i* (Love your country, even if it has done you an injustice).

Maroulla's testimony is confirmed by other sources (Drousiotis, 2000). Apart from the desperate urgency, her account is significant for its vocabulary of protest. For many years relatives viewed themselves, and were encouraged to do so by the Government, as ethnic victims requiring some material recognition by the state. Maroulla's account suggests material entitlement. This is consistent with the humble backgrounds of many of the relatives of the missing. Death through war harvests social classes differently. With an increasing awareness of Government blanket exploitation of the issue, which lumped together those disappeared behind Turkish lines and those whose bodies were buried hurriedly during hostilities, people like Maroulla and Androulla Palma (below) became angry. But the anger primarily against the government is as much for having exploited the issue, and having done so, for not having given enough material recognition to their suffering. By the time this interview was recorded (2000), a different vocabulary was creeping in, partly influenced by Cyprus's 'modernisation'. This was that of 'patient entitlement'. Maroulla's account begins to suggest that the state failed to recognise their entitlement as medicalised victims: 'they should have sent us *psycholoyii*' (lit. psychologists, although she means therapists). As Kleinman, Das, and Lock note 'Cultural responses to traumatic effects of political violence often transform the local idioms of victims into professional languages of complaint and restitution – and thereby remake both representations and experiences of suffering' (1997: x). This tension in the response to the sufferers' perception of their traumas has been far from resolved.

In most accounts it is the mainland Greek officers who sacrifice Greek Cypriot lives, send them to battle, harvest the collection of the dead and bury them in unmarked graves. Here is an interview by Paraskos with a man who witnessed the chaos at hospital in 1974:

'During the days of the invasion an officer telephoned me from Nicosia General Hospital and asked me to go there to collect some dead for burial' Christos Iliofotou said. 'I went to the hospital, I asked for the person responsible, and a Greek captain appeared. He guided me to the mortuary and he showed me a number of dead. I estimated they would have been in the region of forty-five to fifty persons. He told me to take them away for burial. I said that I would take them once I was given details of the dead. He then started swearing at me and said that was not my job. I replied that I knew my job very well, and that during the second world war I had served as a Major in the British Army, and that I had buried many, but none without particulars. I told him when I was leaving that I would return the following day with a photographer of the Press and Information office, and transport to carry the bodies. When I returned to the mortuary the next day they informed me that the dead had been buried by the army.'

Paraskos notes: 'We further investigated this testimony of Christou Iliofotou and learnt from the hospital personnel that the dead, according to what they had heard during those days, were buried at Lakatameia. At Lakatameia they buried twenty-one "unknown dead" who were killed on the 22, 23, and 24 July 1974, and forty-four who were killed on the 15, 16, and 17 August, 1974 [The days of the first and second invasion – PSC]. The other thing we tried to find out was the name of the Captain who was the "officer responsible" for the running of the hospital by fire and steel [i.e. ruthlessly – PSC] during those days. [Loizos (1981: 75) also gives a transcription of an interview that confirms this account -PSC]. The witnesses were many and not difficult to find. Persons dressed in the white garments of a doctor or of a nurse faced during those days a gigantic task, having however at the same time at their temples the pistol of Lieutenant Danos. The witnesses of the happenings and of the days of the Juntist captain confirm that there lies a great part of the responsibility for the "unknown dead". As, indeed, it was otherwise revealed to us, a member of the "custodians" of Lieutenant Danos was the present General Secretary of the Pancyprian Committee of Missing Persons, Nikos Serghides. Nursing staff indeed also remember that General Efthimios Karayiannis, soon after he took command of the GHQ of the National Guard during those days, went to the hospital and in the presence of the hospital personnel "stripped off" the stripes of Danos and his custodians saying: "I apologise. I ask for your pardon. Petty actions from petty men." We were also informed that there are indisputable testimonies about what transpired in the hospital in the hands of the Cyprus Intelligence Bureau (KYP). (Paraskos 1995: *Selides* 207: 46–47)

Hospitals descend treacherously from enveloping sanctuaries to menacing endangerment. There is a hint of this in the account: 'persons dressed in the white garments of a doctor or of a nurse'. Why 'dressed' rather a simple statement about doctors, nurses, etc? The article introduces an element of creeping uncertainty. But whereas Greek Cypriot fears condensed around the armed mainland Turkish soldier, Turkish Cypriots expressed by far the greatest apprehension regarding hospitals. There are (Greek Cypriot) stories of plots to massacre Turkish Cypriot patients in the Nicosia General hospital in 1964, and of Makarios' attempt to save them when he learnt of it, by rushing there and ordering them out of the hospital. There are also reports of the killing of Turkish patients in hospital.[2]

Similar stories appeared in 1974 during the invasion. The hospital figures both as a lens through which fears of genocide are viewed, and as a screen on to which they are projected: a death factory which moves from being a secular counterpart of sacral space for the recuperation /recovery of the body within society through the process of healing, to becoming a treacherous travesty of the ultimate sanctuary of liminal space and vulnerable selfhood. The white coat of the doctor/nurse is transfigured as the last concealment of uniform and the pursuit of genocidal plans through the murderous application of surgical implements. Images of butchery and medicine fuse in mid-1970s Cyprus. EOKA B gunmen are referred to as 'butchers' by other Greek Cypriots (Sant Cassia, 1999), and a short-lived new terrorist group called Eoka-Gamma in 1977 was led by an individual known as *O Iatros*- the Doctor.

In situations of complete lack of trust, where individuals identify both themselves as victims and others as their oppressors in taxonomic terms, an alterity of the monstrous double has to be construed. This alterity comes close to the voluntary projection of oneself onto the other, presented as the appropriation of the closest symbols of identity. Uniform and language are two such Durkheimian symbols of solidarity, which paradoxically re-enforce the threatened self through their appropriation by otherness. Radio Bayrak carried a report in English on 2 August 1974, claiming that National Guard soldiers were wearing Turkish Cypriot fighters uniforms and carried Turkish flags in order to infiltrate Turkish villages (ME/6669/C/7). Inversely, Greek Cypriot villagers in the Paphos village of Pano Arodhes claim that Turkish Cypriot fighters went round their villages in the night speaking Greek to terrify their co-villagers.[3]

Fears emerge out of real experiences of what is potentially imaginable. Peter Loizos has suggested to me (personal communication) that collective fears are characteristic of 'worst case' scenarios about how the enemy might behave in the future if they were to repeat the excesses of their ancestors. Stories about events express very real fears and experiences that are culturally specific and not interchangeable from one community to the other, although they might be mirror images of each other. It is unimaginable that Greek Cypriots could go around a Turkish Cypriot village in the night speaking Turkish because few Greek Cypriots spoke it well. But it is possible that Turkish Cypriots could have known enough Greek to speak it to simulate a threat. Such scenarios therefore are culturally imaginable even if perhaps improbable. It would also have been highly risky for Greek Cypriots to expose themselves in a heavily armed Turkish village, especially in the night. It could therefore seem authentically imaginable for the Greek Cypriot villagers that such a scenario could have occurred, because it corresponds with certain cultural resonances and community experiences, and it fits-in with Turkish Cypriot fears that they were a surrounded minority. Greek Cypriot claims authenticate such fears but simultaneously suggest they were also managed by Turkish Cypriot authorities. Turkish Cypriots give a counter-story: Greek soldiers born in Istanbul, speaking perfect Turkish, drew out Turkish Cypriot civilians in hiding during the night and killed them silently with stones crushing their heads in order not to give their positions away. In both cases each group projects a monstrous double.

The fear of hospitals as inverted sanctuaries is not so much a Greek Cypriot fear, but a Turkish Cypriot one. It corresponds with, and expresses, deep apprehensions about exposure, about being separated from the security of the group, and it expresses a distrust of even the most transparently humanitarian organs of the state. It is in effect saying that there is no security for the individual Turkish Cypriot outside the group in the Greek Cypriot-controlled territorial state. Likewise, Greek Cypriot apprehensions of missing persons kept alive in the depths of Turkish Asia are culturally-specific fears embedded in nationalist history that the 'Turkish soldier', a 'nomad' from the 'depths of Asia', is an 'Attila', not bound by normal cannons of 'civilised' behaviour. But it is also paradoxically about the perverse 'complementarity' of Greek and Turk.[4] As anthropologists we may sometimes have to imagine what we are professionally trained to conceive of as unimaginable: that such stories may be 'true'.

The period between the coup and the end of the invasion was particularly tumultuous and chaotic. Reports of massacres of Turkish Cypriots began coming in soon after the Turks began the second phase of their invasion, although there are reports of attacks on Turkish Cypriot villages beginning after the initial invasion. This occurred in the village of Tochni and others when the Turkish Cypriot villagers were taken away in buses and disappeared. The period between the coup and the invasion does not seem to have been marked by Greek Cypriot attacks on Turkish Cypriots, and Denktash said in radio broadcasts said this was an 'internal Greek Cypriot affair', not to provoke a Greek backlash whilst at the same time suggesting that assistance from Turkey was forthcoming. The fighting involved pro-Makarios forces (including the various *omadhes* such as the Lyssarides' groups) and the National Guard-Eoka B alliance, and lasted a number of days. During this period there was little information on casualties, and various figures were quoted for propaganda purposes.[5] The (Greek) Defence Ministry, clearly interested in minimising losses during the coup, gave impossibly low figures.[6] The chain of command within the National Guard was broken and fluctuating, and there were no parallel civil bodies to monitor events. Movement was restricted and dangerous, martial law and curfews were imposed. It was therefore difficult for individuals to discover the fate of kin, especially if one had a conscripted son in another town, or even to learn what was happening generally. When confronted by inquiring relatives, officers brushed them off. The woman's account above indicates that she obtained more truthful replies from the Turks than the Mainland Greeks. The army prevented people from entering the cemeteries when they brought truckloads of casualties because they feared that that the rage of parents, consequent upon discovering their dead sons, could be directed towards them as the begetters of their personal and national disaster.

In such contexts rumour thrived. Many informants told me of going from one military camp to another to obtain information on kin and employees. The frantic movement of civilians as vulnerable individuals (not as citizens with rights) in besieged and shelled public spaces searching desperately for scraps of information contrasts sharply with the fixed, sealed, and closely guarded military occupations of space, from where little information emerges, and from where bodies are transported out, concealed under tarpaulins in trucks for secret burials.[7] There are reports of sixty-two casualties on the first day of the coup, which were loaded on to military vehicles on 16 July 1974 and taken to the Cemetery of Ayii Constantinos and Eleni at Nicosia.[8]

The state attempted to fabricate a simulation of normality in a state of emergency. The military State was not just involved in a struggle with opponents, initially supporters of Makarios, and later the invading Turks. This was 'merely' a matter of dis/information or propaganda. It was also (interrelatedly) involved in a covert struggle with its own citizens in concealing information that camouflaged its agency and redirected attention elsewhere. The state resorted to proclaiming signs of normality, routinization, and predictability: 'shops are now open', 'flights are leaving normally', 'Telegrammes can now be sent (but only up to a certain word limit)', etc., whereas the content of such messages subverted the veracity of those claims, highlighting the very abnormality of the insistence on normality, and prepared the social ground for the sowing of the dragons' teeth of rumour. At the same time both the military and the post-military state issued warnings that the trading of rumours and false information was a punishable offence, further hastening the widespread scepticism of official accounts and official indifference (see Herzfeld, 1992). As Feldman has observed:

> A public culture of rumors reveals the extent to which the sense of control over reality is finite, and the extent to which control has to be reasserted through exaggeration and imaginative supplementation ... By turning apparently once-stable social structure into provisional and contingent narrative, rumor becomes the production of a counter-society. The social production of rumor is the social production of collective experience in the absence of wide-scale social credibility. Rumor emerges from, and accelerates, the collapse of official organs of institutional depiction, memory, and information dissemination. (1995: 231)

Some women confided that they kept secret notes of information they picked up regarding the events of 1974. One woman confided that she would fear for her life if this information should reach the light of day. From what she showed and disclosed to me, I did not get the impression that her information was more incriminating than what is available to any investigative journalist, but one has to keep in mind that many of these women, coming as they do from humble backgrounds, feel very insecure about they think they are *permitted to know.* Nevertheless it would be foolhardy and arrogant to dismiss such fears. They indicate that the grassroots understands very well Canetti's (1973) suggestion that secrecy lies at the very core of power. Except that by disclosing that she possessed threatening secret information garnered from the public domain, and preventing herself from disclosing it because of fear, she re-enforced not so much the power of the secret but the *secret of power*, which is that we interiorise and apply self-censure, and thus service the religious nature of power.

Rumour in Cyprus was not just what was said, an attribution to an indefinite third person plural, during the coup and the invasion, although it certainly thrived then. It is an ever-present reality when there are gaps in official credibility. Here, a distinction between rumour and gossip is useful. Rumour is disembodied, circulating with no identifiable individual authorship, yet allowing individuals to participate in the production of a social reality that conflicts with official depictions of reality. And whilst it is quite distinct from gossip, in that gossip consists of whispered, confided, progressively disclosed secrets about individuals that most feel they should know, and which punctures the official presentation of the self, gossip can evolve into rumour. It does so when the content has wider social ramifications. An example is the case of the woman who claimed to have exhumed her husband: 'however, I did so, and I know that after me others did so too'. By being incorporated so emblematically in the public domain, by moving from a whispered object of gossiped disclosure to an active self-identifying subject and actor, and by claiming that others did so too, she becomes an active agent in the questioning of official depictions.

The articles by Paraskos helped crystallise public debate about the missing, and highlighted gaps between the official presentation (i.e. the Republic of Cyprus' official position, and the PanCyprian Committee for the Relatives of the Missing), and people's experiences. It also helped force a split between the Government and the PanCyprian Committee for the Relatives of the Missing (CRMP). I begin with the first consequence – the gaps between official presentations and people's experiences. For a long time the various governments of the Republic of Cyprus had permitted the CRMP to dominate public discourse on the missing both locally and in international fora. But it was a simulacrum of certainty.[9] For example, for a long time every Greek Cypriot believed that there were precisely 1,619 missing persons: no more, no less. Numbering losses suggests certainty and a proper accounting. Specificity conjures facticity. It then transpired that the number was far from certain, but had been adopted by the Government on the advice of the CRMP. The complete list had not been submitted to the UN sponsored CMP, and had therefore never been officially claimed. Nor had it been revised, although new information had come to light.

There may have been genuinely humanitarian reasons for this lack of information to the relatives: officials did not wish to further traumatise them, witnesses did not come forward to confirm deaths because of shame or guilt, nor relish becoming messengers of death. July and August 1974 were chaotic months, and individuals who would not normally have known each other were brought together in a chaotic and unrepeatable series of fleeting interactions with little possibility of follow-up, or even subsequent meetings. War or mass violence brings people together like a random encounter of billiard balls. Let us recall Poussin's picture, *The Rape of the Sabines*. During exhumations in 1999–2000, the bones of a 16 year-old boy, Zinon Zinonos, were identified. He had been shot on the Nicosia front line on 21 July 1974 and taken to Nicosia General Hospital where he died. The hospital was already in a chaotic state. No records were kept. The *Cyprus Mail* noted ironically:

> Yet as soon as news broke about the identification of his remains, all sorts of people remembered him and appeared on TV news shows to give their personal account of his story. There were two National Guardsmen who had been with the teenager when he was shot; one had even told him to take cover minutes earlier. Then there was the commander of the battalion who appeared on several stations to say how he had ordered Zinonos to go home but had been ignored. Finally, there was the doctor who had carried the injured boy away from the front line and handed him over to an ambulance crew; he was later told that the teenager was dead.
>
> None of these people apparently thought it necessary to take the trouble to inform the authorities that Zinonos should not have been listed as missing. The doctor said that he had seen the name on the missing list but thought it referred to someone else, as the list said he had been arrested by the Turks. So for twenty-five years Zinonos' family thought he was missing, because the bureaucracy created specifically to handle the

issue was too busy shuffling papers to actually investigate each case properly. How many more such cases will surface with DNA testing now under way?

In addition, there were a number of serious institutional lacunae. First, the Government Service for Humanitarian Affairs relied too heavily on the CRMP for its information, which was unreliable. The CRMP was, and is, dominated by individuals who had political ambitions. Even today, aspiring politicians from small parties attempt to court relatives of the Missing; they represent a small but useful electoral segment. The CRMP has increasingly lost credibility with both the Government Service for Humanitarian Affairs and a considerable number of relatives. Second, although it appeared that there were witness testimonies from 1975 indicating some individuals were dead, the Government apparently did nothing about them. This was the case with the two women, Androulla Palma and Maroulla Shamishi who had broken into the graves at Lakatameia cemetery, and briefly discussed in the first chapter. Finally, individuals may have felt reluctant to come forward because it would have seemed to be questioning official reality. From the perspective of the relatives, the 'evidence' of death available, accounts by strangers rather than 'demonstrable evidence' (*apodihtika stiheia*, related to *apodikseis*: a receipt, an exchange item, a proof, a confirmation of an exchange) are, like all language, potentially suspect as *psemata* – lies designed to damage, to hurt and to gnaw away at certainty. Weber's secular theodicy of suffering is useful here: the fortunate are seldom satisfied with being fortunate. They want to know that they have a right to their good fortune, except in the very act of bearing witness to a death even in an exchange of fire, or a bombing, one inevitably authors oneself to the recipient of the bad news as the deserving fortunate, and the victim as the deserving unfortunate (*atychos*): a guilt inducing exercise. For many relatives such evidence came close to rumour (*fimes*), a social production of reality inimical to, and resisted by the modern bureaucratic state, the very opposite of the legalistic evidence demanded by the relatives, and which is embedded in (and derives from) statist jurisprudential categories. Thus for many years many relatives refused to accept that their missing are dead, asking why, if that is the case, they had not been told so before. When the Government began seriously re-examining its files in the mid 1990s and identified some one hundred and twenty-six individuals for whom there was some evidence that they had died /been killed, this was resisted strongly by the CRMP. On the instigation of Father Christoforos, the Chairman of the Committee, the relatives refused to accept anything except the 'scientific' proof of death. He threatened that if these names were removed from the List of Missing Persons, he would bring out the mothers to demonstrate. The Government backed down, fearful of appearing to want to close the issue. Relatives paradoxically reinforced statist categories of certainty used by the Republic of Cyprus in its campaign to get Turkey to account for the missing. They insisted that if the government now believed the missing are dead, then it must offer them 'tangible evidence' (*apodikhtika stiheia*): bones, exhumations, confessions, sworn statements, ratified by the state, almost as receipts (*apodikseis*) affirming that if these individuals are dead, they did not die in vain and there will be justice for them in the end. Relatives thus turn the very language of emotions and humanitarian rights employed by the Republic of Cyprus in its international campaign against Turkey's occupation, against the certainties of the state itself. Relatives of the missing are therefore not just victims of the state and its propaganda, but paradoxically accomplices with the state in their insistence on certain type of evidence, whilst at the same time engaged in contesting official (un) certainties.

Exhumations

On 31 July 1997, the leaders of the two communities, Clerides and Denktash, met and agreed that (i) they considered the problem of missing persons as a 'purely humanitarian issue the solution of which is long overdue', (ii) 'no political exploitation should be made of the problem', (iii) 'as a first step … to provide each other immediately and simultaneously all information already at their disposal on the location of graves of Greek Cypriot and Turkish Cypriot missing persons'. For a brief period it appeared that the issue was on the way to resolution. The Greek side was optimistic, and the press speculated that investigations would be extended to Turkey, but the UN warned against such speculation. Some nationalist Turkish Cypriot political commentators said this was likely to increase hatred and mistrust between the two peoples, and to fan feelings of revenge. It also subverted the official Turkish Cypriot line that the majority of the Greek Cypriot missing were victims of the coup or were missing in action. Possibly aware of this resistance, Denktash had been careful not to place this agreement within the remit of the UN sponsored CMP, but rather maintain it as a bilateral agreement. On 30 April 1998 the Turkish Cypriot CMP representative stated that he was 'not prepared to discuss the necessary arrangements leading to the exhumation and return of the remains of the Greek Cypriot and Turkish Cypriot missing persons until the Greek Cypriot side, as proof of its sincerity, agree to first look into the fate of the Greek Cypriot victims of the coup d'etat against Archbishop Makarios in 1974. 'This position', noted the Secretary General, 'deviates from the 31 July 1997 agreement … As a result of the position taken by the Turkish Cypriot side, no progress has been made towards the implementation of the 31 July 1997 agreement. The Greek Cypriot side has since decided to begin exhumation and identification of the remains located in graves in the area under its control'. A few months later the two Greek Cypriot women, Androulla Palma and Maroulla Shamishi, referred to at the beginning of this book made a daring attempt to exhume their husbands at Lakatameia cemetery.

In 1999, the Republic of Cyprus decided to proceed with exhumations at two cemeteries. This decision may not have been totally due to Androulla and

Maroulla's actions, but they certainly contributed. A group of courageous young officials in the Ministry of Foreign Affairs and the Greek Cypriot participants to the CMP had also patiently tried to convince the Foreign Minister and various other highly-placed politicians and officials that exhumations and proper identifications of the collective burials would remove any ambiguity about those individuals whose fates were particularly unclear. The exhumations were not officially presented as related to the Clerides-Denktash agreement, but it was popularly interpreted as a unilateral implementation of that agreement, the implication being that it placed an implicit reciprocal obligation on the Turkish Cypriots. There was no reciprocal action by the Turkish Cypriots, partly because this would have probably implicated the Turkish Army.

Greek Cypriot authorities envisaged the exhumations proceeding in three semi- coordinated or *pari-passu* stages. First, the exhumations were planned of those whose fates were particularly unclear and whose names had not been presented to the CMP. There were some 126 individuals out of the total 1,619 missing whose relatives had not been informed due to Father Christoforos' threats. This was meant to absolve the Government for having made political use of the issue, and to strengthen the claim that the rest of the disappearances were genuine and had occurred behind Turkish lines. Second, the Greek Cypriot authorities hoped to provoke or shame the Turkish Cypriots into beginning their own exhumations of their own missing. Finally, and concurrently, they hoped to begin a similar process on the Greek part into exhumations of missing Turkish Cypriots, and thus encourage the Turkish Cypriot authorities into a reciprocal gesture. A bi-communal institution, the Institute of Neurology and Genetics, had been established in 1991 which could provide the necessary scientific backup.[10] DNA testing commenced in 1995 and soon after the collection of blood samples from relatives. The Turkish Cypriot leadership refused to allow Turkish Cypriot relatives to donate samples. Initially, it was not easy for the Greek Cypriots to obtain the samples, as this clearly implied that the authorities considered such individuals to be dead. In a climate where rumours were still being given currency about sightings, [11] this implied that the Government had abandoned any hope of finding such men alive. The most notorious disclosure had been made by Father Christoforos that fourteen people, listed as missing since 1974, were alive and well and living in a third country but could not leave because they were in fear of their lives! Such rumours muddied the waters. To circumvent the resistance of the older relatives (such as parents) who clearly found it particularly difficult to accept the death of their children, and where their donation of blood samples implicated them in the personal recognition and participation in the declaration of their children's 'official' death, the Institute adopted a personal approach. They patiently targeted the youngest and most educated members of the families to convince the closest relatives, the parents, to donate blood samples. According to the Director, this approach paid off. Slowly, the families moved from hearsay (oscillating hope and despair) expressed in the unspoken and unacceptable, to a desire for positive confirmation and closure. He claimed that the relatives pushed Government for exhumations and DNA testing. He added: 'The bones belong to the relatives so we have responsibilities to provide them with correct information. They are asking: don't just tell us that our relatives are dead. Go through a scientific process to prove they are dead'. By August 1997 some 2,000 relatives of 1,380 missing persons had given samples. Some twenty families refused, saying: 'Our relative is alive; we know he is held by the Turks. We shouted our greetings across the Green Line. So leave us alone'.

At the time of writing (2002), the second and third stages of the process had not materialised. The Turkish Cypriots have resolutely refused to conduct any exhumations of Greek Cypriots, or provide blood samples from their own people. They argue that the exhumations have nothing to do with them, and that since the establishment of the CMP in 1981 they had been asking the Greek Cypriots for a full list of the coup casualties and where they are buried, and had not received this information.[12] Over the past year there have been sporadic (and unpublicised) discoveries of Turkish Cypriot remains in the south. Greek Cypriot authorities have stated that they are willing to proceed with identifications of Turkish Cypriot remains, but they cannot do so unless they have permission from the relatives and DNA samples to identify the remains, both of which have not been permitted by the Turkish Cypriot authorities. The bones thus await ownership. This places both leaderships under embarrassment: the Turkish Cypriot leadership because they are preventing their own people from being united with their dead, and the Greek Cypriots for sticking to legalistic criteria.

It is worthwhile to return to our play. On one side (Greek Cyprus), Creon has finally relented and is now passing on the bones to Antigone to bury. On the other side (Turkish Cyprus), Creon refuses to give the body of the hero, Eteocles, to the relatives. The bodies are not of those who *betrayed* the polity, but those who according to the authorities *protected* and fought for it as heroes, and are officially designated *shehitler* (martyrs).

I now take the case of Androulla Palma who together with Maroulla Shamishi attempted to get into the tombs at Lakatameia:

Androulla lives alone in her dowry home in Peristerona. Opposite is a house she built for her daughter Popi, who lives in a restored house in old Nicosia. An open plot belongs to her second daughter Christina. Behind her lives her brother Kyriakos. Her living room is a shrine to her husband and to her efforts to discover his fate. All the photos on her wall show her demonstrating. These are photographs of active kinship. Androulla has commissioned a painting of herself holding her two young daughters one of whom is clutching a small photograph of their disappeared father (Figure 29). It adorns her *saloni*. It is based on a photograph taken from life. I realise this is equally a family representation, of an absence, an attempt to have an idealised united family in a painting which could never be captured by a photograph. People commemorate absences and turn them into presences. Like the shoes, the shirts, that would never be filled by a

Figure 29 'Androulla and her daughters'.

Figure 30 Newspaper cutting dealing with the attempted exhumations by Androulla Palma and Maroulla Shamishi (*I Aletheia*, 18 August 1998).

warm body, or the place left empty at supper (Figure 26). Although these are family photographs, they are ideal representations just the same: of being together. They indicate that her husband, Hambis, is not forgotten, that she is holding up her children to commemorate him. In that respect she is acting out an idealised gender role. It is almost as if we need a *representation* of patriarchy, rather than its enactment, in order to create a space and a role for her to fulfil. I get the impression that this is as much like the role of a daughter who has to bury her father as a wife to discover her husband's body. Indeed as I hope to show during the process of exhumations and burial something more was involved than the attempts by a wife/widow to find her dead husband and lay him to rest. It was a reassertion of obligation, and the obligation of reassertion. Here is her story:

'My husband Haralambos Palma from Livadhia (Larnaca) was captured together with Andrea Palma his cousin from Lefka. Six years ago I read the papers, and I learnt how my husband had been captured. Until then I didn't know anything, nor did they tell me anything'. Until then she still believed that her husband was missing. For example there had been a memorial service for his battalion in 1975 and as her husband's name was not on the list for the memorial service she assumed that he was considered missing. Suddenly all the situation became clear. Newspapers say that they were captured, but not what happened afterwards. According to the reports published in the papers in 1975 (which she did not read then), that then led her to the witnesses mentioned there, who were with her husband at Ayios Pavlou of the outskirts of Nicosia on 16 August 1974. 'They resisted capture for a whole day, being stuck in a Guard Post (*Philakeion*), but then they were surrounded and gave themselves up at 5pm approximately. After capture, Turkish soldiers forced them to go down on their knees and hit them. Two and a half-hours scourging (*vasana*)', she said referring to the witness statements, 'and then, it appears, they killed them. But nobody heard the shots apparently'. According to the newspaper report: 'From that time nobody saw them back at their homes and they are among the 2500 *agnoumeni*' (22 June 1975). Androulla and other women apparently did not read these reports in the newspapers, and were not given access to their files (to which I did not have access). 'The Government said that the witnesses appeared 6 years ago, but they had given their statements way back in 1975', she said. Although this is correct, the account published in the papers was available to both Androulla and the Government, who did not apparently do much with them. Androulla's then husband appeared on the list of 126 people whom the government did not present to the UN committee charged with investigating the disappearances, a clear indication that the Government considered there was sufficient proof he was dead.

'The newspaper didn't give the witnesses' names. When I asked the Government they refused to give me their names but I insisted and I took a lawyer relative and they gave us my husband's file to read. I was crying a lot and I couldn't bear to read it. Andreas said there was no hope. I then traced the witness to Greece with difficulty. I went with Popi, my daughter. The witness refused me to tape him but Popi knew shorthand. We started working with the article. The first statement I had was that the Turks took my husband alive. But later in Greece he told me that he had seen my husband dead. Why didn't the Government then go and find the witnesses if I could do so myself?'

'According to my witnesses my husband was lost on 17 August 1974 during the second invasion'. Here she used the word for lost- *hathike*- (not killed, *skothithike*-or *to eskothosan*- was killed, or *pethane*, died). ' Six bodies were loaded onto a truck. My husband was wearing military uniform. Dentktash said that my husband died in the coup. This is not true and I want you to write this down'. This was a recurrent feature of fieldwork: the anthropologist is seen as a scribe to carry messages. 'Witnesses saw my husband being beaten by the Turks. It is also on the Internet' [the Internet has the same role of photography as confirming and validating a story]. Androulla then obtained photographs from her husband's companions showing him in army fatigues. The photographs show a group of young men holding guns, in postures half way between a soldier and a hunter. They have longer than army-regulation hair, and were it not for the weapons, one would think they were hunters out on an expedition; farmers also wear army fatigues when working. Yet whilst the immediacy of the discoloured 1970s photograph renders the scene almost an intimate one, perhaps the purpose of the photograph was precisely to document not just an intimate group of young men in an unfolding historical situation, but also as a protection following capture. For the photographs demonstrate that they formed part of an army, and therefore required treatment according to the Geneva Convention. Ironically, many men who changed into civilian clothing when facing capture appear to have been treated much more badly by the invading Turkish army.

July 1999

When I visited her in July 1999, exhumations had just begun. The Government had commissioned the renowned team *Physicians For Peace* led by the well-known forensic anthropologist Bill Hagland. Androulla attributed this move to her previous actions, and although Government officials had started their efforts much earlier, nevertheless her actions had precipitated the sense of urgency. She wrote to the Foreign Minister and the Attorney General telling them that she wanted her own pathologist present. She was suspicious of the government:

'For 24 years we didn't know anything, so we lost all confidence. I said to Christopoulos (the Commissioner for Humanitarian Affairs) yesterday: I wouldn't have objected had they given me the bones. But as they didn't, I am afraid that they will trick us (*mas koreiidevoun*). And I don't know why. Christopoulos assured me that things are proceeding well. For the last sixteen years I haven't felt well and because I went everyday to ask about my husband, I couldn't enjoy my children or my grandchildren (*dhen mporousa na zo ta pedyia che t'angonia mou*). The Committee has been tricking us. What is at issue is *to synferon* (interest)'. She explicitly linked the Missing Persons issue to the Cyprus Problem. In contrast to what UN and some sympathetic Greek Cypriot officials say informally, that the relatives are unaware of their exploitation, she had a definite awareness and resentment of this: ' I told the authorities to take me to court (for having broken into the cemetery)', she said defiantly, although she was clearly worried that they might do so. And she continued with some desperate bravado: 'the next time I said, I will go with my husband's kin- they are over 400. I said I would return and raise all the bones'.

Androulla was disturbed and in a highly suspicious mood. 'As soon as they started digging I went with Maroulla and Popi and threw yellow flowers on the graves. They didn't allow me to do so'. She was bitter and angry that soldiers had stopped her. As with most of her interactions with Government, the cemetery became a place of contestation, with Androulla attempting to personalise and symbolise her grief. She said that yellow signified that one becomes pale through grief and pining (*Kitrinizies ap tin marazi*), because it stands for hope, and because it stands for waiting and delay. She added: And the dead person who is pale (i.e. yellow) from having waited for so long (*Che o necros pu ine chlomos che perimeni tosa*).

> 'Yesterday I couldn't sleep. I had to take a pill to sleep. I was feeling very bad yesterday. My daughters feel very bad too. They didn't know their father- now they see his bones'. At another point she prided herself at having brought up her children well and made them courageous and that 'they could accept seeing their father like that'. 'I have been waiting for 25 years. I wanted to know whether he was alive or not. In 25 years I have aged (*yerasa*). Now I am old. I've lost my life'. She then referred to the Turkish Cypriot mothers: ' I also say the *Tourkalles* are also mothers. I also feel their pain. I feel it. They also need to know. And if that means that our people have to do something ... I want *pliri diafania*- full transparency. Both sides are responsible. The Turks for killing them; our people for not telling us and hiding the facts from us. Before you had some hope. Now you lost it all. I will bring him here to Peristerona, to bury him. I think they will find him'. She is extremely suspicious of the authorities: 'I do what I feel. I always want to find out the truth. Let this problem be resolved. So many years. A heavy damage has fallen on us *(Na liksi afto to prama yia mena. Tosa chronia. Megali zimyia ehi girisi mas")* I told my doctor to give me a pill every day to be able to do this. He was number 124 on the list. I never saw him dead and I knew him as a whole person. We are the victims of the war ...'

She claimed government officials called at the houses neighbouring the cemetery telling the residents not to say anything about how the bodies were buried. She got this information from a woman residing there. She is the only woman waiting at the cemetery. Although, or because of, the Government's announcement that nobody should come, Androulla is the only person there. Together with her friend Maroulla she decided to appoint her own pathologist. The pathologist, a well-known nationalist politician with a penchant for dramatic actions, only appears briefly, and Androulla and her family face the exhumations alone turning up day after day in the hot sun, taking water to the team of foreign archaeologists: 'I felt sorry for them working in the hot sun'.

Why is Androulla the only relative of the missing present? The authorities could not exclude her. She had already embarrassed the authorities through her desperate attempts to open the graves. She had asked me to accompany her to Lakatameia Police Station to retrieve her pickaxe. Perhaps she felt that if she had a foreigner who looked Greek but spoke like an expatriate Cypriot, then she would not be harassed. She need not have worried. Androulla can stand up to people in authority. In fact they may need her, almost as character in some drama – to clarify and to bring into the open something which was embarrassing. I discuss this in the concluding chapter. Through radio announcements, the authorities discouraged relatives from attending the exhumations. The Press also did not appear. This is Creon's dilemma. How can the authorities make amends and yet retain some measure of legitimacy among the people they claim to represent?

Androulla is unsure as to the purpose of the exhumations. In her handbag she always carries a lock of hair taken from her mother-in-law before she died, to assist with genetic identification. She believes that the aim is not just to identify bones but also how people died. As I discover later, the latter is not the stated aim of the authorities. She says that if she finds out that her husband was killed in cold blood she will take Turkey to the European Court of Human Rights. At a dinner party that evening, amid songs on an exquisitely-made bouzouki, I chat with a Greek Cypriot diplomat. I decide to fish (*Na psarevo*). I say: Are you aware that some women are saying that if they discover their husbands were killed in cold blood they will go to court? *Sotto voce* he replies: *prepi na proseksoume*. We need to be careful. The world of diplomats is far removed from that of ordinary people in whose name they claim to be doing things. The authorities do not want further complications in the road to a settlement that has eluded them for a quarter of a century and left Nicosia the only divided capital of Europe. They would prefer to close the issue.[13]

When I turn up at Lakatameia cemetery, Androulla is there with her husband's sister who was the most visibly disturbed. She cried at the cemetery: 'To think that his mother came here and didn't know that her son was buried here'. She is wearing black, in contrast to Androulla who has long passed this stage. Her daughter Popi, a bright, recently married young woman, who never knew her father, is also present, as well as Christina her other daughter with her two children, and her parents-in-law who busied themselves with their joint grandchildren.

Androulla and her group spend a few days clinging on to the edge of the cemetery whilst the exhumations proceed. Maps, photographs, levels are taken. National Guardsmen sift soil. The scene resembles an archaeological dig. On one of the last days, an American archaeologist walks over and says that she is about to start the digging. Popi starts talking fluently in English and has a file on her father. She reels off details: his operations, that his dental records were not retained, his shoe size, and his height. Her father's tangibility and existence is there in the file, a proof he existed, that he is not an *agnoumenos*, a person of unknown fate, a disappeared. He is more real to her than many fathers would be to their children through their memory. When Popi and her sister married they each took items of their father's clothing to their new homes. These are *momento mori*, except that they are held to prove that he existed, was alive, and that he should be reclaimed, given an identity, and buried properly with a name, not in some collective anonymous grave. To every detail the archaeologist replies 'OK'. But how could the archaeologist tell Androulla this skeleton is her husband? Surely the whole point is to identify the bones through DNA testing? Androulla and her daughter seem convinced that body is her husband's. They walk up to the pit overlooking the collective grave, and return.

Popi says that no dental records have been kept from the General Hospital. The archaeologist again says OK. Popi shows her a photograph of her Father. Precise information seems to be being offered. The switch to English, and the exclusion of Androulla from the conversation orients the interchange to two younger women who belong to a different, wider, world. The information about the specificities of her father conveyed in English, associated as it is with the higher bureaucracy and the interface between the foreign (*xenos*) world and the local, contrasts with the intimacy of Greek that would normally be used. Androulla's doctor was absent on this and on the previous occasion. He has a political career to cultivate.

Over those few days, Androulla moved from pent-up anticipations of certainty generated through high expectations in the revelatory power of 'scientific' investigation (the term *epistemoniki* , scientific, has a certain legitimacy in Greek which is absent in English), and a suspicious stance towards the authorities' version of the past, to one where her immediate, unarticulated, taken-for-granted world was slowly dissolving. This nudged her towards coming to terms with the fact that her husband was dead. She began moving away from her epistemological certainties of disbelief in official versions of reality to grasping more existential realisations. She reached this in two ways. First, as I show below, there were certain slips, differences in language use between her and others, that slowly implanted the realisation that she had to adopt a different way of imagining and talking about her husband. This included learning about, and accepting, other accounts, other memories of what happened. Until then, her husband held an existential validity and tangibility for her as an *agnoumenos* which specifically excluded her from navigating through his last hours and thus giving shape to his death. There was no aftermath; there was just a closed door, which she could not enter. Indeed, by maintaining him as an *agnoumenos*, which was as much a decision on her part as his inclusion on that list by the authorities, she excluded herself from knowledge.

Her often stated desire for 'full transparency' *(pliri diafania)* kept her in a domain of unknowing for it did not address her husband's last days. That clarity would be ushered in through the senses. In effect, by going over and listening to other witness accounts of the collective burials, Androulla was guided by the markers they set down, especially the senses, to give imaginary shape to what happened, and thus render it more real and experienceable. The restitution of the senses, through others' accounts, was for her a substitution for experience, and the restitution of imagination, through specific shapes and forms. It enabled her to enter the territory of the past which she had been barred from surveying.

By going over the events though newspaper accounts and witnesses from the vicinity that she questioned, Androulla moved from an unwritten chronicle to a relateable history. She was slowly being exposed to and given, as well as making for herself, a story. It was primarily through sharing or slowly being exposed to how others experienced the events of August 1974, and through the senses, that she became to move from considering her husband not just a question mark over which the authorities had refused to give answers, but a knowable entity. By being exposed to what happened to her husband in terms of what she assumed to be his burial (for there was as yet no evidence that any of the remains exhumed were those of her husband), she had a history, an account she could imagine and thus give shape to what occurred. At the same time this sharing suggested that scientific certainty is not transcendent, self-evident, immediate, unambiguous, and authoritative. The questions and the interaction she had had with the archaeologist had left her (and me) confused, with a question we could only partly articulate: was this body actually her husband? As there were many bodies, the archaeologist's initiative in entering a conversation on her husband's specific medical history seemed to suggest some certainty as to the identity of the remains. The suggestion of certainty conjured through the negotiation of information between the two parties could not be confirmed empirically through what she saw, as the remains were slowly being cleaned through brushes and displayed through the paraphernalia of archaeology. What was revealed was clearly not recognisable. Paradoxically the more the remains were exposed through the exhumations, the more her uncertainty as to whether this included her husband increased. I now suspect the archaeologist's initiative was an attempt to provide Androulla, who had been hanging around the site for days in the hot sun, with some form of focussed, if fabricated, closure to her vigil.

During the exhumations it was clear that Androulla still considered her husband as still with her, as still present, and certainly not dead. She humanized him. She used the word *mirizan* (smelt) for the corpses when talking about the reasons why the bodies were buried hurriedly. This was certainly the case: 'We buried them without a proper *khideia* (mortuary ceremony)' said the Papas Andreas Christoforou, 'we only performed the *treisayio*. There were some 190 dead and we couldn't do more than this because of the unrelenting bad smell (*aperandi disodia*)'. (As reported in the *Phileleftheros* 3 June 1999). The term used is a literary one. Androulla by contrast used the word *mirizan*, from *mirodhya*, which could also suggest to smell well, even perfume (although the term aroma covers this).

The term can be applied to smells occurring from the natural world, such as for flowers. The woman at the neighbouring house to whom she spoke used an even more unambiguous term: *vromisan* (they stank): a term used for cesspits, filth, and dirt. The term refers to cultural sources and human putrefaction. Something that is *vromizi* needs to be concealed, kept away from light and air, to be buried. It is a polluting smell. Clearly, what the neighbour meant what that for non-kin, such bodies were mere corpses requiring immediate burial. By contrast when Androulla said '*mirizan, i kaimeni*' ('they smelt bad, the poor ones', literally 'the burnt ones'), she talked about her husband not as a polluting putrefying corpse to be hidden but as someone still recognizable, belonging to the world of the living, such as a hunter returning home (as depicted in his photograph) who had now become the hunted. The persons referred to are objects of pity and compassion, requiring cleansing and washing, not of fear deriving from pollution. They still belong to the world of the living. Thus her husband also required cleansing; his body prepared for the proper burial he never got. It is thus not too fanciful to suggest that women like Androulla assume the symbolic role of an Antigone who fights to bury her brother (husband) against the wishes to the State / Elders / Creon, because he was implicated in a shameful betrayal and civil war, which require a sacrificial scapegoat to uphold the integrity of the city-state or the nation. Clearly Androulla did not see it in such conscious terms. To model herself on a classical heroine was far from her concern. But her defiance, even her harshness and her pride, are features that a careful reader of the play would recognize as not too distinct from the character presented to us by Sophocles.

In the gentle vine-clad Paphos hills, a man went to prison for three years for a homicide. The story goes that his son was one of the disappeared, but the father conducted a secret exhumation a few months after his disappearance in the military cemetery, and discovered his body by his wrist watch and his cross. He retained his son on the list of the missing. The boy was lost at Ayios Pavlos on 17–18th August 1974 the last day of the war, like Androulla's husband. Years later, the father quarrelled with a co-villager who uttered the awful truth: 'We all know that your son is dead and so do you. So, stop pretending'. The father returned home, got his gun, and shot him. After serving his time in prison, he moved to Limassol and never returned to his village. What are we to make of this story? Insensitivity of sentiments that someone could have the gall to tell a man what he should feel? That men could go to such great lengths to maintain a 'lie'? We do not even know whether it is true that the father actually did conduct the awful exhumation, or indeed that he did find his son, although the point of this story is that somehow this man was prepared to defend an illusion with his own life. Clearly there must have been a long history of tension between the two men that other interlocutors consider too unimportant to mention. Perhaps those were in fact the most important. Or is the 'moral' of the story that an item of such importance could not be flaunted in such a disrespectful way in a village and could only be expressed by the state for which that man's son had been sacrificed? If the boy has died, and he had much promise (he had just returned to his family after having studied in the Soviet Union), then at least the authorities should have had the decency to actually identify him as having given his life for his country, rather than having allowed him to disappear in a collective grave to keep the missing issue alive.

Burial

On arriving in Cyprus in September 2000, I learnt that the bones of Androulla's husband (Haralambos) had been identified. Her daughter said that her mother was getting better every day, but when I spoke to her, she sounded subdued. She phoned me up and I arranged to meet her the next day at her home. She had had an operation, was leaner, and her skin was darker. Her eyes were tired. It was as if she was bracing herself for a final encounter with what she had to do. In particular she concentrated on the role of the authorities, and it was now an opportunity to turn the tables.

She repeated a number of times 'I lost my life (on this issue)' (*Ehasa tin zoi mou*). According to the examinations, her husband was shot in the neck from behind or the side, whilst his cousin was treated much more badly. His body was broken in various places and he had been shot in various places. ' I cried for him more', she said. They did not find his cross around his neck but they found his wristwatch and some items of clothing which were synthetic and identifiable. Androulla went to the Phaneromeni Church on the 16 September 2000 to pay the priest to read his name out as a *mnimoseno* (memorial service). This was a clear indication that she considered him dead. This was the first time she had done so. She later learnt that his mothers' *mnimoseno* fell on the same day. Very strange (*periyergo*), she said, but left the discussion empty, although she seemed to be toying with the idea that this was fated.

She was keen to learn why the government hadn't yet published the names of her husband and his cousin, and wanted me to ask why. She noted that it depended on the family whether to accept a Government representative at the funeral. ' I said that my husband fought for his country, Greek and Turks'. Because of Androulla's high profile, media attention was intense, and the authorities tried to impose a news blackout over the *translatio* (movement of bones to a final resting-place). Cyprus is a small place and news travels, so the press and TV channels turned up. Androulla was in two minds whether she wanted the authorities to attend. In the end she relented. Her condition oscillated on different levels and she often talked about her dreams. Her major struggle and reality was defined by and in contrast to the bureaucracy. Given her high profile and her irrepressibility, the authorities were concerned that she would use the opportunity to make some highly embarrassing public statements to the media. She quite justifiably believed that the authorities were withholding information from her, but she managed to ferret it out. 'I have my own sources and blood speaks', she said.

She wanted me to ask a Foreign Ministry official, a friend of mine, on her behalf: 'When are you going to tell the people that you have given back the bones back to the relatives?', and she complained that the authorities seemed to be imposing a news blackout.

'The politicians shouldn't talk', she said. Popi, her daughter was planning to do so. This day will be hers and hers alone. She wanted, in the apt phrase of Seremetakis, to have the last word. 'All the family will be there'; they plan to receive his body, keep him at home and then have a *khideia* the next day. 'I am preparing to receive my husband as he is. Nobody understood our tragedy and us. I am proud that I found him and that he will be a hero for his country'. Another theme she was proud of was that she had acted in the way she did by breaking into Lakatameia cemetery, which forced the authorities to do something.

The next day I phoned up Androulla to see how she was. She seemed extremely distressed. 'The problems have begun' (*Archisan ta provlimata,*) she said. She had been on the phone with various government people and they seemed to be pressuring her. She wanted the Defence Minister to be present whereas they wanted politicians to make the oration. They told her that there were many missing and that it would not be fair that he should speak at this ceremony. She replied that her husband had lost his life for his *patrida*, his country, and therefore it was only right that the Head of the Army should speak. She added that if he would not speak, she would not allow anyone to talk and that Popi would then talk. It seems that the TV stations had been phoning up to find out what was going to happen. I asked her what flowers she would be laying, and she said she would be laying down hyacinths 'because they have a strong aroma' (she did not draw any reference to the *Hyancinthides* or *Parthenoi*, Maidens, a cult title of a group of heroines identified as daughters of Hyacinthus sacrificed for the safety of Athens). *Mas koreideve poly i politeia,* ('the state has tricked us too much') she said, as a justification of having excluded the politicians. She expected to have to face them and was confident of her strength and her abilities to resist the pressures. Yet there was a strong sense of vulnerability just below the surface, in spite of her fighting talk.[14]

Two days later the government had accepted her request for the Defence Minister to give a funeral oration. It appeared that she had changed her mind about excluding government ministers, and politicians, and that as a result 'everything was organised'. As in other cases, the government would pay for the funeral expenses. The authorities laid on a formal handing over of the remains. All her husband's close kin were present including his three sisters and his five brothers (including one who had travelled from the U.K.) The box with the remains was collected from the laboratory, draped with a Greek flag, blessed by a triad of priests, and transported by military cortege to Androulla's home. There it remained for the night and the wake.

'God gave me much strength (*dynami*). When they told me about the death of my husband, that night I had a dream'. She didn't mean the identification but used the word for death (*pethane*). This was the first time she used the most neutral word for death, indicating that until then he was somehow still alive for her. 'I saw my *pethera* (mother-in-law) and next to her was my own mother. My *pethera* said to me "come and sit next to us" and made a sign. And I was glad. But I was also afraid that there would be news from this part of the family. Then the telephone rang.

That day I went to Tzonis in the Ministry of Foreign Affairs. I wasn't happy. Something was eating me inside. My daughter sent Haglund a fax. That other night I had another dream. They opened my mother's tomb, to bury someone. I asked the man digging: "Has my mother dissolved (*elyose*)?" He showed me a bone and told me that this was all that was left. They were about to phone me up. I was warned of this in the dream. Haglund phoned up my daughter and asked for her sister. The other daughter came. He told us that they had found our father (here she used *o pateras mas*). We said it was right to see the bones – *yia na pistepsoume, yia na katalavoume* (for us to believe, for us to fully understand it). Until then I knew and yet I didn't know (that he was dead). We wanted photographs and had to photograph secretly. We wanted photographs to show that it is ended'. She also wanted me to photograph the ceremony. To her it was incredibly important: "It is good to have a video- for the children".

Throughout the late afternoon till the next day, the coffin lay in her *saloni* for the wake (*agripnia*). A village woman proudly read out a poem in dekapentesyllabic verse, which she had composed. This was a praise poem similar to those sung at traditional Cypriot weddings in the 1970s (see Davis 1977). The house was filled with relatives and close friends, including children who milled around oblivious to the gravity of the situation. Women would come in crying, and she would call out "*ela Christoulla mou*, come and see him" The woman would come over crying, kiss her on the cheek, and them move to another part of the room. Another woman lost her husband in Kyrenia and she was clearly identifying with the situation. The women sat around a table on which the box containing the bones had been laid. It was draped with the Greek flag, and mounted with a framed photograph of Hambis. Below the table on the floor a solitary candle flickered. Androulla was seated next to her husband's sister, who appeared more distraught than she was. The sister who clearly identified with her deceased mother cried: "My only complaint is that our mother and father didn't know (that he was dead). He made the wailing in his fields, our father. *(Ekane ta klamata me sta horafia, o tjiris mas)*, a poignant image of a father who cannot cry at home in order not to upset the mother and who was obliged to cry alone in his fields, on the earth which would never be tended by the son he lost. Emotion ebbed and flowed. At times people talked silently and normally. At others, an event might trigger a collective crying. There was thus no single cathartic moment but staccato crying. Androulla who was highly distraught addressed him many times, often not in full sentences but in phrases, when collective emotions were high. When she uttered these words, her voice became deeper and intense but monophonic: "*Dhen se kavalava Hambi*. (Hambi, I didn't recognise you – meaning, I wasn't able to hear you speaking to me when you asked me to find you). Hambi, what have you done? ... Hambi, I had to come and find you ... I took the *kuspo* (shovel) ... That's what they told me, Hambi" It was almost as if she were addressing him and her that she was predestined to find him: "they were afraid. I told you that I would find the place where you were buried, the (wrong) place they had put you, my dear (*eipa sou na kalipso ton topo pou etafis, ton topo pou se evalan mana mou*). … My dear, did you think you would go and fight? (*Chryse mou, nomisis na polemisis?*)". At an early stage in the wake Popi opened the box and displayed her father's personal items in plastic evidence bags (his rusty jammed wristwatch and synthetic socks that had survived the burial), and the women gathered around in a manner reminiscent of the women gathering in Bouboolina's room on her deathbed in Cacoyiannis' film, *Zorba the Greek*. Androulla shouted out "Let them see! So that the people can believe the lies of the Government and the betrayal of the people! (*ya na katalavi o laos ta psemata ton Giverniseon che ton emboron ton ethnon!*)"

The wake was important not just to channel emotions but also for Androulla as a vindication of her struggle. She had been labelled as slightly crazy for having broken into the tombs, and was aware that this required much courage. She had acknowledged to me that such actions were macabre (*makavrio*), but she believed she had to do it. It was also an opportunity to present her own account of her struggle to others. During the wake she also recounted to visitors a logical, sequential, more episodic account of how she had realised that her husband was actually buried in the Greek side, in contrast to her utterances above when she was 'possessed' a word used very easily in anthropology. In this case, she presented matters as if she had been predestined to find him. Yet the two strands of knowledge united literally in an epiphany of disclosure. She repeatedly said, 'the truth was made manifest' (*ephanike I alitheia*). This is what she recounted:

'In 1981 there was a secret agreement whereby they exhumed bodies from Tymvo military cemetery and cleaned them and sent them to Greece. Why did they take them to Greece? Eh, they will tell us. I don't know' [This was a secret agreement whereby some bones were 'identified' by the Greek Cypriot authorities as belonging to mainland Greek army officers and sent to their families. It then transpired that they were the wrong bones, and had to be prised away from their Greek relatives, to much embarrassment. It also transpired that the bones couldn't be identified because they had been cleaned with the wrong chemicals. The situation resembled the Albanian novelist, Ismail Kadare's *The General of the Dead Army* – PSC]. 'In 1981, I was informed of this and I went to the Committee (of relatives of missing persons) and they told me that he wasn't in that group and they exhumed all of them and took them to Tymvos, and he wasn't there. It was from this time that I got angry (*synhistika ego*), and you know, I was gutted (*teliosa*), and I wrote requesting to be informed of all the names. They phoned me up 5 years ago. I didn't know that the *osteophylakia* (sacred place where the bones are retained after exhumation) were a *koinotaphon* (common tomb where bones are reburied after exhumation). But they didn't collect the bones from one place. They got a leg from one place, a head from another. At the end they phoned me twenty one years later to say that my husband was dead, and I asked where? They didn't say. I went to Lakatameia and the sign said 'Previous Military Cemetery Lakatameia', and when I went in there and saw that there were some tombstones with 'Unknown Soldier' on the tombstones, I got alarmed, my blood pressure went up, and I had to take pills for three and a half years, and then I had to do this … It was from other witnesses that I discovered the truth … Government people didn't believe that I would do this, saying, "slowly, slowly", but we had been waiting all these years. … I didn't know which grave was his, only generally as there were many men there … I had dreams: on the day they notified me by letter that my husband had been identified and on the day they informed me to go and collect the body. In it I recognised him from his skull (*kranio*). There were other women who were weaker than I was and they locked themselves up in their homes all these years. But I won – *ime nikitis*'.

The women gathered around can be seen like the Chorus in an ancient Greek play. They expressed collective feelings, social sentiments. Often people would say: 'But can you understand what it means to die and for your loved ones not to know? This is the biggest sin'. The similarity to Aeschelian ancient theatre is more than skin deep. Like theatre the action took place off-stage and was recounted. The gathered women were the Chorus, and there were two main characters present: Androulla and the corpse/remains of her husband. But what is a chorus? According to Lacan, 'the Chorus is people who are moved; they take care of the emotional commentary for us' (1992: 252).

The men stayed outside. I was the only male inside having been asked to come in by Androulla and placed next to her. I did not know what to do, and I felt awkward that I had only white clothing to wear whereas most wore black.

Hambis' brother, Nicos, who came from the UK, had let his beard grow as a sign of mourning. In the courtyard men spoke about how Hambis had always been generous with his family, how he used to help out his father and mother even after he had got married (he married young and Androulla became a widow after seven years of marriage), how he used to send vegetables to his father and other siblings; how he was a type of person who once he decided on something would go ahead and do it (his sister said that had he not been so determined perhaps he would have been saved). Nicos said that the men stay outside 'out of respect to the women … we leave the women to mourn in their own way'. But this did not mean he said that we do not feel. He said that he felt the need to remain alone with his brother, and that he would do so later. Maroulla had come to stay the night- it is considered a sign of good friendship if one spends the night at the wake. But some of his sisters had to return home as they had young children.

Androulla had a son who suffered from cerebral palsy and died at the age of twelve. Her brother, Kyriakos, who lives next to her, went to the cemetery to empty the bones of her son next to whom her husband would be buried. On the Saturday morning Androulla said she wanted to see her son. She took *eau de cologne* to sprinkle on her son's bones that Kyriakos had gathered in a blanket onto which he had placed the son's skull. She went first to his grave and told him, crying as a *miroloyio*, 'we have found your father. Tonight you will sleep with him next to you'. She then went to her mother's grave and told her mother, 'Mother, I have found my husband, Hambis'. She was highly agitated. Maroulla her friend was worried: 'I thought she would faint, and then what will I do? Fortunately, the *colognia* revived her'. 'I will sleep with Hambis tonight', Androulla said, hugging his coffin.

The shovels used to bury him were the same ones she used at her attempted exhumations, she said.

The memorial service at the Church, *praesente cadavere*, was a major event attended by the media, Ministers, the Bishop of Morphou, officials, and repre-

sentatives of the Committee of the Relatives of the Missing. The speeches reinforced the tendency to turn the missing into heroes, something that Androulla
and many other relatives seemed pleased with. This process occurred also in
Argentina (Robben, 2000). Christian symbolism was predominant. The Mayor
of her town mentioned Golgotha, Crucifixion, black exile (*xenitia*), resurrection
(*anastasi*), and freedom (*eleftherosi*). As the names of the organisations and individuals who had presented wreaths were read out, an honest and humanitarianly
engaged man who conducted most of the investigative work for the CMP, snorted
with disgust when the names of the Committee of Relatives of the Missing were
read out, as he considers them to have exploited the issue. Androulla and
Maroulla would agree with him, but they might have similar views about CMP
officials. No officials came to her home after the funeral to take refreshments.
According to Androulla they didn't come 'because they are tired of the whole
business, but they came only to the Church to see the reaction of the family'. The
gathering at the house after the funeral is for insiders.

Androulla's observation was astute. Tensions between political widows and
authorities over burials are not new. They underlie Sophocles' *Antigone* and in
more contemporary times, South Africa. For the latter Ramphele has noted 'the
political widow becomes a valuable resource for the political organisation to
which her husband and /or herself were affiliated. She embodies the social memory that has to be cultivated and kept alive to further the goals of the struggle ... .
[But] she also becomes the embodiment of the brutality of the state which leaves
women like her in a vulnerable liminal state' (1997: 110). The authorities were
apprehensive of Androulla's potential for independent action and the danger
(from their point of view) that she might overstep her passive role as political
widow and condemn them. Initially she wanted to exclude them, but relented
(perhaps as a result of some pressure, which she may have privately negotiated
some compensation, and certainly the costs of the funeral, for she is not a wealthy
woman). Her insistence on the Defence Minister's attendance confirmed her husband's heroic status. Ramphele suggests 'the public role of the political widow
derives from her relationship with her husband; she is not seen as a widow but as
someone standing in for a fallen man ... . Her agency is not completely eliminated but constrained' (ibid: 112). This may apply to South Africa and indeed to
many Cypriot widows on both sides, but is perhaps too uncompromising in its
positing an ideal of unconstrained political agency, a romantic view of Antigone.
The messiness of social life rarely permits such gestures. What was important for
Androulla was the recognition by the authorities that her link with her husband
was more compelling than the scandalous uses they had put him to as a missing
person. In short, she was a political widow *before* his identification and exhumation. His burial returned him to her, much like Phocion's widow who gathered his
ashes from beyond the city's walls (as depicted in Poussin's painting depicted on
the cover of this book). Clearly the authorities attempted to derive political capital out of the public ceremony, but it suited her purposes. Political sponsorship

did not assuage her resentment, nor indeed constrain her possibilities for future action. It may even have strengthened her position. Nor was the charade lost on the public or on the officials present.

Conclusion

Funerals do not end mourning nor rituals a drama. Rosaldo had made the former point (1984); I am emphasising the latter. Sometimes funerals may actually precipitate a tragedy as with Sophocles' *Antigone*. In this chapter I hope to have shown that during the process of exhumations and burial something more was involved than the attempts by a widow to find her dead husband and lay him to rest. It was a reassertion of obligation, and the obligation of reassertion. In situations of extreme stress (versus quotidian existence), kinship reasserts itself not through the enactment of roles but rather through *the enactment and embodiment of sentiment*. Sentiments are not restricted to, and by, roles. Rather, individuals embody their sentiments not as a contingent upon their roles, but as a means to find themselves and define their roles in their own way.

Contemporary anthropological theory finds it difficult to grapple with these notions. Our understanding of kinship is embedded in our treatment of roles – as brother, mother, wife, father, etc. But there is a sense in which emotion transcends these terms and has to be treated as a *sui generis* phenomenon, redefining what we normally understand by these terms. In Greek one could use the *term dhiki mas/dhikos mas*, (our man, and our person) to denote an ascriptive role beyond kinship terms. 'Our man/woman' applies to strict kinship and affinity, patronage, political party membership, even ethnicity. It is opposed to *xenos*. Yet although the term is useful, the sense of recapture, of emotion expressed by Androulla, and how she spoke of her husband, transcended a 'simple' matter of the recovery of a husband. She recovered something more than that. Here I want to make a detour to the classical Greek notion of *philia*. In discussing Greek tragedy, Simon Goldhill (1986) notes that the notion of *philos* (and relatedly *ekthros*) cannot be glossed as friend (and enemy). *Philos / philia* is the language of obligation between one's own, between husband and wife, brother and sister. *Philia* is an obligation to be obliging, versus an equal obligation to be disobliging to ones *ekhthroi*. Sophocles' Antigone upholds the sentiment of *philia* towards her brother above the rules of the city which holds him to be an *ekthros*: 'I am not of a nature to share in hatred (*ekhth-*) but to share in love (*phil-*)'. Modern Greek does not carry that notion. Indeed when a woman refers to her *philos*, it is to an (often-secret) lover. But it is precisely this categorically transgressive term I am suggesting of *philos* here that could give us an insight into the notion that her husband was her *philos* in both the modern Greek sense of 'lover', but also the Classical Greek sense of binding obligation between husband and wife, *and* brother and sister. Androulla's struggle against the authorities in wanting Hambis identified not as an *agnoumenos*, but as her husband, i.e., not as an anonymous person buried secretly beyond the city's walls but as someone with an identity who should be buried *within* the city (i.e. the moral community), was in effect a struggle for recognition of a living, binding, personal, relationship of her obligation, of her *philia*, rather than an imposed, civic, depersonalised, linkage to her husband as a political widow. Her struggle to maintain that bond with Hambis can be seen metaphorically as a bond with a *philos*, i.e. a secret, not socially recognised, bond with an individual, rejecting the role of a passive Penelope for the state. She rejected the waiting or mourning role of a wife /widow, and pursued the action of frequenting Hambis' materiality after his politically imposed 'disappearance', i.e. non-materiality. Through her attempted exhumation, she 'materialised' (*pragmatevthike*, lit. made real /true, her husband). In this sense, until his positive identification, he could be seen in the modern Greek sense as her *philos*, i.e., as someone with whom she maintained a non-socially recognised or openly acknowledged rapport on an ongoing emotive level. I am of course talking metaphorically here, but it is through the use of symbols and hidden levels of meaning that we can understand the subtlety of her utterances and conflicting emotions during the exhumation and burial process. In another sense however, her rapport with her husband can be seen in the Classical Greek sense of *philos*, i.e. as a term in moral discussion or judgement. I am not referring here to the notion of 'friend' but as someone to whom she had an overriding obligation (perhaps *dhikos mou*). It is not too fanciful to suggest because she had not had a material or physical relationship with her husband for some twenty-six years, that he became something 'like' a brother or even a 'father' i.e. somebody whose bond one inherits. She did indeed make the slip to referring to him as *'o pateras mas'* (our father). I am struggling here to try to fit in complex sentiments and representations in extraordinary situations into categories and roles (husband, wife, brother, etc) that *produce* normality. Terms like 'husband', 'wife', etc, do not fully work in such situations. It is because of the situation's phenomenological extraordinariness that we must move beyond the normal embedded meanings of terms. Significantly, she only addressed him as *o andras mou*, my husband, i.e., as a socially restricted role, when talking to officials in public. At home during the wake and at the cemetery, she always referred, and addressed him, by his name, Hambis. Nor could she refer during the wake to any of his characteristics as a husband. He had long ceased to materially disclose himself to her as a person. It was not his identity as an interacting recently departed husband that was recalled, for they had only been married for a short time. She did not have a bank of images to draw upon. Instead she drew incessantly upon his last days: And you thought you would go off to fight, dear Hambi!'. By contrast, it was his siblings who could recall him as an individual prior to his marriage with his personal characteristics, etc. The re-presentation of missing persons is also a struggle against the missing enemies of memory.

One could describe this process of Androulla's recapture of her husband as a *process of recognition*. It is this that gives the process its extraordinary dramatic potency. The various scenes at the cemetery during the exhumations, and at the wake, could be called 'recognition scenes', similar to those found in classical tragedy. Recognition is a process of legitimisation. Antigone recognises Polynices and throws earth over him. Androulla recognises her husband and wants him buried properly. As Goldhill has noted: 'these (recognition) scenes – regarded by Aristotle as one of the two most powerful types of scene in tragic plots – drama-tise not just the moment of a sentimental rediscovery of a family member, but also the reaffirmation of the legitimacy or obligations of a particular tie' (1986: 85).[15] It was precisely because the burial/ritual process here was the *reverse* of normal burials that this type of recognition took place. The normal process of burial $\rightarrow$ exhumation $\rightarrow$ recognition as outlined by Danforth (1982), when women talk or sing to the exhumed bones, is one both of recognition and of untying the bonds between kin. Here by contrast, the following process occurred:

Androulla's desperate first 'exhumation' to draw attention to her unrecognised tie $\rightarrow$ scientific exhumation $\rightarrow$ her 'recognition' of his bones $\rightarrow$ scientific iden-tification $\rightarrow$ burial. It was thus important for her to 'recognise' the bones, to make them hers. Her 'predestination' to find her husband was a reaffirmation of the bond between them. But recognition works both ways. In Lacanian terms it supposes the existence of an Other, a place from where one is heard, one is rec-ognized. Hence, the recognition by Androulla of Hambis was also a position from where Androulla herself was 'recognized' (of course by herself) as a moral person who fulfills her obligations as a wife. In that respect, Androulla's recovery of her husband was also her self-recovery.

Victor Turner had ago identified the dramatic moment to expose the various forces that affect the social structure. The preceding discussion suggests that some insights from classical tragedy can be effective tools in prising open the complex-ities of this particular set of dramatic moments. This can help us recognise Aris-totle's views on tragedy as anthropologically significant when approaching the phenomenon of social suffering. Tragedy is not a condition. It is the working out of the actions of individuals on each other, guided by certain ideas and beliefs, 'often without clearly knowing why' (Loizos, 1975: 6). 'Suffering is an action. It is the outcome of a series of preceding acts. Indeed this plot-centred view holds the promise of cognitive clarifications that may lead to the possibility of personal and social change' (Morris, 1997: 37). The characters discussed here progres-sively achieved some cognitive clarifications through pursuing cultural patterns of action more likely to result in 'closure'. It would be hubristic to identify this western vocabulary of suffering with a return to the situation *status quo ante*. Events etch indelible traces on the lives of individuals. Women like Androulla and Maroulla used the cultural resources available to them against the very authorities that sought to use them for state purposes, not to achieve closure, but to recover their dignity through discharging their gender-informed obligations. *Contra*

Ramphele (op. cit.) I would argue their gender identity as constrained widows enabled them to claim agency. Gender *is* constraint, but those constraints are part of the cracked edifice of society. The Hegelian ideal of a genderless 'full citizenship' may actually *disempower* individuals. The major threat to the recognition of the widows' suffering does not come from their current transparent political exploitation by the authorities on both sides of the Green Line. There is increasing awareness of this in Cyprus (Drousiotis, 2000). It is rather that the national politicization of the issue on both sides conceals an even more fundamental reality, which is the Statist necessity for the appropriation of dead bodies, in short that political order requires representations of suffering, and that this particular political formation requires ethnic representations of suffering. The major threat to the recognition of suffering always comes from the concealment of agency.

If I am right that every political order requires its own specific representations of suffering, we should not be surprised if suffering is redefined in Cyprus, from ethnic to medical. Should a political solution to the island's division be found, suffering may be depoliticized through medicalisation. There certainly was a strong medical conceptualization by Androulla but this is what one could call a 'traditional' mode of assistance-seeking. Post-ethnic (nation) states in a context of globalization transform concepts of subjectivity and accountability. Globalization and modernization, to which the professional classes aspire to in Cyprus, can homogenize the symptoms and vocabulary of suffering to take advantage of the Promethean gifts of modern therapeutic regimes imported from overseas. These may be profoundly unsuited to people's original experiences, but they create new subjects (and thus new citizens) for modern political and medical orders. In the interests of 'national reconciliation', we should not be surprised if medicalisation may offer an 'economical solution' to override recognition of political agency. This has happened elsewhere, but at a cost. Kleinman and Kleinman note the implications: 'increasingly those complicated stories, based in real events, yet reduced to a cultural image of *victimization*, (a post-modern hallmark), are used by health professionals to rewrite social experience in medical terms' (1997: 10). As often occurs, this may be wrought out of the compromised silences of those who have to bear this gagging.

NOTES

1. This was the son of the then President of the Greek Committee of Missing Persons, Theodoros Kritikou.
2. This concerned the story investigated by Commander Packard in 1964.
3. I have no definite means for checking whether such stories of hospital patients' massacres are true. I certainly have my doubts about the veracity of the claims of false uniforms and simu-

lated Greek. On the other hand I was told by a source that would prefer to remain anonymous about a case between 1964 and 1973 involving a highly educated Greek Cypriot in an intelligence unit of the National Guard. The latter wanted to know what the Turkish Cypriots were doing in terms of military protection in one of their enclaves, so they dressed some of their men in blue helmets and other UN insignia, and simply drove into the Turkish-controlled area to have a good look around. I have no means of knowing whether this is true, and it may be argued that these are largely irrelevant concerns from an anthropological perspective, or that one could suspend judgement even about veracity. I do not subscribe to this view. Whilst it may be possible to analyse the significance of such stories from a 'symbolic perspective', whether they are true or not (i.e. 'actually happened') is relevant. And it is also relevant whether the anthropologist believes them because this influences how s/he approaches them. Certainly the fact that one's informants appear to believe them, or wish them to be believed, is important, because this affects their actions, as well as how they present stories to the anthropologist. Even a sceptic must entertain the possibility that such events could have occurred; that they are within the bounds of possibility. It is relevance of one kind if such stories were 'true', and of another kind if they were 'not'. It is therefore difficult to agree with Robben (1995) on this particular case who claims that the prerogative of the anthropologist is not to establish truth or guilt, especially if many of one's informants desire precisely this from a 'neutral' outside observer. Indeed this is why they collaborate with the anthropologist. Yet informants often 'appeal' to and try to 'seduce' (Robben's terms) the anthropologist to their account of events. This is not specific to violence but can encompass anything contested. If we were to accept what informants tell us, but exclude their attempts at seduction/manipulation as 'intended to entice (one) away from where (the anthropologist) is standing' (ibid: 99), then we miss the whole point of our engagement with these societies, and betray not just our engagement with these societies, but also our engagement with our discipline and with ourselves. On a personal level, due to my questioning of people both in 'official' frames and unofficial contexts, I do believe that such atrocities on both sides took place, but I have difficulties with the word 'genocide', now evoked perhaps too easily to describe such situations. I accept that such killings may have been perceived as such by certain Turkish Cypriot political segments keen to feed the very real fears of the Turkish Cypriots to justify partition.

4. Therefore just to deny them paradoxically merely reinforces the fear, rather than addressing it.

5. Ankara Radio, undoubtedly in a bid to soften up resistance prior to its invasion on 20 July 1974 and to legitimate its intervention as upholder of the Constitution, claimed on 17, 18 July 1974 that 300 members of the National Guard had died (ME/4655/c/3 SWB 19 July 74).

6. They gave the following casualty figures: 2 officers, 27 men, wounded: 7 officers, 56 men' (SWB ME/4657/C/15-Broadcast 22 July).

7. There was another contrast, which is not often brought out. Men who were conscripts in the National Guard then have told me about apparently aimless orders, and of the chaos that were 'battles' (*mahes*). One case (probably far from atypical) involved a platoon who thought they were being shot at in downtown Nicosia. They proceeded to fire indiscriminately around them at buildings with their machine guns, and only after a couple of hours shooting did they realise that they had been shooting at nothing. There had been no attack. Here again the facade of purpose, of order, of marching, of power-claiming directionality that characterises military organisation is perhaps exposed as indiscriminate destruction through chaotic fear and self-preservation.

8. According to Drousitis 'a man who worked there (Michalis Klangides) was ordered to dig pits for four bodies at a time. Later other police cars came with bodies of dead Presidential Guards and civilians. When we got ready to bury them the Greek Major, Th. threatened us with a pistol, saying: "What are you doing, idiot? Do not bury these dogs close to our heroes". They obliged us to fill in the pits and they showed us another place, far away from the rest of the graves in a corner of the cemetery (for the presidential guards)' (Chronicle, p.82).

9. I use the word simulacra rather than simulation because the former suggests a precipitation of an imaginary situation, in an 'object' in a 'reality', rather than a process, a doing. And a simulacrum suggests that the substitution is much more complete. There is no definite class of individuals who are manipulating the signs of substitution /deception and others being 'taken in'. Rather, everybody participates in its construction.

10. It was established to research genetic disorders.

11. There was one notorious case in 1998 where Father Christoforos, the head of a splinter organisation representing the Missing, set in motion a chain of bizarre allegations claiming that thirteen people people, listed as missing since 1974, were alive and well and living in a third country. The *Cyprus Mail* noted 'This was not Father Christoforos' only incendiary claim of the week. Speaking on a radio show ... he said he had heard (again the source remained secret) that the remains of the US citizen missing since the summer of 1974 found by the Turks in Ashia in the occupied north had actually been found in Turkey and been brought to Cyprus before being handed over. Once again, we were supposed to believe this claim, merely because it came from the mouth of this irresponsible, sensation-seeking priest ... It is becoming exceedingly difficult to believe anything this man says regarding the missing ... Three months after the death of Leandros Zachariades, who had served as Commissioner of Humanitarian Affairs, Father Christoforos claimed that Zachariades had reached a secret agreement with the Turks accepting that all those listed as missing were dead. Zachariades had allegedly summoned him to his office a day before he died and told him all this during a 'confession'. But nothing of the sort had happened ... Zachariades had many public clashes with Christoforos and would never have made a confession to him, (his) brother said. Father Christoforos apparently had no misgivings about defaming a dead man and attributing to him words he never said. Subsequent events showed that the late Zachariades, a decent and honest man, had never reached any agreement with the Turks about the missing. So what is Father Christoforos trying to achieve with these latest outrageous utterances, for which he has recruited the help of an equally irresponsible Cypriot living in Canada? We can only assume that his main objective is to thwart the efforts that were set in motion by last year's agreement between President Clerides and Rauf Denktash to tackle the issue of the missing. It is alarming to think that he may have been using the same disingenuous ploys with the people for whose interests he is supposedly campaigning – the relatives of the missing persons. How could anyone knowingly raise false hopes among a particularly vulnerable group of people, who have suffered pain and anguish over the fate of their loved ones for more than 20 years, simply because his own personal agenda seems to mandate it? What irony that Father Christoforos unstintingly promotes himself as a champion of the rights and interests of the relatives of the missing. His actions seem to suggest that the last thing he cares about are the feelings of these people.' (*Cyprus Mail* 20 March 1998)

12. Interview by Rustem Tatar to the *Cyprus Mail* on 2 June 1999.

13. In July 2001 Androulla took the Cypriot Government to court.

14. Her sister-in-law confided to me that perhaps it wasn't that right that Androulla criticised the present government so harshly, as actually they had been these people who had the courage to begin the exhumations.

15. The French psychoanalyst André Green says much the same: 'The tragic space is the space of the unveiling, the revelation, of some original kinship relation, which never works more effectively than through a sudden reversal of fortune, a *peripeteia*' (1979: 7–8).

9
POWER, COMPLICITY, AND PUBLIC SECRECY

Creon: 'For it is a fact that this whole business is nothing but politics: the mournful shade of Polynices, the decomposing corpse, the sentimental weeping and the hysteria you mistake for heroism – nothing but politics … It's vile; and I can tell you what I wouldn't tell anybody else: it's stupid, monstrously stupid. But the people of Thebes have got to have their noses rubbed into it a little while longer. My God! If it was up to me, I should have had them bury your brother long ago as a mere matter of public hygiene. But if the feather-headed rabble I govern are to understand what's what, that stench has got to fill the town for a month!'

Anouilh's *Antigone* (1960: 48)

Throughout this book I have been concerned to do two things: to explore the issue of missing persons in Cyprus as a complex interplay of memory, projection, and recovery on both the individual and collective levels, and secondly to illuminate the dilemmas raised by reference to variations in the Antigone tragedy. I hope the reader will have been inclined to consider this was not a mere literary conceit, but has some genuine heuristic value.

The Turkish invasion and continuing occupation of Cyprus was so traumatic (for Greek Cypriots) that it became the most important transforming event in the past century. It influenced all aspects of life, from the economic ethic of Greek Cypriots to their popular art. One could divide Cyprus' modern political history into pre-Invasion and post-Invasion periods. Papadakis (1994) has noted how Greek Cypriot historiography, which by its nationalist nature must aspire to linearity, cannot deal with 1974 because it represents a regression and a defeat of history, and is thus a fundamental threat to national identity. Within this context of a damaged collective subjectivity, The Missing can be seen as a set of representations operating on what Lacan would call the Imaginary Order. 'The Imaginary is the order of mirror-images, identifications and reciprocities … The Imaginary is the scene of a desperate delusional attempt to be and to remain 'what one is' by gathering to oneself ever more instances of sameness, resemblance and replication' (Bowie 1991: 92). Within contemporary Greek Cypriot society, the Missing are considered *ieromartyres* (Saint-heroes), they have to be laid to rest, and their relatives and the wider society are involved in complex transactions with them, such as through their attempted recovery through art, demonstrations for their return, bureaucratic procedures that ghost them as legally recognised characters by the state, and obligations to be activist on their behalf. The recovery of the Missing thus represents a recovery of the situation *status quo ante*, a utopian state whereby on an Imaginary level the relatives are reunited with their relatives, and the society achieves closure and healing. This is of course impossible but because politics cannot satisfy this need, except to feed it through an elaboration of the issue, Christian symbolism offers resolution of this *aporia*. As Lacan noted, 'Desire is not a mere drive; it is pursued through representational practice' (1977: 189). He further suggested: 'the structure of representation is present in the very process of the drive' (ibid: 189). The murals discussed in Chapter 7 do not just reflect desire; they shape it.

I want to conclude by looking at the public secret, for I believe this can provide us with a key as to how need, desire, and complicity are wrought out on a collective level. This issue raises important questions regarding the extent to which we as anthropologists (in our roles either as observers or witnesses), the relatives of missing persons, and the officials that make up the state, might well be implicated in a more complex and subtle drama.

Heirs of Antigone

When Androulla Palma and Maroulla Shamishi broke into Lakatameia cemetery in Cyprus, they were clearly engaged in a dramatic and desperate act of questioning the official presentation of reality. Like modern Antigones, they took on the duty to their relatives to give them a proper burial, and they bravely challenged the laws of the state, or at least the official presentation of reality, that assigned the Turks to hold the answers to the fate of the missing Greek Cypriots. They exposed the public secret that many 'knew' but feared to articulate: that the state had manufactured a simulacrum of knowing which held that all the missing are missing as a result of Turkish action whereas in fact the politicians knew that some of the missing may have been buried on the Greek side. These particular individuals were the real missing because the state held them hidden from their relatives whilst dissimulating that the Turks were responsible for this lack of knowledge. This was Antigone's doubt, and like Antigone they could be proud that they had challenged Creon. Like Antigone, this transgressive act exposed them to both criticism and sympathy by the chorus, i.e., the public's social conscience.

When Father Christoforos made his fantastic and irresponsible claim that some missing persons might be alive in a third country some twenty-five years after their disappearance, something different happened. Cypriot society was shocked and he was forced to resign his position as representative of the relatives of the Missing. It is hard to disagree with many that felt that he had long exploited the issue. But here I am interested in something else. How can we precisely locate the shock value? The claim was so fantastic that it did not bear entertaining. And yet what seemed to occur was the making of the claim, its airing in the media, signalling it as 'fantastic', and at the same time condemning it as 'irresponsible' and 'cruel'. There is no doubt that it was all this. But what I would suggest a different interpretation. The shock value of this assertion lay not in what it said, but rather by being so implausible it brought the society too close to the public secret: that all the missing are /were in fact dead, but that (fantastically) we have known /suspected this all along, and that we have known that the authorities knew that we, the public, have known this all along. This may have been the real scandal. Baudrillard would call this a simulacrum: 'The transition from signs which dissimulate something to signs which dissimulate that there is nothing, marks the decisive turning-point' (1988: 170). Although there are problems with Baudrillard's notion, he suggests that the 'traditional' system of signs accepted a correspondence of sorts between the sign and what was signified, the signifier and the signified, even if sometimes signs were planted to conceal or dissimulate existing realities. However, where signs are put into place, which refer to nothing but themselves, we are in the presence of a simulacrum. Religion is of course the ultimate simulacrum, which does not mean that it is either false or an illusion. Signs are there to sustain faith and vice-versa, and religion facilitates the human transformation of chance into necessity and thus has socially necessary effects and is 'true' in the Durkheimian sense of having a social reality over and above private illusions. But the parallelism between the 'truth' of the simulacrum in traditional religion and the simulacrum of reality that seems to occur in contemporary politics bears further exploration. In Anouilh's *Antigone*, Creon disassembles and reassembles the bodies of Eteocles and Polynices from the mashed pulp they originally were. This is the beginning of the making of a simulacrum and Creon's disclosure to Antigone shatters her faith:

> Creon: 'What else could I have done? People had taken sides in the civil war. Both sides couldn't be wrong: that would be too much. I couldn't have made them swallow the truth … Would it have been better to let you die a victim of that obscene story?'
> Antigone: 'It might have been. I had my faith'
>
> Anouilh: *Antigone*, (1960: 54–55)

The conniving contempt of politics in the real world often shames the cynical artistry literature can conjure. In 1978 the Yasukuni Shrine, the memorial containing Japan's war dead, received the remains of more than a dozen people executed in the late 1940s after their trials as war criminals. By mingling the war criminals' remains with those of other war dead, the shrine's authorities presented subsequent leaders with a problem: neglect the soldiers who died in the war, or honour the war's masterminds along with them (*The Economist*, 27 April 2002).

Anouilh's Creon destroys the principle of representation. He shatters the link between the signifier and the signified, and substitutes it by a system of free-floating signs. Creon conjures up a principle of (state) morality out of a rearrangement /manufacturing of bodies as signs, through a ruthless disregard not just of which body belonged to whom, but of any correspondence between the post-mortem treatment of the body and ethics. Furthermore, although Creon does not say so, they could be the bodies of anyone. This results in Antigone's dejection: 'I had my faith'. In short, there is no correspondence between the signifier and the signified, except the sign that it is a signifier.

What seems to be happening here is not just the shattering of the link between the signifier and the signified, but that the signifier achieves an autonomous importance. What I mean is the following. We can distinguish between The Missing as Signifier, and the Signified as a set of Representations. We have established that these Representations (Signifieds) are various: Occupation of Cyprus by Turkey, her violation of the rights of the relatives to be united with their loved ones, heroism and sacrifice, loss, and a whole complex of social emotions. When the authorities held on to information that some of the Missing were in fact buried in the Greek side, they were in effect maintaining not just a fiction, but still retaining their investment in the power of the Signifier (that there are people who are missing), and insinuating the fiction that everybody was still unrecoverable, because of 'Turkish intransigence'. Or to put it bluntly, the authorities *lied*, which is what Androulla, Maroulla, and others concluded. But a lie can be a simple denial, or it can be more, and more was involved here. When Androulla perceptively noted 'The state deceived us, made fun of us' *(mas koroyideve i politeia)*, she was indicating there was an element not just of denial but of a masquerade; a pretence at suggesting a different order of things, and involving us not just as spectators but as participants. An alternative reality was being offered, and it was being sustained by the fiction in its real sense, not of 'not true' (i.e. a 'lie'), but of a relatively integrated and mutually sustaining convincing alternative reality, sustained by a entire social scaffolding, much like fiction-as-literature. As Aristotle observed, a convincing improbability is preferable to what is unconvincing even though it is possible. A non-sign as sign (the absence /concealment of bodies) insinuated that the Missing were held elsewhere by the enemies of the polity. The notion of recoverability was sustained through the scaffolding of legal rights, ghosted representation, investigative procedures, political demonstrations, and performances of grieving which were crafted out of very real experiences of loss. This is not to say that this is a complete fiction or fabrication. Far from it. Many missing Greek Cypriots disappeared behind Turkish lines in murky circumstances. It was the careful crafting of what was known with what was not known that conjured up a persuasive verisimilitude, even if improbable. What began as confusion in 1974–76, increasingly turned into strategy, and with the passage of time many of those who should have known better have, in some cases, selectively remembered the facts as they knew them. Inchoate confusion turned into extemporising strategy, and finally cohered into belief, which was not aware of its own contradictions. And it was sustained by deep cultural and social needs, in which everybody had an investment.

Lacan has suggested the signifier could become more important than the signified. Signifiers are public property, they belong to everyone. In some cases individuals may become so attached to them that they press them into uses for which they may be ill fitted, even contradictory. Those 'slips' may themselves be significant. Let me offer an example. At another funeral oration (*Khideia*) for a soldier whose remains had been identified in 2001, the Defence Minister referred to the twenty-seven years of 'unjust, inhuman and unethical punishment' (*timoria*) of the dead. These were the 'sacred bones (*iera osta*) of the dead who had been sacrificed'. He used his speech to appeal against 'the reappearance of divisions that could lead to fratricidal anguish (*adelphochtonos sparagmos*) in our country, and that united we should liberate our enslaved lands'. He then emphasised that it was part of Greek culture to take care of our dead pointing to the Antigone story! Let us recall it was the authorities that prevented proper burial and it was the relatives who struggled to have them identified and buried properly. The Minister, an educated man, surely knew the Antigone story, but the irony must have escaped him because 'as a Greek' he identified with Antigone. To him, 'Creon' was the evil Other, the Turks perhaps. This is an example of the signifier (Antigone as a representative of 'Greek' identity) overcoming and indeed conflicting with the signified.

Androulla's hint that we were in the presence of a masquerade merits further exploration. I believe we are witnessing the creation of religious value fashioned out of real human experiences of loss. Here I think Taussig's re-working of Simmel's notion that secrecy magnifies reality may be useful. Canetti (1973) had also suggested that secrecy is the very core of power. Taussig asks: 'Are not shared secrets the basis of our social institutions, the workplace, the market, the family and the state? '(1999: 2). He defines a public secret as 'that which is generally known but cannot be spoken' (ibid: 50). This can provide an insight into a critical question that puzzled me during fieldwork and one that I (and others) never had the courage to ask. Like ethnographers working in 'simple' societies where the women cannot appear to question that the 'Spirits' are the men dressed up to frighten them, I found it impossible and insensitive to pose an analogous question to the relatives of the missing, viz.: Did they 'really believe' that their husbands were still in custody by the Turks as a means to torture them? This was a question neither other Cypriots, nor I, could pose for a long time, certainly until the mid 1990s. On reflection, the really critical issue was that something so fundamental was occurring in Cypriot society such that, with the encouragement of the state, none of us ever questioned this whole façade of not wanting to ask certain questions. We all 'knew' that the *Agnoumeni* were dead, they (i.e. the state officials and the representatives of the relatives of missing persons) 'knew' we (i.e. the rest of the society, including the relatives) 'knew', but it was virtually impossible for it to be expressed in this way. Later, I want to suggest some reasons why this was the case, but at this stage it is worthwhile to further explore Taussig's suggestion. He calls the public secret, the labour of the negative: 'Knowing it is essential to its power, equal to the denial. Not being able to say anything is likewise testimony to its power' (ibid: 6) This is exactly what happened with the *agnoumeni*. It was not something that the society knew and concealed. It was rather that the society did not want to face recognising that they did not know this. Taussig suggests 'this negativity of knowing what not to know lies at the very heart of a vast range of social powers and knowledges intertwined with those powers, such that the clumsy hybrid of power /knowledge comes at last into meaningful focus, it being not that knowledge is power but rather that active not-knowing makes it so' (ibid: 6–7).

We can thus re-approach that act of Androulla and Maroulla. When they attempted that mock /desperate exhumation they were performing something more than an act of transgression and of resistance. They were doing two related things. First, they were attempting to establish a new relationship between bones (matter) and the symbol. They wanted DNA testing because they intuited that the authorities (Creon) had put on a macabre display that was a simulation for political purposes. 'Behind the baroque of images hides the grey eminence of politics' (Baudrillard, ibid: 170). Second, paradoxically, they were at the same time upholding and recreating the sacred, and thus of the state's self-insinuation in the whole process of the creation of sacrality. For the state had to be re-involved in the re-investment of bones with sacred power, through DNA testing. It was thus not just an attempt at the private recuperation of sacred rituals and of their loved ones they were denied by the state. They were not so much challenging the state, but challenging the social understanding of the situation, because as discussed above, the signifier is a social artefact. They were not so much challenging the idea that the *agnoumeni* were dead, but rather that the political authorities together with society's passive complicity had decided that none were recoverable. This explains why the authorities felt unable to prosecute them. Similarly, when Fr Christoforous made his preposterous claim that some 13 *agnoumeni* were still alive in a third country, he unwittingly punctured the public secret that they were unrecoverable, rather than they might be alive. By suggesting that they could be alive (together with unsourced witness statements as rumours so very similar to those actually used by the State and by the Relatives' Committee), his claim projected the un-sayable secret that they were dead. What was un-sayable was not that they could be alive, but they were dead, i.e. unrecoverable, and therefore that the loss had ultimately to be recognised as an absence.

We can thus appreciate that in this contemporary version of Antigone, it is not a matter of the state embodying one set of values and Antigone another (as Sophocles' version is often interpreted); nor that Creon begins the modern process of state deception by dressing bodies whose identity he is ignorant, as symbols (Anouilh's version). It is also that Antigone 'knew' this as a public secret and yet was still implicated in the enterprise. Taussig raises the question:

> How do you destroy a charade that is not a secret but a public secret (something that is known by everyone but not easily articulable)? For it would seem that such a phenomenon has built-in protection against exposure because exposure, or at least a certain modality of exposure, is what, in fact it thrives upon. Might it not be, then, that the drama of exposure … did not destroy the secret, but became instead the raw material for new myths and modernist rituals along the same lines as before? (1999: 216).

One could apply this suggestion to the notion that it is still the state that unites the relatives to their missing through DNA identification etc. Could not one see the emphasis on genetic identification and new notions of ownership and belonging as new powerful myths and modernist rituals that have very real effects in society? Having denied relatives access to the mortal remains of the dead, the state on both sides of the Green line (in its dual forms of the Republic of Cyprus and its alter, the TRNC), i.e. modern Creon, is now engaged in a complex political choreography with the relatives accessing and /or denying them ratification of their links with their dead, but this time through the modern rituals of kinship and belonging through DNA identification conjured through scientists as the ultimate verifiers of reality rather than through sacred rituals over the corpse. In my Introductory chapter I suggested that the ultimate ambition of political power has always been a transcendental one: the manipulation of dead bodies as the ultimate sanction of power and, like Cerebus, as a means to control access to the underworld. DNA testing and identification can be seen as another version of this. In this respect therefore the old conflict between power of the state (*recht*) and of kinship is still real.

We have to ask why we are faced with what seems to be a 'complicity' in this staging of power; why 'we' as heirs of Antigone are participants in this drama. Here we ought to return to art and ponder on a perplexing fact. In the Republic of Cyprus, until the time of writing, there have been very few public works of art that have contemplated the disaster of 1974 in any fundamental sense. There are no memorials to the 1974 events, because it is too painful and because this is an unfinished story from the perspective of Greek Cypriot society. In the Turkish-occupied North there are many monuments to what has been called 'Liberation by the Turkish army'. Arthur Danto has written: 'We erect monuments so that we shall always remember, and build memorials so that we shall never forget' (1985: 152). But memorials are constructed after events have achieved a closure. Even if that might be an illusion as the debates over the Vietnam Veterans Memorial have shown (Sturken, 1998), the act of materialisation may aid that process, although good art always does so in an ambiguous way. As in literature, including our *Antigone* , where the debate will continue. Instead, Greek Cypriot society memorialises its traumas and losses, which is one way of fighting the cruel finality of the memorial. This is why everybody seemed to be implicated in the public secret that could not accept presentation in this way. One main projection of this process of memorialisation is through the relatives of the missing. It is the women as relatives, as Antigones, who have become living memorials. For some twenty years they became the performers in the state's staging of loss and redemption, crafting the sacred out a labour of loss. As Georges Bataille observed 'sacred things are constituted by an operation of loss' (1998: 70). According to him, sacrifice is the highest form of expenditure that involves a consecration of pure loss. The events of 1974 are always referred to in Cyprus as *I Thisies tou Evdominda Tessera*: 'The Sacrifices of Seventy Four', a clear example of the inconceivability of the events except in religious terms. There could be nothing more appalling for a society than the loss of one's children on a mass scale.

When I began this research I naively thought I would be investigating politics. I then began to realise that I was looking at kinship, because the Missing represent ancestors who have not yet been put to rest both for the society and for the relatives concerned. There is also an element of religious representation for a society that has experienced a real and tragic trauma. Concurrently, I began suspecting politics was a secondary issue, because I believed that once the political manipulations were exposed, then that would be the end of my struggle with the material I encountered during fieldwork. I finally realised that there was a much deeper political reality behind this, which a reading of Taussig and Canetti helped me discern. This is how we are inevitably complicit in the realities we try to describe. Throughout my engagement with Cypriot society I had skirted the issue of relations between Greek and Turkish Cypriots for various reasons, yet here I was, exploring the most oppressive area of relations between the two groups. It has not been an easy matter to look at such expressions of pain, and I have tried to be truthful and sensitive to the suffering of the people who took generously me into their confidence on both sides of the ethnic divide, hoping that I could 'do something' for their predicament (and what could I do except write a book that has taken some four years of my life and which will be read by few?).

The issue of The Missing in Cyprus is a good example of what ancient Athenians called a *mnesikakein*, the brandishing of memory in an offensive manner, the active remembering of past wrongs to your opponent. To circumvent the disasters inherent in such vindictive recollection, ancient Athenians instituted an oath of *amnestia*, a ban on recalling misfortunes, taken by all citizens. Creon is an agent of *mneme*, memory, but so is Antigone. Through taking that oath, Athenians prefigured by some twenty-five centuries Renan's famous observation that a nation is a group of people united by a common remembering and forgetting. Yet amnesty is anything but value-free (Loraux, 1998). The official erasure to anticipate the benefits of forgetfulness in the modern nation state is wrought out of two intertwined processes. First, the selective memorialisation of the past sometimes uses that very same material offensive to the other group: the Turkish Cypriots against the Greek Cypriots, the Greek Cypriots against the Turks. These memories are essential components of the construction of ethnic identity. Creon has an investment in such memories. Second, paradoxically, programmes of political memory often involve the suppression of individual memories and experiences of loss and suffering, especially among the weakest members of society, much as Paulina's sacrifice in Dorfman's *Death and the Maiden*.

Kant once famously wrote that 'If ethics without politics is empty, then politics without ethics is blind'. This still seems to hold for anthropology. It has been claimed that if Antigone is pure ethics without politics, Creon is pure politics without ethics. In this book I hope to have shown that this dualist interpretation is not quite true. Antigones are quite aware of politics and Creons suffer from the pricks of conscience. Let us return briefly to Anouilh's *Antigone*. Creon not only destroys the principle of representation, but he also displays this concealment to Antigone, and he asks her to connive in a public secret to which only she is to be an unwilling captive, polluted by that knowledge. He wants Antigone to connive with him, even if for a short time: 'and I can tell you what I wouldn't tell anybody else'. He recognises the absurdity, but confides it has a purpose, a political purpose devoid of ethics, or a different form of 'ethics' gutted of any acknowledgement of the importance of human links, sentiments and emotions. Could not we as anthropologists see ourselves as Antigone's heirs, privileged through the limited insights of our endeavours, but often disclosed to us through, and after, the practice of fieldwork and writing-up? Antigone rejects the awfulness of the active connivance at this disclosure. But in so doing she reinforces the deadliness of the public secret that 'it is all politics' which, 'like all public secrets, cannot in the final analysis be exposed yet insists we keep trying, thereby provoking a storm of theatricality in which the unmasking of deliberate deception stokes the fires of spiritual plenitude' (Taussig, ibid: 149). That is Antigone's, and our dilemma. We need to go beyond this because in the real world Creon does not connive with us like a Santa Claus (Taussig's last autobiographical example). He may himself also be a prisoner on probation of that public secret. That is Creon's dilemma, and we are also Creon's heirs. That is also our dilemma.

Nancy Scheper Hughes exhorted anthropologists to engage in a committed, grounded anthropology, and become 'anthropologists, comrades and *companheiras*' (1995: 420), Attractive as these sentiments are, I believe her particular stance is flawed because it does not fully take cognisance of the fact that our own subjects, just as we are, are also covertly engaged in the theatrics and secrets of power. This is the sly venom coursing through the veins of the body politic. A committed, socially engaged, anthropology could start from this premise. We, too, as heirs of Antigone, assist Creon in the secret masquerades of power, and we, too, often become aware of our intrication after the event.

BIBLIOGRAPHY

Abbot, G.F. 1969. *Macedonian Folklore*. Chicago: Argonaut.

Anderson, B. 1991. *Imagined Communities*. London: Verso.

Anouilh, J. 1960 (originally published 1951). *Antigone*. London: Methuen Drama.

Aristotle. 1920 *Poetics*. (transl. Ingram Bywater). Oxford: Clarendon Press.

Barthes, R. 1984. *Camera Lucida: Reflections on Photography*. London: Fontana.

Bataille, G. 1998. *Essential Writings*. (Edited by Michael Richardson). London: Sage.

Baudrillard, J. 1988. *Selected Writings*. (Edited and Introduced by Mark Poster). London: Polity Press.

Beard, M. and J. Henderson. 1995. *Classics. A Very Short Introduction*. Oxford: Oxford University Press.

Berger, J. 1984. *About Looking*. London: Writers and Readers Publ. Co-op.

Biggs, D. and J. Smith. 1995. 'The Cyprus Tragedy. A Narrative about Modern Cyprus', in P.W. Wallace (ed.) *Visitors, Immigrants and Invaders in Cyprus*. Institute of Cypriot Studies, New York: University of Albany. S.U.N.Y.

Black Michaud, J. 1975. *Feuding Societies*. Oxford: Blackwell.

Bloch, M. and J. Parry (eds). 1982. *Death and the Regeneration of Life*. Cambridge: Cambridge University Press.

Blok, A. 1972. 'The Peasant and the Brigand: Social Banditry Reconsidered'. *Comparative Studies in Society and History*. 14: 4, 494–503.

Blum, R. and E. Bloom. 1970. *The Dangerous Hour*. London: Chatto and Windus.

Bowlby, J. 1961. Processes of Mourning. *International Journal of Psychoanalysis*. 44: 431–453.

Bowie, M. 1991. *Lacan*. London: Fontana.

Campbell, J. 1964. *Honour, Family, and Patronage*. Oxford: Clarendon Press.

Canetti, E. 1973. *Crowds and Power*. Harmondsworth: Penguin.

227

Caraveli, A. 1986. 'The Bitter Wounding: The Lament as Social Protest in Rural Greece', in J. Dubisch (ed.) *Gender and Power in Rural Greece.* Princeton: Princeton University Press.

Clerides, G. 1989. *Cyprus: My Deposition (Vol. 1).* Nicosia: Alitheia.

Constantinou, C.M. 1995. 'Memoirs of the Lost: The Dead and the Missing in the Politics of Poetry', *The Cyprus Review.* 7, 2: 59–73.

Crapanzano, V. and V. Garrison (eds). 1977. *Case Studies in Spirit Possession.* New York: John Wiley and sons.

Crowther, R. 2002. Intergenerational outcomes of 'missing' parents – A Greek Cypriot case study. Unpublished B.A. thesis, University of Durham, U.K.

Cuddon, J.A. 1991. *Dictionary of Literary Terms and Literary Theory.* Harmondsworth: Penguin.

Danforth, L. 1982. *The Death Rituals of Modern Greece.* Princeton: Princeton University Press.

De Certeau, M. 1998. *The Writing of History.* New York: Columbia University Press.

Danto, A. 1985. 'The Vietnam Veterans Memorial'. *The Nation,* August 31, 1985.

Derrida, J. 1993. *Aporias.* Stanford: Stanford University Press.

Dorfman, A. 1991. *Death and The Maiden.* A Play in Three Acts. London: Nick Hern Books.

Doka, K. (ed.) 1989. *Disenfranchised Grief.* Lexington, Mass.: Lexington Books.

Drusiotis, M. 2000. *1619 Enohes.* Nicosia: Diafaneia.

Dubisch, J. (ed.) 1986. *Gender and Power in Rural Greece.* Princeton: Princeton University Press.

Englund, H. 1998. 'Death, Trauma and Ritual: Mozambican Refugees in Malawi', *Soc. Sci. Med.* 46, 9: 1165–74.

Evdokas, T. *et al.* 1976. *Refugees of Cyprus. A Representative Socio-psychological Study.* Nicosia: Socio-psychological Research Group.

Fabian, J. 1983. *Time and the Other. How Anthropology Makes Its Object.* New York: Columbia University Press.

Feher, M. *et al.* (eds). 1989. *Fragments for a History of the Human Body.* New York: Zone.

Feldman, A. 1991. *Formations of Violence.* Chicago: Chicago University Press.

_____ 1994. 'From Desert Storm to Rodney King via ex-Yugoslavia: On Cultural Anaesthesia', in C. Nadia Seremetakis (ed.) *The Senses Still.* Boulder: Westview Press.

_____ 1995. 'Ethnographic States of Emergency', in C. Nordstrom and A. Robben (eds) *Fieldwork under Fire.* Berkeley: University of California Press.

Fisher. J.A. 1989. *Mothers of the Disappeared.* London: Zed Books.

Freud, A. 1989. 'About Losing and Being Lost', in A. Freud (ed.) *Indications for Child Analysis and Other Papers, 1945–1956.* London: Hogarth Press.

Freud, S. 1959. *Collected Papers of Sigmund Freud,* Vol. 4. New York: Basic Books.

_____ 1984 (originally published 1917). 'Mourning and Melancholia', in S. Freud *On Metapsychology*, Vol. 11, The Pelikan Freud Library. Pelican: London.

Gambetta, D. (ed.) 1988. *Trust: Making and Breaking Cooperative Relations.* Oxford: Blackwell.

Gibbons, H.S. 1997. *The Genocide Files.* London: Charles Bravo.

Girard, R. 1988. *Violence and the Sacred.* London: Athlone.

Goldhill, S. 1986. *Reading Greek Tragedy.* Cambridge: Cambridge University Press.

Goody, J. 1997. *Representations and Contradictions.* Oxford: Oxford University Press.

Gorer, G. 1965. *Death, Grief and Mourning.* Garden City, NY: Doubleday and Company.

Green, A. 1979 (originally published 1969). *The Tragic Effect. The Oedipus Complex in Tragedy.* (transl. A. Sheridan). Cambridge: University Press.

Guest, I. 1990. *Behind the Disappearances. Argentina's Dirty War against Human Rights. and the United Nations.* Philadelphia: University of Pennsylvania Press.

Herzfeld, M. 1992. *The Social Production of Indifference: Exploring the Symbolic Roots of Western Bureaucracy.* New York: Berg.

Hitchens, C. 1984. *Cyprus.* London: Quartet Books.

Hobsbawm, E. 1985. *Bandits* (2nd edition). Harmondsworth: Penguin.

Holst-Warhaft, G. 1992. *Dangerous Voices Women's laments and Greek Literature.* London: Routledge.

Hornblower, S. and Spawforth, A. (eds). 1996. *The Oxford Classical Dictionary.* (3rd Edition). Oxford: University Press.

Klass, D. 1989. 'The Resolution of Parental Bereavement', in R.A. Kalish (ed.) *Midlife Loss: Coping Strategies.* Newbury Park, CA: Sage Publications.

Kleinman, A., Das, V. and M. Lock (eds). 1997. *Social Suffering.* Berkeley: University of California Press.

Kleinman, A. and J. Kleinman. 1997. 'The Appeal of Experience; The Dismay of Images: Cultural Appropriations of Sufferings in Our Times', in A. Kleinman, V. Das and M. Lock (eds). *Social Suffering.* Berkeley: University of California Press.

Kristeva, J. 1982. *Powers of Horror: An Essay on Abjection.* New York.

_____ 1989. *Black Sun. Depression and Melancholy.* New York: Columbia University Press.

Lacan, J. 1977. *Four Fundamental Concepts of Psychoanalysis* (Transl. A. Sheridan). London: Hogarth.

LaCapra, D. 1999. 'Trauma. Absence, Loss', *Critical Enquiry.* 25, 4: 696–727.

Lemprières Classical Dictionary, 1984 (originally published 1778). London: Routledge and Kegan Paul.

Lewis, C.S. 1966. *A Grief Observed.* London: Faber.

Loizos, P. 1975. *The Greek Gift. Politics in a Greek Cypriot Village*. Oxford: Blackwell.

_____ 1981 *The Heart Grown Bitter. A Chronicle of Cypriot War Refugees*. Cambridge: University Press.

Loraux, N. 1998. *Mothers in Mourning*. Cornell: Cornell University Press.

Loraux, P. 2001. 'Les Disparus', in J.-L. Nancy (ed.) *L'Art et la Memoire des Camps*. Paris: Seuil

Machiavelli, N. 1993. *The Prince*. Ware: Wordsworth.

Metz, C. 1974. *Film Language: A Semiotics of the Cinema*. New York: Oxford University Press.

Miller, J.A. (ed.) 1992. *The Ethics of Psychoanalysis, 1959–1960. The Seminars of Jacques Lacan, Book VII*. London: Routledge.

Morris, D. 1997. 'About Suffering: Voice, Genre and Moral Community', in A. Kleinman, V. Das and M. Lock (eds). *Social Suffering*. Berkeley: University of California Press.

Neidig, J.R. and P.P. Dalgas. 1991. 'Parental Grieving and Perceptions Regarding Health Care Professionals' Interventions', *Issues of Comprehensive Pediatric Nursing*, 14, 3: 179–91.

Nordstrom, C. and A. Robben (eds). 1995. *Fieldwork under Fire*. Berkeley: University of California Press.

Packard, M. 1996. 'Cyprus 1964: Subversion of a Mission', in D. Bourantonis and M. Evtiviadis (eds) *A United Nations for the Twenty-First Century*. Amsterdam: Kluwer Law International.

Paine, R. 1995. 'Behind the Hebron Massacre, 1994', *Anthropology Today*, 11, 1: 8–15.

Panteli, S. 1984. *A New History of Cyprus*. London: East-West Publications.

Papadakis, Y. 1993. 'The Politics of Remembering and Forgetting in Cyprus', *Journal of Mediterranean Studies*, 3, 1.

_____ 1994. 'The National Struggle Museums of Nicosia', *Ethnic and Racial Studies*, 17: 400–19.

Parkes, C.M. 1995. (originally published 1972). *Bereavement. Studies of Grief in Adult Life*. (new edition). London.

Patrick, R. 1976. *Political Geography and the Cyprus Conflict, 1963–1971*. Dept of Geography Publication Series No 4. University of Waterloo.

Pavlides, A. n.d. (probably *circa* 1980). *Cyprus 1974, Days of Disaster, In Black and White.*. Text for a Photographic Essay with photographs by D. Partassides, Text by A. Pavlides, Chronicle by D. Andreu. Nicosia: no publisher.

Perera, S. 1995. *Living with Torturers and Other Essays*. Colombo: International Centre for Ethnic Studies.

Pitt-Rivers, J. 1977. *The Fate of Schechem, or The Politics of Sex*. Cambridge: Cambridge University Press.

Ramphele, M. 1997. 'Political Widowhood in South Africa: The Embodiment of Ambiguity', in A. Kleinman, V. Das and M. Lock (eds). *Social Suffering.* Berkeley: University of California Press.

Report of the Chilean National Commission on Truth and Reconciliation. Vol. 2. 1993. (Transl. P. Berryman). Indiana: Center for Civil and Human Rights.

Ricoeur, P. 1981. 'Narrative Time', in W.J.T. Mitchell (ed.) *On Narrative.* Chicago: Chicago University Press.

_____ 1992. *Oneself as Another.* Chicago: Chicago University Press.

Robben, A. 1995. 'The Politics of Truth and Emotion among Victims and Perpetrators of Violence', in C. Nordstrom and A. Robben (eds) *Fieldwork under Fire.* Berkeley: University of California Press.

_____ 2000. 'The Assault on Basic Trust: Disappearance, Protest, and Reburial in Argentina', in A. Robben, Antonius and M. Suarez-Orozco (eds) *Cultures under Siege Collective Violence and Trauma.* Cambridge: Cambridge University Press.

Rosaldo, R. 1984. 'Grief and a Headhunter's Rage: On the Cultural Force of Emotion', in E. Bruner (ed.) *Text, Play, and Story.* Illinois: Waveland Press.

Rose, G. 1996. *Mourning Becomes the Law. Philosophy and Representation.* Cambridge: Cambridge University Press.

Roussou, M. 1986. 'War in Cyprus: Patriarchy and the Penelope Myth', in R. Ridd and H. Callway (eds) *Caught up in Conflict. Women's Responses to Political Strife.* Basingstoke: Macmillan.

Rubin, S.S. 1992. Adult Child Loss and the Two-track Model of Bereavement', *Omega*, 24: 183–202.

Rycroft, C. 1972. *A Critical Dictionary of Psychoanalysis.* Harmondsworth: Penguin.

Sant Cassia, P. 1983. 'Patterns of Covert Politics in Cyprus', *European Journal of Sociology*, XXIV, 1983: 115–35.

_____ 1993. 'Banditry, Myth and Terror in Cyprus and Other Mediterranean Societies', *Comparative Studies in Society and History*, 35, 4: 773–95.

_____ 1999. 'Martyrdom and Witnessing *(Martyria).* Narratives of Violence and Memory in Cyprus', *Terrorism and Political Violence,* 11, 1: 22–54.

Sarris, M. 1995. 'Death Gender and Social Change in Greek Society', *Journal of Mediterranean Studies*, 5, 1: 14–32.

Sauna, V.D. 1974. 'Psychological Effects of the Yom Kippur War', *New York State Psychologist.*

Schapiro, M.J. 1997. *Violent Cartographies. Mapping Cultures of War.* Minneapolis: University of Minnesota Press.

Scheper-Hughes, N. 1992. *Death Without Weeping. The Violence of Everyday Life in Brazil.* Berkeley: University of California Press.

_____ 1995. 'The Primacy of the Ethical. Propositions for a Militant Anthropology', *Current Anthropology*, 36, 3: 409–20.

Schwenger, P. 2000. 'Corpsing the Image', *Critical Enquiry*, 26, 3: 395–413.

Seferis, G. 1973. *Collected Poems, 1924–1955* (Translated Edited and Introduced by Edmund Kelly and Philip Sherrard). London: Jonathan Cape.

Segal, C. 1981. *Tragedy and Civilization. An Interpretation of Sophocles*. Cambridge Mass.: Harvard University Press.

Seremetakis, N. 1991. *The Last Word. Women, Gender, and Divination in Inner Mani*. Chicago: Chicago University Press.

Skuktans, V. 1998. *The Testimony of Lives. Narrative and Meaning in post-Soviet Latvia*. London: Routledge.

Slater, D. 1997. 'The Object of Photography', In J. Evans (ed.) *The Camerawork Essays*. London: Rivers Oram Press.

Smyrli, A. 1989. *I mana tou agnoumenou, kai alla diigimata*. Athens: Pendadactylos.

Sontag, S. 1978. *On Photography*. Harmondsworth: Penguin.

Sophokles. 1947. '*Antigone.*', in Three Theban Plays, (Transl. by E.F. Watling). Harmondsworth: Penguin.

Steiner, G. 1984 *Antigones*. Oxford: Clarendon Press

Stewart, C. 1991. *Demons and the Devil*. Princeton: Princeton University Press.

Sturken, M. 1998. 'The Wall, the Screen and The Image: the Vietnam Veterans Memorial', in N. Mirzoeff (ed.) *The Visual Culture Reader*. London: Routledge.

Suarez-Orozco, M. 1992. 'A Grammar of Terror: Psychological Responses to State Terrorism in Dirty War and Post-Dirty War Argentina', in C. Nordstrom and J.A. Martin (eds) *The Paths to Domination, Resistance and Terror*. Berkeley: University of California Press.

SWB (Summary of World Broadcasts). London: BBC (1994).

Taussig, M. 1992. *The Nervous System*. London: Routledge.

_____ 1999. *Defacement. Public Secrecy and the Labour of the Negative*. Stanford: Stanford University Press.

Taylor, C. 1975. *Hegel*. Cambridge: Cambridge University Press.

Verderey, K. 1999. *The Political Lives of Dead Bodies*. New York: Columbia University Press.

Volkan, V. and G. Ast. 1997. *Siblings in the Unconscious and Psychopathology*. International Universities Press, Madison: Connecticut.

Volkan, V. and N. Itzkowitz. 2000. 'Modern Greek and Turkish Identities and the Psychodyanamics of Greek-Turkish Relations', in A. Robben and M. Suarez-Orozco (eds) *Cultures under Siege. Collective Violence and Trauma*. Cambridge: Cambridge University Press.

Werbner, R. (ed.) 1998. *Memory and the Postcolony*. London: Zed Books.

Winter, J. 1995. *Sites of Memory. Sites of Mourning. The Great War in European Cultural History*. Cambridge: University Press.

Zelizer, B. 1998. *Remembering to Forget. Holocaust Memory through the Camera's Eye*. Chicago: Chicago University Press.

Zur, J. 1998. *Violent Memories. Mayan War Widows in Guatemala.* Boulder: West-view Press.

(forthcoming) 'Remembering and Forgetting. Guatemalan War-Widows' fordidden memories', in K.L. Rogers and S. Leyderdorff (eds) *Trauma and Memory.*

Greek and Turkish Cypriot Media and Popular Sources

AKEL. 1975. *Chronicle of the Contemporary Tragedy of Cyprus.* Nicosia.

CRTCMP (Committee of Relatives of Turkish Cypriot Missing Persons). 1993 (September). *Question of Missing Persons in Cyprus. Myth and Reality.* Cyprus: Nicosia.

The Cyprus Weekly, Lifestyle supplement: 9–15 February 1996.

Pancyprian Committee of Parents and Relatives of Undeclared Prisoners of War and Missing Persons, n.d. (but post 1994). *The Case of Cypriots Missing since the Turkish Invasion* (4th ed.)

Pancyprian Committee of Parents and Relatives of Undeclared Prisoners of War and Missing Persons, n.d. *Disappearances. The Case of the "Missing" Cypriots.* (3rd ed.)

Selides Periodical, 1995. Issues 203, 204, 207, 210,211,212.

Stephen, M. 1997. *The Cyprus Question.* London: British-North Cyprus Parliamentary Group.

TCHRC (Turkish Cypriot Human Rights Committee), December 1995. *Greek Cypriot Media on Greek Cypriot Missing Persons, 20/7/1995–10/12/1995.* North Cyprus.

TCHRC (Turkish Cypriot Human Rights Committee), May 1979. *Human Rights in Cyprus.* Lefkosha: Turkish Federated State of Cyprus.

TCHRC (Turkish Cypriot Human Rights Committee), April 1996, *Fact Note on Missing Persons in Cyprus.* Cyprus.

Turkish Cypriot Network News, Voice of Turkish Cypriots. September 1996, Issue 7. Barnet (U.K.)

Turkish Cypriot Network News, Voice of Turkish Cypriots. December 1996. Barnet (U.K.) 10, 1.

APPENDIX I
SELECTIVE CHRONOLOGY OF
MODERN CYPRIOT HISTORY

Cyprus: Population approximately 650,000 of which 80 per cent are Greeks, 18 per cent are Turkish, and the rest, Latins and others.

1192–1489 CE: Lusignan Period.

1489–1571: Venetian occupation.

1571–1878: Ottoman occupation. Settlers from Turkey.

1878–1960: British occupation.

1931: October uprising against British rule.

1950: Election of Makarios as Archbishop of Cyprus.

1951: Britain rejects for strategic interests an overwhelming Greek Cypriot referendum vote for Enosis (Union with Greece).

1955: Secret landing of George Grivas to start armed underground campaign for *Enosis.*

1955–59: EOKA (Greek Union of Cypriot Fighters) armed guerrilla campaign against Britain in favour of Union with Greece. EOKA is right wing and excludes left wingers. Some left wingers eliminated by EOKA.

1956: Establishment of *Volkan* (The Volcano), an underground Turkish Cypriot armed group, later renamed TMT (Turkish Defence Organization), opposing Greek Cypriot plans for union with Greece. Turkey suggestion for *Taksim* (partition) of the island between two communities, rejected by Greek Cypriots. Localised violence between the two communities.

1960: Zurich Agreement establishing the Republic of Cyprus, with a bicameral system of Government. Cyprus to have a Greek Cypriot President, a Turkish Cypriot Vice-President. Turkish Cypriots to have 30 per cent government posts. Archbishop Makarios elected President, Dr Fasil Kuchuk Vice-President. Britain, Greece and Turkey to be Guarantor Powers. Britain retains sovereign bases. Greek and Turkish army contingents stationed in Cyprus. Ex-EOKA gunmen given major Cabinet posts and government positions.

1961: Grivas leaves Cyprus for Greece. Makarios becomes a major figure in the Non-Aligned Movement.

1963: Disagreements over the working of the Constitution and administrative paralysis lead Makarios to propose constitutional amendments to Dr. Kuchuk who rejects them.

December 1963: Serious inter-communal violence erupts. Hostage taking between two communities. First disappearances. Makarios unable to control ex-EOKA gunmen who murder and disappear Turkish Cypriot civilians. Turkish Cypriots interpret this as an ominous plot to eradicate them.

1964: Beginning of gradual physical separation between the two communities. Turkish Cypriots withdraw into armed enclaves. Approximately 25,000 Turkish Cypriots become refugees. Dr Kuchuk supports partition. Mass grave of Turkish Cypriots discovered at Ayios Vasilios. Turkey threatens to invade. ICRC delegation arrives. Arrival of UNFICYP (UN Peacekeeping Force). Violence gradually subsides. US begins to view partition of island as a 'solution' to Makarios' non-aligned policy, to protect NATO bases in the face of vociferous opposition by a popular grassroots left wing movement (AKEL), and as a means to bring Cyprus within its sphere of influence. 'Acheson Plan' for Partition of island, resisted by Cyprus and Greece. Cyprus seeks to internationalise the issue through the UN as a means to prevent a NATO imposed solution which would involve *de facto* partition.

1966: Turkish Cypriot Kavazoglou and Greek Cypriot Misiaoulis trade unionists murdered by separatist Turkish Cypriot organisation TMT.

1967: Military officers stage coup in Greece. Turkish Cypriot leaders announce formation of 'Provisional Turkish Cypriot Administration'. Violence between the two communities. Turkey bombs island and threatens to invade, but is dissuaded by US President Johnson. Turkish Cypriot population, threatened by maverick ex-EOKA gunmen, progressively comes under the domination of hard-line Turkish Cypriot nationalists and TMT gunmen who are in turn supplied and dominated by Turkey. Greek Cypriot embargoes on Turkish enclaves further encourages this drift.

1968: Inter-communal talks begin between Glavkos Clerides (Greek Cypriots), and Rauf Denktash (Turkish Cypriots). Presidential elections: Makarios re-elected gaining 97 per cent of the votes.

1971: Grivas returns secretly to Cyprus to start EOKA-B in armed uprising against Makarios' government, and is supported by Greek Army officers stationed in Cyprus. Various plots and unsuccessful attempts on Makarios' life. Three Greek Cypriot bishops, supporters of Junta-dominated Greece, unsuccessfully attempt to remove Makarios from Archbishopric. Makarios re-elected President.

1972–74: Greek Cypriot society splits between pro-Makarios and pro-Grivas EOKA-B groups, the former reluctant on Union with Greece (as this goes against the Constitution), the latter in favour and supported by the Greek Junta with arms and money. Violence and bombings common.

1973: Grivas dies in hiding.

1974: (2 July) Makarios sends open letter to Greek President General Gizikis demanding the withdrawal of Greek troops stationed in Cyprus and accusing Greece of being behind various attempts on his life.

(15 July) Greek Officers lead National Guard in a coup. Archbishop's palace bombed. Nikos Sampson, a notorious ex-EOKA fighter proclaimed President. Greek Army strongman Ioannides telephones Sampson for 'the head of the bearded Muskos (Makarios) on a plate'. Makarios narrowly escapes, is spirited away from Cyprus by British forces. Heavy fighting between pro-Junta and pro-Makarios groups.

(20 July) Turkey, which had already moved troops to Mersin-Alexandretta areas close to Cyprus since June (*before the coup*), invades Cyprus to 'restore Constitutional order'. Troops land in Kyrenia. Britain, the other Constitutional Guarantor Power, does nothing. Massacres of Turkish Cypriots from three villages (Aloa, Maratha, Sandallar) by EOKA-B gunmen, discovered on September 2 by Turkish forces. Massacre of Turkish Cypriot male inhabitants of Tochni (in Republic of Cyprus territory) by extreme Greek nationalists.

(22 July) UN Security Council calls for cease-fire and withdrawal of foreign troops from Cyprus.

(23 July) Greek junta falls. Restoration of democracy in Greece.

(24 July–12 August) Peace conference in Geneva rejected by Turkey, which starts second offensive in August. Turkey occupies 35 per cent of Cyprus and most Greek Cypriot inhabitants evicted. July–August is the major period of disappearances of Greek Cypriots. Nearly 200,000 refugees forced to leave their homes by Turkish army.

(1 November) Unanimous UN General Assembly resolution (including vote of Turkey) calls for withdrawal of foreign troops from Cyprus, and return of refugees to their homes under conditions of safety. Turkey subsequently refuses to act, considering 'The Cyprus Problem' to be 'solved'.

(December) President Makarios returns to Cyprus.

1975: Establishment of the Pancypian Committee of Relatives of Missing Persons.

1976: Population swap-over: Greek living in the North move South, Turks living in the South of island move North. *De facto* partition of the island. Turkish Cypriot administration appropriates Greek Cypriot properties in the North for Turkish Cypriots, and begins changing toponomy of the North.

1977: Beginning of intermittent (and so far unsuccessful) inter-communal talks under UN aegis till today. Death of Makarios.

1981: Establishment of UN Committee to investigate the fate of Missing Persons.

1983: Establishment of TRNC (Turkish republic of Northern Cyprus) condemned by UN Security Council which calls on member states not to recognise it and to respect the sovereignty of the Republic of Cyprus. TRNC begins encouraging settlers from Turkey. This progressively alarms Turkish Cypriots who migrate abroad due to a collapsed economy, as the TRNC becomes increasingly dependent on Turkey.

1988: US prevails upon Turkey to permit exhumation in the North of two US civilians of Greek Cypriot origin in unmarked graves, who had disappeared during Turkish invasion. Ambassador Dillon Report to US Congress confirms these men had been murdered. No similar rights to return of remains extended by Turkey to Greek Cypriots.

1991: Perez de Cuellar's final report on Cyprus. Security Council: 'The mere maintenance of the status quo does not constitute a solution'. The Republic of Cyprus applies for EU membership. Turkey threatens to annex the North.

1997: Agreement between Clerides and Denktash (leaders of the two communities) to begin exhumations, later reneged by Turkish Cypriots.

1998: Two Greek Cypriot women attempt to break into collective tombs which they believe contain the unidentified remains of their husbands.

1999: Cyprus Government charges the renowned Physician for Peace to begin exhumations in its territory.

2002: Identification of remains of some 126 Missing Persons in the South, the remainder have not been found, and assumed to be in the Turkish Occupied North.

APPENDIX II
DRAMATIS PERSONAE

Glavkos Clerides (b. 1919). Greek Cypriot. Barrister and politician. Led Inter-communal talks with Denktash in 1968. Formed *Dymokratikos Synayermos* Party in 1976. Elected to Presidency of the Republic of Cyprus in 1993–2003. An astute experienced politician commanding wide respect.

Pater Christoforos. Greek Cypriot. President of the PanCyprian Committee of Relatives of Missing Persons from 1976–1999. Forced to resign after his 'disclo-sure' he had 'reports' that Greek Cypriot Missing Persons were still alive in a third country. Has a son, Alexandros, who disappeared in 1974. Established a Foun-dation and Church in memory of The Missing..

Takis Christopoulos. Lawyer. Greek Cypriot. Presidential Commissioner for Humanitarian Affairs.

Rauf Denktash (b. 1924). Turkish Cypriot barrister and politician. Led Inter-communal talks with Clerides in 1968. Replaced Fasil Kuchuk as leader of the Turkish Cypriots. President of the TRNC. Major politician who dominates Turk-ish Cypriot affairs, a tenacious fighter with a wide popular following in Turkey, and an opponent of any unitary state.

George Grivas (1898–1974). Greek Cypriot. Leader of a shadowy right-wing group in Greece during second world war. In agreement with Makarios, landed secretly in Cyprus in 1955 to establish EOKA and led a successful guerrilla war against the British in favour of *Enosis* (Union with Greece). With the establish-ment of the Republic of Cyprus relations between him and Makarios cooled as he suspected the latter to have lost the enthusiasm for *Enosis*. He left Cyprus for Greece in 1961 but returned briefly to reorganise the National Guard and the informal armed groups of fighters engaged in inter-communal violence. Returned to Cyprus secretly in 1971 to form EOKA-B, in favour of immediate *enosis*. Died in hiding.

Fasil Kuchuk (1906–1971). Turkish Cypriot medical doctor, and politician. Led the *Cyprus is Turkish* Party and later the *National Front Party*. Moderate. Served as Vice President of Cyprus in 1960.

Xenophon Kallis. Greek Cypriot. Member of the Greek team for the UN Committee for Missing Persons (CMP). A committed humanitarian.

Archbishop Makarios (1913–1977). Greek Cypriot. Archbishop of Cyprus from 1950–1977. *Ethnarch* (national leader) of Greek Cypriots he was exiled to the Seychelles by the British when he led a successful political campaign against British rule in favour of *Enosis* (Union with Greece). In 1960 he was elected President of Cyprus. One of the founders of the Non-Aligned Movement with international stature, he commanded wide popular devotion and support among Greek Cypriots. Astute and tenacious, he survived numerous attempts on his life.

Androulla Palma. Greek Cypriot. Wife of a Missing Person. In 1998, with Maroulla Shamishi, she attempted to break into some collective unnamed tombs of soldiers who died in the 1974 in an attempt to force the authorities to begin exhumations.

Nikos Sampson (d.2001). Greek Cypriot. Originally a newspaper reporter in the troubles of 1955–59, he doubled-up as a covert EOKA fighter. A extreme rightist and anti-communist, he established the newspaper, *Machi*, and led some bravado attacks on Turkish Cypriot enclaves in the 1967 troubles for which he earned their natural enmity and fear. He was 'appointed' President of Cyprus after the coup by the Greek Junta in 1974. Served only a short time of his prison sentence after the coup. Widely blamed in Cyprus for doing the Junta's bidding which led to the catastrophe of the Turkish invasion and occupation.

Maroulla Shamishi. Greek Cypriot. Wife of a Missing Person. In 1998, with Androulla Palma, she attempted to break into some collective unnamed tombs of soldiers who died in the 1974 in an attempt to force the authorities to begin exhumations.

Rustem Tatar. Turkish Cypriot. Accountant. Member of the UN Committee for Missing Persons (CMP).

Polykarpos Yorgadjis (d.1970). Greek Cypriot. Originally an *agonistes* (fighter) in Grivas' EOKA, he established a reputation as a powerful and ruthless individual. Appointed as Minister of the Interior in 1960 from where he dominated many of the armed groups of disbanded fighters still operating in Cyprus. He was reputed to have his own men in every village. A right-winger and anti- communist, he was reputed to have had links with British Intelligence and the CIA. He was forced to resign his Ministry after he was linked to an assassination attempt on Greek Dictator, Papadopoulos. It is believed that Greek army officers stationed in Cyprus then assassinated him in mysterious circumstances.

INDEX

❧